D0392277

The Essential Retirement Guide

The Essential Retirement Guide

A CONTRARIAN'S PERSPECTIVE

Frederick Vettese

Published by John Wiley & Sons, Inc., Hoboken, New Jersey.
Published simultaneously in Canada.

For general information on our other products and services or for technical support, please contact our Customer Care Department within the United States at (800) 762-2974, outside the United States at (317) 572-3993 or fax (317) 572-4002.

Wiley publishes in a variety of print and electronic formats and by print-on-demand. Some material included with standard print versions of this book may not be included in e-books or in print-on-demand. If this book refers to media such as a CD or DVD that is not included in the version you purchased, you may download this material at http://booksupport.wiley.com. For more information about Wiley products, visit www.wiley.com.

Library of Congress Cataloging-in-Publication Data:

Vettese, Fred, 1953–
  The essential retirement guide : a contrarian's perspective / Fred Vettese.
   pages cm
  Includes index.
  ISBN 978-1-119-11112-2 (hardback) – ISBN 978-1-119-11114-6 (epdf) –
  ISBN 978-1-119-11113-9 (epub)
1. Retirement–Planning. 2. Finance, Personal. I. Title.
  HQ1062.V48 2015
  332.024'014–dc23

                              2015029018

Cover Design: Wiley
Cover Images: Tug of War © Mark Evans / iStockphoto;
                grasshopper © songqiuju / iStockphoto

Printed in the United States of America

10 9 8 7 6 5 4 3

To Michelle

Contents

Preface

The grasshopper watches the ant working diligently all summer long, making a home and gathering food for the winter. Thinking the ant a fool, the grasshopper spends his summer days playing in the sun and consuming whatever food comes his way. When winter arrives, the ant is cosy and well-stocked in the shelter she has constructed while the ill-prepared grasshopper starves in the cold.

Aesop's fable of the Ant and the Grasshopper

A recent study by the Employee Benefit Research Institute (EBRI) reports that 20.6 percent of Americans who died at age 85 or older had no housing assets at the time of death and 12.2 percent had no assets at all. Corresponding percentages for Canada are not available but would probably be comparable.

It seems there are two ways to spin these data. The obvious conclusion is that the 20.6 percent group or the 12.2 percent group were classic Aesopian grasshoppers who failed to prepare adequately for retirement and received their comeuppance at the end of their lives. If this is the spin I thought you should put on it, this would be yet another retirement book exhorting you to save more.

There is another way to interpret the same facts. Given that fewer than 70 percent of Americans or Canadians own their home, it is remarkable that only 20.6 percent had no housing assets when they died. Some would have been too poor to own a home and would have been lifelong renters; there is no shame in that. Others, in King Lear fashion, would have given up their home to their grown-up children years earlier. Finally, some would have sold off their home to finance long-term care in their declining years. And yet nearly 80 percent *had* housing assets at the time of death. Equally amazing is that nearly 88 percent of all persons dying after age 85 had not exhausted their assets yet; many of them would not have expected to live that long.

What I take away from this is that we are not as ill-prepared for retirement as some people would have you believe. The majority will be more or less retirement-ready. Still, there is no question we can do better and do so with less pain and uncertainty during the accumulation process.

If we revisit Aesop's fable, maybe the real moral is more subtle than it appears. Nobody in his right mind would want to suffer the grasshopper's fate, but how appealing was the ant's life, really? She had no time for fun when the days were long and the sun warm—that is to say, during her youth—and while she may have been comfortable in the winter of her life, she was also old and stiff, with a diminished capacity for joy. The grasshopper, on the other hand, had enjoyed his days in the summer sun and yes, he did eventually die in the cold, but at least he had the solace of fond memories to assuage the harshness of approaching winter.

This is not to suggest that you do not need to prepare financially for retirement but it helps to be aware of the mindset you are bringing to the act of preparation. The very fact you are reading this book suggests you are more likely to be an ant than a grasshopper. In fact, both statistical and anecdotal data indicate that the majority of Canadians are ants (Americans apparently less so). As an ant, you are apt to oversave, to be unduly anxious about your retirement prospects, and to accept too readily any news story declaring the country is headed for a full-blown retirement crisis.

In this book, you will find a variety of evidence that, for the most part, should make you feel better about your retirement prospects. You will learn that your retirement income target is less daunting than you might have been led to believe; that government sources of pension are not going to vanish when you need them; and that if you make any reasonable effort at all to save, you will most likely find that finances are going to be the least of your worries in retirement. The trouble is, you will have a difficult time believing the evidence. There are three reasons why.

First, as the ant that you probably are, you are naturally inclined to give credence to pessimistic forecasts while regarding good news with a great deal of skepticism.

Second, the good news I will present—though I should warn it is not all good news—runs contrary to the vast majority of newspaper articles you will read on the subject. It is hard to change perceptions.

This brings to mind an observation by Daniel Kahneman in his book, *Thinking Fast and Slow,*

> A reliable way to make people believe in falsehoods is frequent repetition because familiarity is not easily distinguished from truth.

The astute reader will be quick to point out that even if Kahneman's remark is true, frequent repetition alone does not make a statement false. In the context of whether our retirement anxiety is unfounded, that case still needs to be made.

The third reason why you will find it hard to believe in a positive prognosis for retirement is that supporting evidence for the most part is statistical in nature, whereas refutation tends to be anecdotal. Unfortunately, our brains are wired such that anecdotes carry more weight than statistics, even though the latter are no more than a compilation of the former. "When one man dies it is a tragedy; when thousands die, it's statistics."[1]

I have encountered this phenomenon myself many times. A woman once told me she would never wear a seatbelt because she had an uncle who escaped from a car accident virtually unscathed; he wasn't wearing a seatbelt at the time and had the good fortune of being "thrown clear." (I have always wondered how that works.) My pointing out to her that *not* wearing a seatbelt is 50 times more likely to end badly failed to change her mind. Indeed, any statistic seems less compelling than a pithy anecdote to most people, male or female. My hope is that the reader is not most people.

In case the reader is wondering, the author himself is a closet ant. Yes, I ended up saving much more for retirement than I will realistically ever spend. In my defense, it happened because of fortuitous circumstances that I could not have foreseen. One event in particular that occurred in the latter part of my working life markedly improved my financial situation at a point when it was too late to "un-save" in an orderly fashion. By the way, our tendency will always be to err on the side of caution, and not just because we are more like ants than grasshoppers. We do so because we need to protect ourselves if the downside risk is high, but we cannot afford to do nothing merely because we can see some upside potential.

If you are a fellow ant, I hope the information in this book will alleviate your anxiety about your financial future without tipping you over into outright profligacy. If, by chance, you are one of those rare grasshoppers who got a hold of this book (maybe as a gift or you picked it up in a dentist's office out of boredom), I hope it will mitigate the guilt you may have felt up until now and help you to mend your ways without fundamentally changing who you are.

This book makes no claim to being a beginner's guide, but at the same time it attempts to avoid professional jargon. While some of the ideas explored are fairly sophisticated, I try to describe them in layman's terms.

One distinguishing characteristic of this book is that it is intended to be equally relevant to both Americans and Canadians. This precludes delving into the details on retirement vehicles or tax strategies, and I am happy to acknowledge that there are many other books out there already that do this admirably well. What this book can do is address the perennial retirement questions such as how much you need to save and how fast can you draw down those savings. These big retirement questions transcend borders.

Finally, the reader may be wondering about how the contrarian perspective promised in the title manifests itself within the book. When it comes to some of those perennial questions, my conclusions can differ markedly from many others in the field. Fortunately, corroboration from certain experts I respect has reinforced my own convictions. The challenge is in explaining how I got there without being too ponderous. I leave it to the reader to judge whether I have been successful.

Frederick Vettese

Note

1. Attributed to Stalin. From the book, *The Time of Stalin, Portrait of Tyranny* by Anton Antonov-Ovseyenko.

Acknowledgments

I want to thank the senior management team at Morneau Shepell—Alan Torrie and Bill Morneau in particular—for giving me the time, the resources, the encouragement, and the intellectual latitude to write this book. The book literally would not have been possible otherwise.

I am also grateful to my many colleagues at Morneau Shepell for their help, especially the actuarial team in Montreal consisting of Jerome Dionne, Philippe Guay, and Maude Trudeau-Morin. Using their stochastic modeling tools, they provided invaluable insights regarding asset mix and investment risk. Francine Pell and Martine Vadnais also helped by frequently pointing me in the right direction when I needed information, and Micheline Bougelet produced some wonderful graphics.

Sun Life Financial, a Canadian leader in insurance products, played a critical role in helping me to understand the state of the art with respect to annuities, longevity, critical illness, and long-term care. A team of specialists at Sun Life—most notably, Paul Fryer, Eric Hafeman, Jeffrey Gomes, and Laurel Pederson—were exceedingly generous with their time and knowledge.

There were many others who contributed ideas, time, and expertise:

- My good friend, Haviva Goldhagen, for planting the idea of writing a retirement book that could transcend borders,
- Rona Birenbaum, the most trustworthy financial planner I know,
- Malcolm Hamilton, the undisputed retirement guru in Canada, who offered useful comments on some key chapters, which assured me I was on the right track,
- Fabrice Morin of McKinsey & Co., who has shown leadership on the subject of the retirement readiness of Canadians and who was generous in sharing his findings on post-retirement spending habits,

- Franco Barbiero and the research team at RBC Phillips Hager and North, who diligently researched some investment themes,
- Bob Francis, founder of Medcan, for opening the doors to Medcan's expertise in the exciting area of personal genome testing, and
- Alex Melvin of Cannex Financial, for his insights and data on the annuity market.

PART

I

THE RETIREMENT INCOME TARGET

CHAPTER 1

The Road to Retirement

Take a good look at Figure 1.1. For those of you who have had to watch a loved one succumb to a critical illness, this chart might not surprise you. For others who assume they will sail through their first decade or two of retirement with no problem more serious than how to pay for the next Caribbean cruise, the chart may be a wake-up call.

In a time when we are constantly being told that we are living so much longer than we used to, it may be hard to believe that the average person has little better than a 50–50 chance of making it from age 50 to age 70 without dying or incurring a critical illness. By critical illness, I mean something really serious, such as a life-threatening cancer, cardiovascular disease, or kidney failure. (The full list is given in Chapter 21.) We might be living longer, but we humans continue to be a fragile species.

So why dwell on the morbid? These statistics are an important part of one's retirement planning. If we can change our focus from how many years we will live to how many years of healthy living we have left, it will better inform our actions while we still have the time and ability to act.

If you are age 50, for example, you might be thinking you have 35 to 40 years to go and possibly more. On the other hand, if you can expect to enjoy only 20 more disability-free years (or less), it might very well affect when you retire, what you do in your 60s and how quickly you draw down your retirement savings. Healthy life expectancy is just one of the issues we will consider in this book. But I am getting ahead of myself.

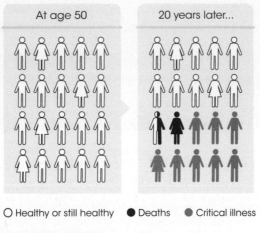

O Healthy or still healthy   ● Deaths   ● Critical illness

Figure 1.1   The Fragility of Life
Source: Canadian Critical Illness Tables (2008), reconfigured by Morneau Shepell

I will let you in on a little secret. Retirement planning can be as straightforward as following these six steps:

1. Save 10 percent of your pay each year.
2. Invest it in low-cost pooled funds, weighted toward equities.
3. Keep the asset mix the same, through good times and bad.
4. Apart from the mortgage on your home, avoid going into debt.
5. Pay off your mortgage by the time you retire.
6. Buy a life annuity at retirement.

This road map sounds rather simple, and it is. If you are able to follow it to the letter for your entire working lifetime—and experience no long-term unemployment or critical illnesses along the way—you will not go far wrong. In fact, you will fare better than most of your contemporaries. So why do you need this book, or any book on retirement planning, for that matter?

If arriving at your retirement goal was analogous to traveling to a destination, then the above six steps might get you to the right country but possibly not the right state or province. Moreover, the route may not be the cheapest, the shortest, or the most pleasant way to get there. At the risk of beating this metaphor into the ground, you might not be able to recognize the potential hazards along the way without a little more knowledge to guide you.

In this book, I try to define your retirement goal as well as the possible ways to reach it. I will use the following process to do so:

1. Define your retirement income needs as a percentage of your final employment earnings. We will call this your retirement income target.
2. Using your retirement income target, determine how much money you will need to have saved up as of the day you retire. We will call this your wealth target. Knowing this figure makes it much easier for you to monitor your progress toward becoming retirement-ready.
3. Having established your personal wealth target, consider the possible savings strategies that will get you there.
4. Assuming you arrive at your wealth target by the time you are ready to retire, you now need a strategy for drawing it down in a sensible and sustainable fashion throughout your retirement years.

My intent is not so much to be prescriptive as it is to provide useful and hopefully interesting, information. Along the way we will learn these realities:

*   Saving 10 percent a year is not a bad rule of thumb if you could follow it, but the odds are, it will be too difficult to maintain in the early stages of your career and it might not even be advisable that you try.
*   Retirement planning is as much about how you manage your cash flows during your working career as it is about accumulating wealth for your retirement.
*   Most people never spend more than 50 percent of their gross income on themselves before retirement, which is why the retirement income target is usually much less than 70 percent.
*   Interest rates will probably stay very low for the next 20 years or longer, which will affect how much you need to save.
*   A constant asset mix for your retirement savings such as 60 percent equities and 40 percent bonds is not bad, but you can improve the odds of reaching your wealth target with a more advanced strategy.
*   Your lifestyle can materially affect how long you will live and how many healthy years you can expect.

- You can withdraw 5 percent or more of your retirement savings each year in retirement, even if your total investment return is a little less than 5 percent.
- As people reach the later stages of retirement, they become progressively less capable of managing their finances, even though they grow more confident of their ability to do so.
- Annuities have become very expensive, but they still make sense for a host of reasons.

Detours

Although it is important to optimize your retirement planning strategy on the basis that everything goes smoothly, you will also need to be able to deal with adversity. When the preparation process takes as long as 30 or 40 years, you are bound to encounter some problems along the way. Below are a few of the events that can complicate your life:

- Losing your job and not finding another for a prolonged period
- Incurring a significant investment loss
- Suffering a business setback that forces you to draw down your life savings
- Being exposed to high inflation after you retire
- Having to help a family member in financial need
- Experiencing a serious illness or an accident involving yourself or someone within the immediate family
- Getting divorced, requiring you to split your assets

I wish I could tell you how to avoid trouble, but the truth is that we are not in as much control of our lives as we think. Yes, we can insulate ourselves from some of these calamities, but ultimately, success in retirement planning is best measured not by how adept or lucky we are at avoiding trouble, but rather, how we respond to trouble when it arises. Your best protection against misfortune is knowledge.

Of course, unforeseen events are not always bad news. Sometimes, good things happen that bring you that much closer to your retirement goal. It could be a big promotion, an inheritance, or an unexpected capital gain from an investment. It could even be something less dramatic like joining the pension plan in your workplace, which you might not think of as good news when you are 25, but you will eventually come to appreciate it.

Just as negative events in life call for a change in retirement strategy, so do the positive events. Either way, the key is to modify your planning appropriately whenever something happens. The better you understand the science behind retirement planning, the greater your chances of success.

Doubts about the 70 Percent Retirement Income Target

Y ou will no doubt have heard that one's retirement income target should be 70 percent of final pay, if not more. This widely accepted target was already common knowledge more than 30 years ago when I was starting out in the pension consulting industry.

As a pension actuary, I have spent much of my career helping organizations establish defined benefit pension plans for their employees. The design process usually started with the 70 percent income target from which one subtracted the portion that was deemed to be the employee's individual responsibility. The balance would then be spread over 35 or 40 years to determine a formula for the amount of pension earned each year. In the case of public-sector plans, for example, the employee was not expected to shoulder any individual responsibility, so it was a matter of dividing 70 percent by 35 years to get an annual pension accrual of 2 percent of final earnings for each year or service.[1]

When a rule of thumb is so integral to the process of determining the pension for millions of participants, you would think it would be unassailable. Over my career, the 70 percent pension target was rarely challenged, and certainly not by a young actuary like me when I was first starting out in the business. Indeed, no one to my knowledge seriously questioned the 70 percent rule until the 1990s when a few voices in the wilderness, led by pension actuary Malcolm Hamilton, made themselves heard.

Those voices were drowned out, though, as constant reinforcement by banks, insurance companies, financial planners, and investment advisors about the need to save enough to reach the

70 percent target kept the rule alive. It continues to underpin virtually every public-sector pension plan in Canada and the United States, and surely what was built to serve millions of civil servants could not be wrong. Or could it?

Niggling Doubts

For me, the doubts started to creep in a little over a decade ago. In the case of workers who earned above average income, a 70 percent target made less sense the more I thought about it. Not that there was any one smoking gun. My misgivings stemmed from a number of sources.

For starters, consider how a typical hard-working middle-income married couple divides up their paycheck. We will assume that they:

- are both working,
- raise two children,
- buy a house and spread the mortgage payments over their working careers,
- avoid going into debt, other than the mortgage,
- save 7 percent to 10 percent of pay for retirement every year, in addition to making Social Security contributions, and
- retire at 65.

If we broke down their gross income year by year into the major categories, it would look something like Figure 2.1.

After paying for all the big-ticket items including taxes, the percentage of their gross pay that remains for personal consumption dips as low as 25 percent during their 30s and never gets higher than 45 percent, something that occurs only in their last 10 years of working. If they wanted to continue spending at the same rate in retirement, they would need retirement income of 50 percent of gross pay to produce after-tax income of 45 percent. That is 20 percentage points less than the conventional target, so something appears to be amiss! Perhaps this example does not fully capture reality, so let us consider other evidence that puts 70 percent into question.

Fewer private-sector workers remain covered by a group retirement arrangement in their workplace, especially in Canada. That arrangement could be either a *defined benefit* (DB) pension plan or a *defined contribution* (DC) plan. In the United States, about half

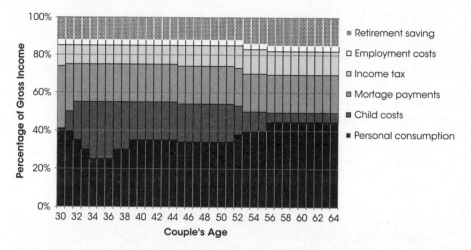

Figure 2.1   Breakdown of Expenditures in a Steady Saving Scenario

of all private-sector workers have no pension coverage at all. In Canada, the figure is closer to 70 percent. That's right. Between 5 and 7 private-sector workers out of 10 have no formal pension coverage other than Social Security, and that is meant to cover only the most basic spending needs. For anyone earning much more than the average wage, the gap between the 70 percent target and the pension from Social Security would be so huge that it makes a disastrous retirement seem inevitable. Why, then, were we not reading more stories in the papers about former middle-income workers being reduced to penury in their retirement years? Yes, the newspapers do report often on a retirement crisis, but almost always from a high-level, abstract point of view, not how Joe the retired engineer is living in a shabby bachelor apartment and eating mac and cheese.

Defined benefit versus defined contribution plan

A defined benefit (DB) pension plan provides a pension benefit that is defined by a formula based on length of service and possibly earnings. The pension does not depend on how the investments in the pension fund perform. The benefit is a predictable amount, at least in terms of earnings. An example is a plan that provides a pension of 1 percent of average earnings in the last 5 years of employment for each year of service.

In a defined contribution (DC) pension plan, the pension benefit is whatever income can be generated after retirement with the account balance that accumulates over the employee's career. Hence, the benefit is uncertain and the employee takes the risk. The employer and often the employees as well contribute a well-defined amount such as 4 percent of pay. A separate account balance is maintained for each employee, who can usually select the funds to invest in. Examples of DC plans are 401(k) plans in the United States and DC pension plans or group RRSPs in Canada.

Social Security

The term *Social Security* in this book includes basic government pensions whether in the United States or in Canada. A fuller definition is given in Appendix B.

In addition, more workers who are lucky enough to have any workplace pension coverage at all are now covered by DC plans. Actuaries were dismayed when DC plans first took hold about 25 years ago because those plans did not seem to meet the pension adequacy test. The employer contribution to DC plans is typically only half what it is for defined benefit pension plans. This was not nearly enough, the actuaries said, and that was at a time when future investment returns were expected to be in the 8 percent to 10 percent range, not the paltry 4 percent to 6 percent as is the case today. The typical DC plan, combined with Social Security, comes nowhere close to reaching the 70 percent target.

The consensus was that once these DC plans had been around long enough for a significant number of workers to retire from them, their shortcomings would become self-evident. Actuaries referred to them as *ticking time bombs.* Yet, here we are, after more than 25 years of living in a DC world, after the perfect storm of 2001–2002 that decimated account balances in DC plans, and after the worst financial meltdown since the Great Depression, and DC plans continue to thrive.

There were other indications that the 70 percent target was unrealistically high. For instance, I have tried more than once to poll retirees in large pension plans to learn more about their spending patterns and financial situation 10 or 20 years after retirement. The intent was to determine what portion of their pension they give as gifts to other family members, how much they continue to save, and what they spend on consumer-durables such as furniture, big appliances, or cars.

The sponsors of the plans that I targeted were sympathetic to the purpose of my investigation, but there was a problem. They needed the consent of the pension plan's retiree association to proceed but the leaders of the association would invariably stonewall the request. Apparently, they were afraid that the data gathered would be used by the employer to justify granting smaller pension increases in the future.

It would seem the retirees knew they had a good thing going and did not want to jeopardize it by disclosing their financial situation. Had their pensions been deficient, which they should have been since most of them retired on considerably less than 70 percent, one would have thought the retirees would welcome a survey to make their plight better known, but this was never the case.

A survey commissioned by the Canadian Institute of Actuaries asked people both before and after retirement how confident they felt about their financial future. You would think the retirees would feel less confident than the pre-retirees because, having retired with retirement income less than 70 percent, they would now be in full panic mode. The survey result, however, showed just the opposite. Only 44 percent of the pre-retirees were confident about their financial future versus 62 percent of those already retired. Among retirees who had paid off their mortgages, 74 percent were confident. In case you are wondering if the people surveyed were unusually affluent, at least 57 percent said they had total investments of under $250,000.[2] Could it be that the retirees learned from actual experience what pre-retirees could not yet know—that they would make out just fine with less than 70 percent?

Another survey, this one conducted by Statistics Canada, asked recent retirees how their financial situation had changed in retirement versus the year before retirement.[3] Of those retirees, 54 percent said it was "about the same," 13 percent said "it had improved" and just 33 percent said "it had worsened." Why wasn't that last group larger?

Even the public-sector pension plans themselves made me question the 70 percent target. To reach 70 percent requires 35 years of participation in a public-sector plan, but relatively few civil servants work that long. Their average retirement age is only 60 and has dipped as low as 58 in recent years. Many of them leave the workforce by age 55. Since they may have had other jobs before settling into public service, this translates into an average of just 25 to 30 years of service by retirement, which suggests their pension is more typically 50 percent to 60 percent of final average pay rather than 70 percent. If public-sector workers are retiring with inadequate pensions, it is curious that no one is making that claim, even the plan participants themselves. They are not demanding higher pensions; they just want to keep what they have.

Saving for Retirement Is a Two-Dimensional Problem

The turning point for me was a paper written by former Bank of Canada governor David Dodge and others[4] declaring that people needed to save 10 percent to 21 percent of their income each year over their working careers to be able to retire with a 70 percent pension. I recall having an epiphany while sitting in a conference room and listening to Mr. Dodge explaining this. It was at that moment I realized that saving for retirement was generally tackled as a one-dimensional problem whereas in fact it was two-dimensional.

The one dimension that everyone in the financial industry fixates on is the post-retirement period and the need to amass the necessary retirement income at any cost. The forgotten second dimension is the pre-retirement period where disposable income has to be sacrificed if we are to feed the post-retirement income monster.

When one considers both dimensions simultaneously, saving in order to build up retirement assets is essentially a balancing act; the more one saves to achieve a 70 percent pension, the lower one's disposable income before retirement. Push that far enough and workers do not have enough to live comfortably before they retire. In some exceptional circumstances, disposable income before retirement would dip below 30 percent of gross income in order to save enough to produce disposable income after retirement of 70 percent. As we saw in Figure 3.1, the circumstances may not even have to be that exceptional for this to happen.

The Macro Case Against 70 Percent

If any more reasons were needed to reject the 70 percent target, consider this. Half a century ago, when our grandparents retired later and lived shorter lives than we do now, they used to work 4 to 5 years for every year that they spent in retirement. Today, most people work just 1.5 years or so for every year of retirement. In the public sector, the ratio is closer to 1:1. To keep the math simple in the following argument, we will assume one year worked for each year of retirement.[5]

Assume that all the money you need for retirement is coming out of your own pocket. In a way, this is what actually happens; it is just that some of that money takes a circuitous route before it is converted into retirement income. Some of it, for instance, will come from Social Security and some more might come out of a company pension plan, but ultimately it is really being funded by you in your role as (a) a taxpayer, (b) a consumer of goods, or (c) an employee who is receiving lower income than he would otherwise.

If we ignore tax, inflation, and investment earnings for a moment, you would need to set aside $1 today for each $1 you eventually receive as income in retirement. If you save at a steady rate, you can think of it as the money you set aside at age 30 provides income for one year when you reach 60. What you save at 31 provides income at 61 and so on. In this way, you can see that the only way to achieve a 70 percent retirement income target is by saving 70 percent of your pay each year, which of course would leave you with just 30 percent of pay to meet all your living expenses over your working lifetime. This obviously makes no sense. In the absence of tax, inflation, and investment returns, the bottom line is that you cannot have both a 70 percent target and work just 1 year for every year that you spend retired.

Assume now that inflation is 2 percent a year and retirement savings earn an investment return of 4 percent a year until retirement, but just 2 percent a year after retirement (a time when you should take on less risk in your portfolio anyway). Assume also that wage increases including promotions average out at 4 percent a year. None of these assumptions is perfect but they are close enough to current reality to serve our purposes here, and more important they will simplify our calculations.

On this basis, we get to the same answer as when we assumed no inflation, tax, or investment earnings. You would still have to contribute 70 percent of gross income each year during your working lifetime to accumulate a pension of 70 percent. You can see the problem.

The conclusion is that the retirement income target cannot be 70 percent if we are working just one year for every year of retirement. We have to work a lot more years and receive pension for a lot fewer years—which means retiring much later than the norm, which is between age 60 and 65 right now. Alternatively, we need to settle for less than 70 percent, which is what the example in Figure 2.1 suggested we should be doing and in fact what most retirees do anyway.

Low-Income Workers

To be clear, this entire chapter, as well as most of this book, is focused on the needs of middle-income and upper-income savers. Low-income workers, defined here as the bottom 30 percent or so of the workforce, definitely need retirement income that exceeds 70 percent of their final pay. Doubts about the need for a 70 percent retirement income target relate only to the higher-income groups.

There are two reasons why this book focuses on the higher income groups. First, they will tend to be the ones who will actually be able to save for retirement and could make use of a retirement planning book. Second, the low-income workers are already well taken care of with pensions from government programs alone, at least in Canada where the poverty rate among seniors is very low, even if they were previously low-income workers. I concede that poverty rates among seniors in the United States are much higher but this is a problem that can best be fixed by income-tested government programs, not by saving more; a solution to that problem is outside the scope of this book.

Conclusions

In summary, the 70 percent retirement income target seems to be wrong, at least as a general rule. The majority of the workforce has no formal pension other than a modest amount of Social Security benefit and yet most retirees are confident about their retirement prospects. Civil servants who have what they themselves acknowledge are generous pensions usually fall short of the 70 percent target, but no one is complaining. Attempts to find out more about how retirees with workplace pension plans are doing are usually rebuffed by the retirees themselves, even though they should welcome the attention if they were struggling. And finally, a simple mathematical scenario based on the premise of a 70 percent target produces an absurd result.

Consider, then, the possible reasons why we continue to give the 70 percent target any credence in spite of all the evidence against it.

One possible reason is a simple lack of understanding that the real target is less than 70 percent.

Another possibility is that the majority of us are being bailed out by inheritances. The flimsy data on inheritances suggest otherwise, but even if this were the reason, it begs the question of how the people who are dying managed to leave so much money behind if they needed 70 percent themselves.

A third possibility is that 70 percent really is the target but only in exceptional situations, and we have decided to apply it to all situations for the sake of conservatism or convenience.

Regardless of the reason, enough doubt exists to warrant further scrutiny. In the next chapter, we will consider some detailed examples that will put the 70 percent retirement income target to rest.

Notes

1. This was usually integrated with government-sponsored pension plans (Social Security) so the employer-sponsored plan would provide a little less than 2 percent for each year.
2. Potentially up to 78 percent had total investments under $250,000 since 21 percent replied they didn't know.
3. 2002 General Social Survey, conducted by Statistics Canada.
4. Dodge, Laurin, and Busby, *The Piggy Bank Index: Matching Canadians' Savings Rates to their Retirement Dreams*, C.D. Howe e-brief, March 18, 2010.
5. This argument is a variation of a similar argument put forth in a speech by Bill Robson (2014), president of the C.D. Howe Institute.

CHAPTER 3

Homing in on the Real Target

In the last chapter, the 70 percent retirement income target came under serious attack. In this chapter, I will try to show that the real retirement income target is usually much lower than 70 percent. This will lead to a new set of targets that can be useful later on. Without a good target, you cannot know what percentage of your income you should be saving for retirement or when you have saved enough.

Setting the Ground Rules

Before we can derive the right retirement income target, we need to establish how our spending needs are expected to change after retirement. Most of us want to have enough retirement income to maintain the same standard of living as we enjoyed before retirement. Not only is this the aspiration of the average individual, large organizations also think along similar lines when commenting on the retirement programs they sponsor for their own employees.

In a 2010 survey, Morneau Shepell asked 217 large to medium-sized employers to identify the most appropriate retirement income target for employees in their organization. 50 percent indicated the target should be high enough to enable employees to maintain their pre-retirement standard of living while 49 percent felt the target should provide a "decent" standard of living in retirement, implying it would be acceptable to make do with a little less. Only 1 percent thought the target should provide a higher standard of living after retirement.

When it comes to individuals, the people I know who oversave are not consciously looking to better their situations after retirement;

they are simply trying to accumulate a sizable sum and are erring on the side of caution, sometimes to a fault.

I concede there is a smallish minority of people (obviously not employers) who subscribe to the belief that spending needs will rise in retirement. They contend they will have more time, as well as pent-up demand, to travel and to spend money on hobbies.

On the other hand, an even greater number of people are prepared to get by on a little less income after they retire. It might be for philosophical reasons, based on their reaching a point in their lives when they are less materialistic or a little less able to get around and spend money the way they used to. Or perhaps they expect to spend less since they have more time to prepare their own meals, do their own work around the home, and avail themselves of the many seniors' discounts.

I will take the middle ground and assume that we would generally be content to continue spending the same amount in real terms, even if the basket of goods we buy at age 65 might differ from what we bought when we were 40. Expressed more precisely, I would argue that our retirement goal is to maintain the same level of *personal consumption*. Table 3.1 shows what that term means in this context:

While this categorization might seem a little arbitrary, notice that everything on the "Included" list can be characterized as immediate

Table 3.1   Defining Personal Consumption

Included in personal consumption	Not included
Food	Expenses related to one's children
Rent (if one does not own)	Saving, especially for retirement
Home maintenance costs including insurance and property taxes	Buying a home or making mortgage payments
Household furnishing and equipment	Employment expenses
Clothing	Gifts of money
Transportation costs, including insurance	Income tax
Health care and personal grooming	
Travel	
Recreation, hobbies, and entertainment	
Education	
Tobacco and alcohol	
Games of chance	
Insurance (but not whole life)	

consumption, whereas almost everything on the "Not Included" list is an investment in the future in one way or another: an investment in your children, your retirement security, your home, or your career. Personal consumption continues for a lifetime, whereas investments tend to taper off by the time of retirement, if not before.

The "Not Included" list has two items that are not strictly investments. One is gifts of money, which can be loosely considered an investment in one's grandchildren, if they are the beneficiaries. The other is income tax, which could be characterized as a type of negative personal consumption. It is on the "Not Included" list since it can drop very significantly after retirement, and personal consumption could not be said to be the same before and after retirement if income tax is included.

Now that we have defined personal consumption, we can proceed onto some examples of how it relates to our gross, pretax income.

Howard and Barb

When the expenditures on the "Not Included" list finally drop off, our income needs drop as well. An example can show how significant the expenditures on the "Not Included" list can be. I asked a fee-only financial planner, Rona Birenbaum, to provide details on a real-life situation. Rona's example involved a young professional couple whom I will call Howard and Barb.

Howard and Barb got married when they were 30 and 27, respectively. They immediately purchased a home with some financial help from their parents. As a junior lawyer in a successful practice, Howard was already making $100,000 a year by age 30. Barb gave birth to their first child at age 32 and their second at 37. At this point, the couple decided they needed help with their financial planning, which is why they went to Rona.

It was also at this time that they traded up to a bigger home and took out a bigger mortgage to match. Even though Howard was now 40, they figured their mortgage payments would not shrink as a percentage of pay any time before age 65 since they expected to do some home renovations from time to time and maybe even trade up one more time. Still, their plan was to be mortgage-free by age 65.

If we chart the breakdown of their expenditures at the point when Howard is age 42, it would look like Figure 3.1. Their hefty

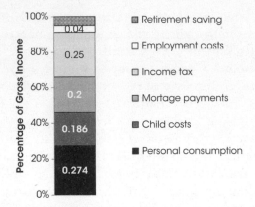

Figure 3.1   Expenses at Age 42

mortgage payments and the additional expenses due to having a second child have left very little room at that point in their lives to save for retirement. In fact, the "Not Included" expenditures are so large so that only 28 percent of gross income is left for all aspects of personal consumption.

With Rona's help, Howard and Barb broke down their expenditures from prior years in a similar manner and also projected future expenditures to age 65. This is charted in Figure 3.2.

Howard and Barb were able to allocate an increasing percentage to retirement saving in their later years as child-raising costs started to drop. The mortgage payments remained high, at about 25 percent of income, right up until age 65 when the last payment was made. The most interesting aspect of the chart, perhaps, is that Howard and

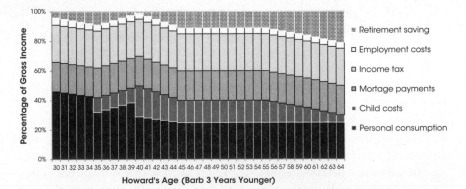

Figure 3.2   "Investments" Keep Personal Consumption Low

Barb do not expect to spend more than 30 percent of their gross income on personal consumption at any time between now (when they are 40 and 37 respectively) and retirement. This makes them a little unusual compared to the average couple but not as much as you might think.

When Howard turns 65, the mortgage should be fully paid off and child-raising costs should also drop to zero. Similarly, employment-related costs and retirement saving would cease. The only expenditure that is not personal consumption that continues will be income tax and the tax bill will be much lower in retirement. To maintain their pre-retirement personal consumption, Howard and Barb need retirement income equal to 30 percent of final pay plus something extra to take care of the income tax payable. That something extra in their case is about 5 percent of final pay, so their retirement income target is 35 percent.

It is easy to see how this situation is unusual in some respects. Howard's pay was about three times the national average even at age 40, and it continued to grow after that. Mortgage payments were high and stayed that way right up until retirement, something not every household faces. All of their extra disposable income that materialized once their children becoming self-supporting was funneled into retirement saving, whereas many couples would have spent at least a portion of it on personal consumption.

Let us consider a more typical example.

Steve and Ashley 1.0

Steve is a supervisor in a call center and Ashley (who is the same age) is a part-time assistant manager at a local hotel. Neither one participates in a workplace pension plan. In their peak earning years, which occur close to retirement, they earned a combined income of $90,000, making them a little better off than the average two-earner household.

They got married at 30 and immediately started saving for a house. The first child came along when they were 33 and the second at 35. Ashley took some time off with each birth but arranged for daycare so she could return to work full time within 6 months. They bought their first house at age 35 and traded up to a bigger place at age 45, which is where they would stay until they retired.

Throughout their working lives, they lived within their means. They still tried to put something aside every year for retirement because the experts said they should. Even during the children's preschool years, when they were saddled with daycare expenses, Steve and Ashley managed to salt away 5 percent of pay in their retirement account, over and above the contributions they make toward Social Security. The amounts they set aside for retirement remained modest until their final few years before retirement.

After buying the second home at age 45, they made every effort to pay down the mortgage as fast as they could, and as a result they managed to be mortgage-free by age 57. By the time of their 60th birthday, the children had both left home and were self-supporting. Eliminating the mortgage and the child-related costs meant that Steve and Ashley now had a lot more disposable income to ramp up their personal consumption and their retirement saving in the last 7 years before they retired at 65. They started increasing their retirement saving at age 58 after the mortgage was paid off and increased it again at 60 after the children had left home.

On the surface, Steve and Ashley seem to be paragons of fiscal responsibility. One might wonder whether they were a little too frugal early on and whether it was worth the financial pain for the sake of being mortgage-free at a relatively young age, but that is a question for a later chapter. The question at hand is whether they need retirement income equal to 70 percent of final pay.

Figure 3.3 breaks down their annual cash outlay the same as we had done previously for Howard and Barb. Based on this breakdown, they lived off of only 32 percent of gross income on average from the time they were married up until the time they paid off the mortgage at age 57. In their early 30s, personal consumption actually dipped to only 25 percent of gross income, which would have put them near the poverty line.

Things improved markedly once the children were gone and the mortgage was paid off. Comparing age 56 to age 60, 35 percent of gross pay is freed up, part of which will be used to increase retirement saving and the balance toward higher personal consumption. For the last 5 years before retirement, 57 percent of gross income is available for personal consumption and after taking income tax in retirement into account, it means Steve and Ashley would need retirement income equal to about 63 percent of final pay to maintain that lifestyle for the rest of their lives.

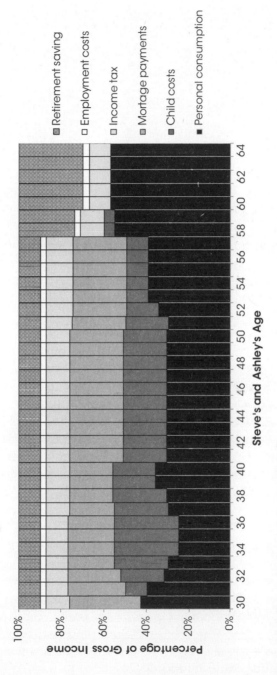

Figure 3.3 Save Early and Party at 60?

Why Even 63 Percent Is Too High a Target

This is a good place to pause for a reality check. Steve and Ashley needed to deprive themselves for decades in order to artificially boost personal consumption to new heights for a few fabulous years before retirement, and even then their retirement target is still only 63 percent of pay rather than 70 percent.

There is no good case to be made for a 70 percent retirement income target for Steve and Ashley, and I would argue that they should not even be shooting for 63 percent. There are several reasons why their target will be lower than that.

First, consider what type of expenditures they would be contemplating in their late 50s after a lifetime of moderation. People tend to increase permanent spending only when they are confident they have the means to maintain that higher spending pattern over the long-term. When the ability to spend more is new and perceived to be short-lived (because retirement looms), people will focus more of their new spending on extraordinary, nonrecurring items rather than on trying to elevate themselves to a lifestyle they cannot maintain.

With the mortgage paid and the children gone, Steve and Ashley may well decide to go on a spending spree to satisfy their pent-up demand. The shopping list, however, will be heavily weighted toward one-time big-ticket items like buying a new car or boat, taking a world cruise, purchasing a long-coveted Rolex watch or fur coat, or perhaps installing an in-ground pool. These are all examples of purchases that, for the most part, do not translate into a need for higher regular spending for the rest of their lives. It is highly likely that Steve and Ashley will *not* try to increase regular consumption from 39 percent of gross income to 57 percent like Figure 3.3 suggests. It is much more likely that they will split the extra 18 percent of disposable income into two buckets, with maybe half representing purchases that they do not plan to repeat in retirement and the other half leading to a permanent increase in regular personal consumption. This means sustainable personal consumption is closer to 48 percent rather than 57 percent. After taking tax into account, 48 percent consumption translates into a retirement income target of 52 to 53 percent of final pay.

Second, not everyone, and maybe not even most people, will pounce on a sudden and temporary increase in disposable income to change their lifestyle too drastically, especially after a lifetime of practicing moderation. I know my parents couldn't do it, even though they had ample financial resources to make the change on a permanent basis. When it comes to spending habits, inertia is a powerful force. I will not try to quantify this factor, but it encourages us to round down rather than up.

Third, while the idea of paying off the mortgage by age 57 is quite realistic, it is harder to embrace the notion that perennially responsible parents, now flush with spending cash, will cut off their grown-up children and spend every cent on themselves. With much more disposable income than they had ever previously enjoyed, Steve and Ashley are likely to continue helping their children after they become young adults; it might involve helping to pay for weddings, contributing to an education fund for the grandchildren, or helping out with the down payment on a starter house. This factor might translate into several percent of gross income continuing to be lavished on children even when it is not absolutely necessary.

You might be thinking that Steve and Ashley should have saved more for retirement in their early working years so they would not have to save so much in their last 7 years of work. That would simply have made a bad situation worse in their early years. As we saw, their personal consumption had dipped below 30 percent of gross income in their 30s, and it could really not have gone any lower.

The conclusion is that even if Steve and Ashley make personal sacrifices to frontload expenses like mortgage payments so that they can artificially bump up their personal consumption for a few brief years, their retirement income target is still in the vicinity of 50 percent.

Steve and Ashley 2.0

The above adjustments that got Steve and Ashley's retirement income target down from 63 percent to 50 percent need to be made a little more precise to take into account the fact that a lower retirement income target means less money needs to be saved for retirement in the last few years. Let us take all this into account with one more illustration. To be clear, we will assume the following:

- Mortgage payments end at age 57.
- Financial support to grown-up children continues at 2 percent of gross income per child (maximum 4 percent) rather than ending completely.

- The increase in personal income that results from the elimination of mortgage payments and the reduction of child-raising costs will be split three ways: part goes toward a one-time spending spree that will not have to be repeated in their retirement years, part goes toward a permanent and sustainable increase in their personal consumption, and the remainder goes toward higher retirement saving.
- This three-way split will be calculated by trial and error until we find the retirement savings rate that enables the extra regular spending to continue for life.
- The goal is to give Steve and Ashley a chance to satisfy pent-up demand for spending after a lifetime of frugality, to reach a level of sustainable personal consumption that is higher than they ever enjoyed before the mortgage was paid off, and to be able to continue that consumption after retirement.

On this basis, their sustainable personal consumption is 48 percent of final pay, which translates into a retirement income target of approximately 52 percent of gross final pay. This is shown in Figure 3.4. Steve and Ashley should be happy since their modest spending habits have been rewarded with retirement security at the highest level of personal consumption they have ever enjoyed.

By the way, Steve's and Ashley's income is very close to the national average for households. If their income had been higher,

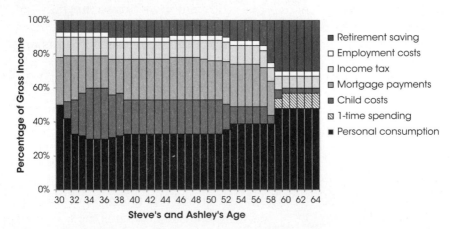

Figure 3.4   Steve and Ashley 2.0

their retirement income target would have been lower. There are various reasons for this, including the leveraging effect of Social Security pensions, the progressive income tax system, and the need for higher-income individuals to save at a higher rate.

> **Quintiles**
>
> Quintile is the mathematical expression for dividing a population into five equal-sized tranches. If they are household income quintiles, for example, it means that each tranche would contain 20 percent of all households with comparable incomes. Middle-income households like Steve and Ashley would fall in the third quintile.

The last point bears repeating—the higher the savings rate, the lower the retirement income target. This seems counterintuitive. How can the target be lower, you might ask, when a higher saving rate produces more retirement income? Earlier we broke down expenditures into personal consumption and "investment." Any type of investment, including retirement saving, reduces personal consumption dollar for dollar. So if the objective is to match in retirement the same level of personal consumption one enjoyed while saving for retirement, saving more lowers the target.

Unlike paying off the house or raising children, saving for retirement is a special type of investment since it has a double impact: Not only does it reduce the retirement income target, it also generates more retirement income to be able to reach that target. This is why a relatively small rate of saving goes a long way.

Expressing Consumption in Dollars

The foregoing examples express spending on each category in terms of a percentage of gross income. If we express all amounts in dollars instead, we will see that disposable income for Steve and Ashley rises even more in real terms than we thought. That is because employment income tends to rise faster than inflation as a result of promotions and general productivity gains. As long as spending remains the same percentage of employment income, then real spending must be rising.

Nominal versus real

A nominal amount does not take inflation into account, whereas a real amount does. For example, if you spent $100 a year for 10 years on golf balls, then your spending remains the same in nominal terms but it decreases in real terms because those golf balls are getting more expensive each year due to inflation. If price inflation was 2 percent a year and you increased your spending on golf balls by 2 percent a year then your real spending remains constant.

In the example of Steve and Ashley, I assumed that their salaries would rise by 3.5 percent a year versus price inflation of 2.25 percent a year. Let us recast the example in dollar terms to see what happens to income available for personal consumption in their last few years before retirement.

We will take the same percentages from Figure 3.4, convert them into dollar amounts, and then strip out the effects of inflation to express them in constant dollars. If golf balls cost $20 a dozen 10 years ago and rose gradually by the inflation rate to $25 today, we would say the price in constant dollars over that period remained unchanged at $20 (using 10-year-old prices as our benchmark).

The results of this exercise are shown in Figure 3.5. This is essentially the same chart as Figure 3.4 except that it shows only sustainable personal consumption and is expressed in constant dollars instead of percentages. Note that personal consumption rises by more than 100 percent in real terms from the low reached at age 34 to age 60. It then remains at that high level until retirement, and we arranged it so that Steve and Ashley saved enough to generate retirement income at that same high level for the rest of their lives. This is why Steve and Ashley should be very comfortable if they hit their 52 percent retirement target.

Conclusions

We have seen that the retirement income target can be as low as 35 percent for a couple that spent a considerable amount on housing and child-raising throughout their working years. The target can nudge above 50 percent for a middle-income couple who paid off their mortgage early and then started to spend much more on themselves in their last few years of employment. The reader

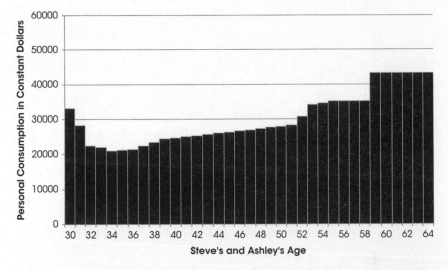

Figure 3.5   Real Personal Consumption Doubles Between 34 and 60

should be starting to gain some comfort that for a middle-income to upper-income household with mortgage payments and/or child-raising expenses, the typical target is significantly lower than 70 percent.

While we have been presenting evidence that suggest the retirement income target may be closer to 50 percent, but we haven't looked at enough data points yet to be sure that 50 percent, or any fixed percentage, is a better rule of thumb. We also have not explored situations where people do manage to spend more than 50 percent of gross income on personal consumption. They do exist. We will save this for the next chapter.

CHAPTER 4

A New Rule of Thumb

In the previous chapter, I used a few examples to show that a surprisingly small percentage of our gross income is spent on personal consumption during our working lifetimes. It is important to formalize those results to determine the average percentage, especially close to retirement age, because that is going to lead us to a better retirement income target.

We haven't seen enough situations yet for us to arrive at a firm conclusion, nor do we know yet if there are any exceptions where the retirement income target might be much higher. Here is what we do know at this point:

- When you are making ongoing "investments" in your home (mortgage payments) or the future generation (raising children), they crowd out personal consumption and thus lower your retirement income target.
- Retirement saving is a special type of "investment" in that it has a double effect: not only does it reduce personal consumption, hence lowering your retirement income target, it also generates retirement income to meet at least part of that target.
- If you make no such investments (i.e., a single renter without children), your personal consumption, and hence your retirement income target, will tend to be higher.
- Some people will have freed themselves of mortgage payments and child-raising expenses well before retirement age. If so, they can boost their personal consumption in their last few years before retiring; this will increase their retirement income target, but not dollar for dollar, because some of the increased

consumption is on one-time items that will not carry over into retirement. Also, some of those consumption dollars have to be redirected into saving more to meet their new higher target.

Viewed from 30,000 feet, the "investments" you make during your working lifetime—paying off a mortgage, raising children, and saving for retirement—take up a very substantial amount of your gross income and in the process, they depress your personal consumption for a considerable length of time.

You can frontload your "investments" to some extent, especially the mortgage payments, but this strategy cannot be carried too far without triggering undue hardship. Do you really want to live off less than 25 percent of gross income in your early working years, when income is low, in order to produce retirement income decades later at 60 percent or more of a much higher income figure?

Guiding Principles

As we work to develop a better rule of thumb, it helps to have some underlying principles to guide us. I propose the following:

- If possible, personal consumption should stay above 30 percent of gross income at all times. This may limit how fast we can pay off the mortgage or how much we save for retirement, especially in the early part of our working careers when income is lower and family expenses are high.
- Since we always want to see progress, personal consumption as a percentage of pay should be highest just before retirement, and into retirement.
- We will assume that the serious child-raising expenses will have ended by the time the primary wage earner in the household is age 60 but that parents will continue to provide some modest ongoing financial support to grown-up children for a few years longer.
- If you are fortunate enough to eliminate mortgage payments or child-raising expenses before retirement, the sudden increase in disposable income will be split as follows:
  - 20 percent of the increase will be allocated to one-time expenditures (cruises, Rolexes) in those final years before retirement as a reward for having spent so modestly in the earlier years.

- The rest will go toward increasing personal consumption on a permanent basis and toward saving more for retirement. The amount that goes toward increased saving depends on how much more retirement income is needed to cover the permanent increase in personal consumption.

In the last chapter, we already showed an example of these principles in action with Steve and Ashley 2.0.

Retirement Income Targets under Different Scenarios

The next step is to determine retirement income target for a broad range of households. From the last chapter we know the retirement income targets might depend on income level since marginal tax rates are different and the impact of Social Security programs is also different. We can also guess that the extent of our "investments" (mortgage, children, etc.) will make a difference. To this end, I ran calculations for 18 household types that vary by income, number of children, and home ownership status. Here are the details:

Income level (average in the last 5 years of employment in today's dollars):

- *Middle income household:* $96,000 for a two-earner couple, $60,000 for a single person
- *Upper-middle income household:* $160,000 for a two-earner couple, $100,000 for a single person
- *Upper income household:* $250,000 for a two-earner couple, $175,000 for a single person

Number of children in the household:

- 2 or more
- 1 child
- None

Home ownership status:

- Owns
- Rents

I had also considered investigating how the retirement income targets depended on marital status but found that, for various reasons, it makes very little difference to the income targets so I left it out.

Scenario 1: Mortgage Freedom Only at 65

Having settled on the 18 sample household types, I then had to make an assumption about when mortgage payments would end. In this first scenario, I assumed that the homeowners would be paying their mortgage at the rate of 20 percent of income right up until retirement age but not beyond. This seemed reasonable, since many people do keep on paying off their mortgage until they retire and also because a longer term of payments meant that each year's payment could be a little less (20 percent of income instead of 25 percent). This ensured that personal consumption in the early working years would not fall to unrealistically low levels.

Starting with the households that own their homes, the resulting retirement income targets are shown in Table 4.1.

The example of Howard and Barb in the previous chapter gave us a hint of how small a percentage personal consumption represents of gross income. Table 4.1 definitely reinforces that notion as almost all households that are making mortgage payments have retirement income targets in the 40 to 50 percent range. Note that all of these households would have had even less income available for personal consumption earlier on when child-raising expenses were higher. With the type of percentages we see in Table 4.1, they will be ending their working careers and going into retirement on a high note.

As low as the retirement income targets in Table 4.1 are, they could have been even lower for a variety of reasons. Mortgage payments in the final years could have higher than the 20 percent of income that I assumed. Significant child-raising costs could have continued into one's 60s, something I assumed is not the case. The savings rate in the last few years before retirement could have been higher which would have depressed personal consumption as well as the income target. A higher savings rate, by the way, would be more

Table 4.1   Retirement Income Targets under Scenario 1: Homeowners

	2 or more children	1 child	No children
Middle income	47%	51%	55%
Upper-middle income	44%	48%	52%
Upper income	40%	44%	49%

Table 4.2   Retirement Income Targets under Scenario 1: Renters

	2 or more children	1 child	No children
Middle income	63%	67%	71%
Upper-middle income	62%	66%	71%
Upper income	60%	65%	70%

likely than someone contributing the same percentage of pay every year since age 32.

As shown in Table 4.2, renters have much higher retirement income targets than homeowners, very close in fact to the conventional 70 percent target if they have less than 2 children. Renters enjoy higher levels of personal consumption since mortgage payments do not take a bite out of their disposable income.

Scenario 2: Mortgage Freedom 5 Years Earlier

Now we will see what happens to retirement income targets if mortgage payments end 5 years before retirement age. Freedom from mortgage payments allows households to spend more on themselves, and having done so for a few years, they may very well want to maintain this newfound spending habit into their retirement years.

At first blush, this second scenario is seemingly less rational than the first. It requires that the occupants of a household live below their means for decades in order to be able to enjoy a higher level of spending in the last 5 years of their working lives, as well as after retirement. From another perspective, this is maybe not so crazy. Paying off certain major expenses early gives them a buffer to better be able to weather adverse circumstances that might befall them. Moreover, many households dream of a better life and know it will take some sacrifice to make it happen.

The results for homeowners are given in Table 4.3. What is noteworthy is that the targets vary only slightly by income level. Given the number of ways in which we could have varied the results by 2 or 3 percent, we can say that for all practical purposes, the retirement income targets for homeowners who pay off their mortgage early is basically the same at all income levels. This is convenient for purposes of devising a general rule of thumb.

If we want to see how much difference it makes to the retirement income target if one pays off the mortgage early, it helps to

Table 4.3   Retirement Income Targets under Scenario 2: Homeowners

	2 or more children	1 child	No children
Middle income	47%	53%	58%
Upper-middle income	46%	52%	57%
Upper income	43%	49%	56%

Table 4.4   Difference in Targets, Scenario 2 vs. Scenario 1

	2 children	1 child	0 children
Middle-income	0%	2%	3%
Upper-middle income	2%	4%	5%
Upper income	3%	5%	7%

compare the figures in Table 4.3 to Table 4.1. Rather than having readers flipping back and forth between the two tables, I have created Table 4.4, which shows the *difference* between the retirement income targets for homeowners under Scenario 2 (Table 4.3) versus Scenario 1 (Table 4.1).

We see that the retirement income targets in Table 4.3 are higher than the corresponding figures from Table 4.1, but not by much. The average difference is under 5 percent. There are two reasons the differences are so small. The first is that some of the spending by the early mortgage payers was one-time spending (as discussed earlier) and did not factor into the retirement income target. The second reason is the increase in personal consumption for the early mortgage payers was tempered by the need to save more to finance that higher level of personal consumption after retirement. Once again, the fact the differences are small is going to make it easier to devise a rule of thumb.

General Rule of Thumb

We have seen that personal consumption as a percentage of gross income varies by household type. It is important to know this statistic, which we will call the personal consumption rate, since it dictates our retirement income target.

What we would like to do now is to generalize the foregoing results to see if we can come up with a simple rule of thumb. From the above tables, we can conclude the following:

- There is a very big difference in the personal consumption rate between lifetime renters and homeowners, about 15 percentage points on average.
- Having children can reduce the personal consumption rate by about 4 to 5 percent per child (for conservatism, I have capped this effect at 10 percent).
- The difference in personal consumption rate between upper-income levels and middle-income levels is small, typically less than 5 percentage points, and can practically be ignored.[1]
- Paying off the mortgage early does allow for the personal consumption rate to increase but not by much.

If we want the simplest rule of thumb possible, we would say the retirement income target is 70 percent for renters and 50 percent for homeowners. This is perhaps a little too general, so let us classify households by the level of "investment" they have made, as defined in Table 4.5.

The proposed rules of thumb for retirement income targets (as a percentage of gross final pay) are then given in Table 4.6.

Let me stress that the targets under this new rule of thumb are on the high side for people with higher income. The targets would be lower if mortgage payments extended right up until retirement and lower again if the costs related to children were higher in the last few years before retirement than I have assumed. For many people, the true target is 40 percent. This is illustrated in Appendix C, which shows retirement income targets under a number of alternate scenarios.

The vast majority of the readers of this book will be in the "significant investment" category, meaning they will have a retirement income target of around 50 percent and possibly less. Statistics show that 95 percent of 50- to 59-year-olds in the top income quintile are

Table 4.5   Size of "Investments" Made

Significant	Raised at least one child and made mortgage payments for an extended period
Moderate	Made mortgage payments *or* raised children, not both
Minimal	Rented their entire lives and never raised children

Table 4.6   New Rule of Thumb for Retirement Income Target*

Significant investment	Moderate investment	Minimal investment
50%	60%	70%

*Annual retirement income from all sources as a percentage of gross final earnings.

homeowners and most have families. Even in the third income quintile (the middle-income households), 77 percent are homeowners.

According to Statistics Canada data, renters who have no children and who earn more than $85,000 a year in household income make up only 2.0 percent of all households. Among above-average income households, it is just this 2 percent that would have a 70 percent retirement income target. It is strange that the best-known rule of thumb for a retirement income target would have such a small fraction of the total population in mind.

As mentioned previously, there is another more significant-sized group that has a retirement income target of 70 percent or even higher. That group includes everyone in the bottom 20 to 30 percent of the population in terms of income. Ironically, this low-income group, which actually has a 70 percent or higher income target, is not the audience that is sought out by the banks and financial planners who are recommending a 70 percent target in the first place!

Conclusions

While it would have been preferable to produce a one-size-fits-all rule of thumb for the retirement income target, that proved not to be possible. Among the middle-income to upper-income households, the target tends to be 50 to 70 percent, depending on how much of the total paycheck in the final years of employment goes toward child-raising, mortgage payments, and retirement saving. A significant majority will be at the bottom end of this range and the higher-income households might even have a target below 50 percent.

Note

1. I do want to point out that the retirement income targets would be much higher for the very low-income households, but that is not our focus here.

PART II

THE WEALTH TARGET

Quantifying Your Wealth Target

Now that you have an idea of your retirement income target, you will want to convert that percentage figure into something more useful. If your retirement preparation consists of saving on your own or through a defined contribution plan at your workplace, what you really want to know is how much wealth you need to amass by the time you retire. I will call that your wealth target. This is your most important indicator of your retirement-readiness and the easiest way to monitor your progress.

A Rough-and-Ready Estimate

We will try to approximate your wealth target using an iterative method. Each iteration is a little more sophisticated than the last and should ultimately bring you reasonably close to the right answer, to the extent one exists.

To start, you will need to estimate your final average employment earnings, which you will multiply by the appropriate retirement income target as given in Table 4.6 in the last chapter. For guidance, you might also want to take a look at the additional calculations of the retirement income target that are tabled in Appendix C.

For example, if your final employment earnings were $100,000 and you estimate that your retirement income target is 50 percent, then the question becomes, how much money do you need to generate $50,000 a year in retirement income? By the way, it is the same question for a single person as for a married couple, except that the married couple would take their combined employment earnings and combined Social Security pensions into account.

Using $50,000 as the retirement income target, we will calculate the wealth target in various different ways, starting with the simplest and then slowly building in some refinements:

1. Ignore any calculations and simply save until you have an account balance of half a million dollars. Why half a million? It is a round number and you may have heard other people use a number of that magnitude. You might have even been tempted to target $1 million but at your earnings level, that figure could be very hard to reach. A back-of-the-envelope calculation indicates that half a million dollars is an amount that a reasonably diligent saver with final income of $100,000 could accumulate over a working career. **Estimate 1: $0.5 million**

2. You know that Estimate 1 cannot be correct in every situation. Someone earning twice as much over an entire working career will also want twice as much retirement income. Still, it does provide us with a starting point. Keeping Estimate 1 in the back of your mind, let us try again. This time, estimate the pension you and your spouse will get from Social Security first and subtract it from the $50,000 retirement income target. You need to be fairly accurate in estimating Social Security pension if this exercise is going to be useful. For the sake of example, let us assume that the combined Social Security pension for you and your spouse is $30,000 a year; all you need to worry about is funding the other $20,000 a year. You might not want to buy an annuity but the cost of an annuity is a good proxy for your wealth target. After all, if the wealth target were higher than the cost of an annuity, then why take the risk of managing your own money? Ask an annuity broker or use an online annuity calculator to find out what the single premium would be to buy a $20,000 life annuity with tax-sheltered money. A recent quote by CANNEX Financial Exchanges Limited showed that a male age 65 could buy $20,000 per annum of lifetime annuity for $320,000. For a single female the same age, the premium would be about $350,000. If you have a spouse, you should probably buy a joint and survivor annuity, meaning one that continues to pay out until the death of the second spouse. If the spouses are both age 65 and the annuity reduces by one third on the death of the first spouse, the

annuity premium is also $350,000. **Estimate 2: $320,000 for a single male, $350,000 for a single female or a married couple**

What is an annuity?

In its most common form, a life annuity is a contract in which a person pays a lump sum amount (a single premium) to a life insurance company and in return receives a series of monthly payments for life. The payments either start immediately or at some future age like 65, in which case it is known as a deferred annuity. This chapter deals only with life annuities.

Sometimes, there is a death benefit attached to the annuity, such as a guarantee that 60 or 120 monthly payments will be made regardless of when the individual dies. The residual payments would be paid to a designated beneficiary or estate. Another type of death benefit involves making continued monthly payments for the lifetime of the surviving spouse, in which case it is known as a joint annuity.

3. If your savings are held in a tax-sheltered account, you will be subject to income tax on withdrawals from that account, including tax on annuity payments. This is taken into account already with the retirement income target. If your savings take the form of after-tax monies, you can adjust your wealth target downward to reflect this. At this level of wealth target, the downward adjustment would be about 10 percent. For purposes of this wealth target estimate, however, we will assume that income from your retirement savings is taxable.

4. If you plan to retire at an extreme age, be it high or low, you need to adjust your wealth target to reflect it. If we consider the normal range for retirement ages to be 60 to 65, then retiring at 55 or 70 would be extreme but is certainly in the realm of possibility. The math we will need to adjust the wealth target for retirement age will be developed later in this chapter so we will skip this refinement for now.

5. Then there are all the contingencies in life that can have an adverse impact on either your spending needs or your wealth. Divorce and long-term care are two examples. You might choose to ignore these contingencies but more likely you will want to keep something in reserve, just in case. Without being scientific about how much more is going to be enough, let's agree that an extra $100,000 would help you to sleep better.

Final estimate: $320,000 to $450,000 (in tax-sheltered savings) but it could be more if you retire very young or you are really concerned about the unknowns.

As a result of this back of the envelope approach, we can tentatively conclude that for every $10,000 or so of retirement income, one needs roughly $160,000 to $225,000 (or perhaps more) in tax-sheltered assets. This helps to demystify the wealth target a little, but it is too vague and involves too much actuarial sleight of hand for us to stop there. By accounting for various contingencies with arbitrary buffers, we have essentially piled uncertainty on top of uncertainty. Such a situation fosters anxiety, which is something we can do without when we are about to retire. We therefore need to move beyond these fuzzy numbers and inject a little more actuarial science into estimating the wealth target.

A More Actuarial Approach

Imperfect as it is, the foregoing does at least highlight many of the factors that can affect the wealth target. We will now look at these factors a little more closely to see if we can arrive at a more precise figure. To the extent uncertainty remains, we will try to quantify it.

Employment Income

The connection between the wealth target and pre-retirement income is obvious. The two are not exactly proportionate, however, because of the leveraging effect of Social Security pensions, which are of greater importance at lower income levels but constitute a progressively smaller percentage of our overall retirement income as we move up the pay scale.

For instance, if we establish a retirement income target of 50 percent of final earnings and agree that we need $210,000 of assets for every $10,000 of income, then Table 5.1 shows our estimated wealth target at various income levels. You will notice that the wealth target as a multiple of income rises with income level.

Social Security Pensions

When forecasting your retirement needs and assets, the one thing you can estimate with a high degree of certainty is your Social Security

Table 5.1   How Wealth Target Varies by Income Level

Income level:	$100,000	$200,000	$300,000
Retirement income target	$50,000	$100,000	$150,000
Social Security pension	($30,000)	($36,000)	($36,000)
Net retirement income needed	$20,000	$64,000	$114,000
Approximate wealth target	**$420,000**	**$1,344,000**	**$2,394,000**
Wealth target as a multiple of income	**4.2**	**6.7**	**8.0**

Assume a 50% retirement income target and maximum Social Security pension of $30,000 a year.

pension. Using online tools, federal agencies can help you make that estimate, whether in the United States or Canada.

From the headlines that arise from time to time, you might be worried that these government pensions will not be there when you retire or that they will be reduced because of inadequate funding. This worry is not totally unfounded given that the starting age for Old Age Security (OAS) pension in Canada was recently changed from 65 to 67 with effect from 2029 or that the age for full Social Security pension in the United States is gradually increasing to 67 as well. Other developed countries around the world have also been pushing back their normal retirement age for full Social Security pensions, with 67 becoming the new normal.

Nevertheless, the reader of this book is unlikely to have to worry about further changes in the pensionable age or other cutbacks in Social Security pension occurring any time soon. These types of changes tend to be announced decades before they take effect, as happened with the change in normal retirement age in the United States. Moreover, the backlash from an outright reduction in benefits would almost certainly be greater than any political party would be prepared to face. If there are going to be any adverse changes to these programs in the foreseeable future, they would more likely take the form of gradual increases in the required contribution rates rather than any headline-grabbing takeaways.

How Will You Save?

Most people save for retirement in tax-assisted vehicles. They get the tax deduction in the year a contribution is made and pay tax only when they withdraw money. This tax treatment is applicable to RRSPs and DC pension plans in Canada, and to 401(k) plans and IRAs in the United States.

More and more, people are using special savings vehicles in which they contribute after-tax dollars but pay no tax on the investment earnings nor when they withdraw their money. This applies to Tax-Free Savings Accounts (TFSAs) in Canada and Roth IRAs in the United States.

Finally, some people will have built their wealth in vehicles that are not tax-sheltered at all, such as brokerage accounts, employer-sponsored stock purchase plans, and bank accounts. Once again, withdrawals from these types of vehicles are not subject to tax, other than possibly capital gains tax.

When it comes to determining how much money you need to retire, the difference between monies that are subject to tax when they are withdrawn and monies that produce taxable income can be significant. If retirement savings are the main source of retirement income other than Social Security, the retirement income may straddle more than one tax bracket so we should think in terms of average income tax rates rather than a marginal rate. If the average income tax rate after retirement is 10 percent, then $400,000 in a tax-assisted vehicle is equivalent to about $360,000 in after-tax dollars. The difference is greater at higher wealth targets.

What Investment Return Can You Expect?

Having diligently saved for 30 or more years and reached retirement with what you think is a big enough account balance, it may seem almost unfair that you have to continue to worry about how your investments will perform. You can of course make the problem go away by buying a life annuity from an insurance company, but as we will see later on, few people do. For everyone else, the savings balance they need to accumulate depends heavily on the investment return their monies will earn after retirement.

Given the low-interest-rate environment that we have become mired in, your investment return over the next 25 years can be as low as nil or as high as 10 percent a year. Where you land in that range depends on three factors:

1. *Equity weighting.* In spite of concerns about stock markets becoming overheated, a higher equity weighting in your portfolio is your best bet for achieving higher returns over the long run. With interest rates on long-term bonds in the 2 percent range, you cannot expect bonds to provide a good return in the years to come. To do better, you will need

to take risks. This is why investment experts like Morneau Shepell's Rob Boston are saying that 70–30 is the new 60–40 (equity–bond asset mix).

2. *Investment management fees.* Unless the firm that is managing your monies (if you have one) can demonstrate they consistently achieve higher returns than the benchmark indices, you should expect that your own returns will just match the benchmarks, less whatever fees you are paying. Those annual fees will range from about 25 basis points (1/4 of 1 percent) for ETFs to as much as 3 percent in the case of some high cost equity mutual funds.

3. *Luck.* Sometimes equities underperform for long periods of time. The Dow Jones reached 1,000 for the first time in 1966 but then went into the doldrums and did not breach that threshold again for another 17 years. The fact that the S&P 500 index has more than tripled in the past 6 years probably increases the chances of a substantial correction and/or a prolonged sideways move. You have to hope you are not caught in a downdraft.

To estimate the possible range in average annual returns more precisely, I called upon the actuaries in Morneau Shepell's Retirement Solutions practice to perform a Monte Carlo simulation. If we assume a 60–40 equity/bond asset mix for the portfolio, the simulation reveals that the return over the next 25 years is likely to land between 2.8 percent and 9.1 percent but with some residual risk of an even lower return. Nothing in the investment world is ever totally certain.

My sense is that this is too much risk to be taking over the rest of your life. In a later chapter, we will reduce that risk by adopting a slightly more conservative asset mix and assuming the purchase of an annuity at age 75 or 80.

How Safe Is Your Marriage?

Splitting a household into two is expensive. While retirement experts might dispute the income needs of a typical household after retirement, they all agree that consumption does not fall in proportion to the decrease in the number of occupants in the household. Instead, they would say that household spending is proportional to the *square root* of the number of occupants. For example, if there are 2 people in a household and total spending equals 200 units, then a household with just 1 occupant would need about 140 units to maintain the same standard of living (since the square root of 2 is about 1.4).

Consequently, married people are more vulnerable to coming up short of their wealth target than single people. They are especially vulnerable if a marriage breakdown occurs close to the time of retirement. Household assets get divided in half (I am assuming an equal split) while income needs decline only 30 or maybe 35 percent based on the square root principle. What was enough money before divorce becomes inadequate once former spouses are living separately.

As an example, let us take the $200,000 employment income scenario from Table 5.1 and see what happens to the two spouses after a marriage breakdown. If we assume an equal split of both assets and Social Security pensions upon divorce, the result is shown in Table 5.2. Each spouse following divorce is about $315,000 short of the assets needed to maintain their pre-divorce standard of living. To avoid this deficit, they would have had to maintain an asset buffer equal to 40 percent of the wealth target in contemplation of a possible marriage breakdown, but suffice it to say that few people do this.

In spite of the significant shortfall in assets triggered by a divorce, there are several reasons why you are not going to pad your wealth target by 40 percent. First, how would you square that with your spouse as you do your retirement planning together? Second, if the marriage does survive, that buffer ends up being a rather large amount of cash to be lying fallow over your lifetime. Finally, the financial consequences of divorce can be mitigated to some extent without the

Table 5.2   How Income Needs Change after Divorce

	While married	Spouse A after divorce	Spouse B after divorce
Retirement income target	$100,000	$65,000	$65,000
Social Security pension	($36,000)	($18,000)	($18,000)
Net retirement income from savings	$64,000	$47,000	$47,000
Wealth target	$1,344,000	$987,000	$987,000
Actual assets	**$1,344,000**	**$672,000**	**$672,000**
Shortfall	**Nil**	**$315,000**	**$315,000**

This assumes $200,000 in employment earnings before retirement, a 50% retirement income target while married, and same standard of living to be maintained after divorce.

buffer. For instance, one or both spouses might return to work at least part time or simply postpone retirement if they are still working at the time of marriage breakdown. If they had already retired and a return to work is not possible, they may have other assets to fall back on.

If that backup plan fails as well, and they are not prepared to accept such a large drop in their standard of living, then perhaps an explicit buffer is necessary after all. Each situation will differ.

When Will You Retire?

The earlier that you retire, the more money you will need, simply because you would be expected to live that many more years in retirement. Table 5.3 shows how the amount of money you will need varies with retirement age. These particular numbers are based arbitrarily on the wealth target at age 64 being $400,000. The variability in the wealth target by retirement age is breathtaking. It varies almost sevenfold between retirement age 58 versus 70.

The reason why it varies so much is the leverage created by the Social Security pension. In this particular example, it was assumed that the total retirement income was $50,000 with $30,000 of that

Table 5.3 How the Wealth Target Depends on Age (Target at age 64 = $400,000)

Retirement age	Wealth target
58	$616,000
59	$582,000
60	$546,000
61	$510,000
62	$474,000
63	$437,000
64	$400,000
65	$362,000
66	$310,000
67	$257,000
68	$203,000
69	$148,000
70	$92,000

Based on an underlying annuity interest rate of 2.5 percent, total income of $50,000 and Social Security pension at 65 of $30,000 for 2 people, increasing 8% a year for delayed retirement.

coming from Social Security pensions (for both spouses) at age 65. If pension commencement is delayed until age 70, Social Security pension climbs another 40 percent,[1] so it becomes an even greater proportion of the overall retirement income target. That is why the wealth target becomes so small for people who delay retirement. If we crunched the numbers for a household with higher retirement income or for a single person, this leveraging effect is less pronounced. That is because proportionately less pension income would be coming from Social Security.

How Long Will You Live?

When it comes to saving for your own retirement, longevity risk has nothing to do with how long the average person will live but everything to do with your own life expectancy, something we cover in Chapter 9. Individual longevity risk stems from not knowing whether you will live another 40 days or 40 years. We will learn that the matter is not totally outside of your control; you may be able to extend your life span significantly by making some lifestyle changes.

You do not have to worry about outliving your savings if you purchase an annuity, but it is a real concern if you are going to try to manage your retirement savings on your own after retirement. To give an idea of the potential variability, let us take a 63-year-old male whose life expectancy reflects the average of the general population. If we ignore the 5 percent chance he has of dying before age 70 and the 5 percent chance of living beyond 100, this person's death can realistically occur anytime between age 70 and 100. That makes for a thorny retirement planning challenge in the absence of purchasing an annuity.

Next Steps

In the next few chapters, we will delve more deeply into the above issues, as well as a few others, before we can conclude on the wealth target. As a result, the estimate of the wealth target described above should be regarded as little more than a rough approximation.

Note

1. This varies slightly between the United States and Canada.

CHAPTER 6

Why Interest Rates Will Stay Low (And Why You Should Care)

Unless you participate in a defined benefit pension plan, your standard of living in retirement will depend on how much wealth you can accumulate before you retire. It is quite likely that your wealth target has increased sharply in the past few years, and all because of what is happening to interest rates. The lower that rates are, the more money it takes to generate a given level of income, and unfortunately for savers, interest rates are not only very low right now, they will almost certainly be staying low for many years to come.

In the aftermath of the Great Recession of 2008–2009, interest rates in most developed countries sank to record lows, where they continue to languish. In both the United States and Canada, yields on 10-year government of Canada bonds are hovering in the 2 percent range. By comparison, the average yield over the 50-year period ending in 2008 (when the financial crisis hit) was close to 8 percent.

One would think that interest rates fell so far because the recession prompted companies to conserve cash instead of borrowing to expand their businesses. Central banks flooded the monetary system with liquidity to force interest rates lower and thereby stimulate an economic recovery. The US Federal Reserve Board in particular pushed longer-term rates lower in dramatic fashion with their trillion dollar *quantitative easing* program.

Quantitative easing (QE)

This involved the Federal Reserve buying longer term US Treasury bonds and mortgage-backed securities in large volumes. In the third tranche, known as QE3, the Federal Reserve was buying $85 billion of securities a month until June 2013, when the Fed announced it would be tapering its bond buying. The program ended in October 2014.

If this is indeed why interest rates fell, how then to explain the fact they are not rising again more than 6 years after the global economies hit bottom and a year after the biggest injection of liquidity in history? Given the size of the monetary stimulus, we would have expected to see long-term government bond yields well on their way back to normal levels. This is not happening.

Interest rates did start to climb for a while when the Federal Reserve hinted in early 2013 that QE3 would be coming to an end. Yields on 10-year US Treasuries rose from 1.4 percent in May 2013 to 3 percent by December 2013 just on the prospect of a tapering off of the Fed's bond purchases. By the start of 2014, almost everyone finally bought into the prospect of a continued and pronounced rise in interest rates. At that point, though, the bond market perversely went in the other direction. By January 2015, yields fell to a new all-time low and that happened without any new intervention in the markets by the Federal Reserve.

Could it be that another factor was responsible for keeping rates so low? If so, is it possible that interest rates will not be returning to so-called normal levels for a long time to come?

As highlighted in a paper by Michael Walker,[1] another powerful force is indeed at work: demographics. The aging of the population has been slowly changing the balance of borrowers and savers for the past 25 years and reached what appeared to be a tipping point around 2010, at least in North America and Europe. That trend will continue for decades to come, and as a result, any increase we do see in interest rates in the foreseeable future is likely to be minor and to take the form of a short-term aberration. This is bad news for retirees.

The Rise of the Savers

Viewed from 30,000 feet, interest rates depend on supply and demand—the demand by borrowers for funds in the form of a mortgage on a house or a car loan, for instance, and the supply of funds from the banks to allow that loan to happen. In reality, the bank is only a middleman in these transactions, as the funds emanate from other people, the savers, who are looking for a place to invest their money. When we are trying to forecast where interest rates are going over the long term, it ultimately comes down to whether there will be more borrowers than savers.

Of course, people of any age might save, be it for retirement or to buy a car, and people of almost any age might borrow. That being said, it is younger people who do most of the borrowing and older people who have most of the assets. For the sake of simplicity, we can adopt the dividing line proposed by Walker and consider people under 50 to be net borrowers and those who are age 50 to 75 to be net savers.[2] It helps to define a ratio, which I will call the *saver ratio.*[3]

$$\text{Saver ratio} = \frac{\text{Total population between ages 50 and 75}}{\text{Total population under 50}}$$

A lower saver ratio means fewer savers and hence higher interest rates as funds that are made available for borrowing are scarce. In 1990 for instance, the saver ratio was 27 percent in both Canada and the United States. In hindsight, we can say that 27 percent is relatively low, which largely explains why interest rates were so high at the time.

Not only were nominal interest rates high in 1990, so were real rates. The real rates on risk-free federal government bonds, for instance, were in the 4 percent range. Table 6.1 shows the saver ratios for highly developed countries in 1990 (the Eurozone, which consists of 27 countries, is lumped together).

As long as the population is growing at a fairly steady pace and average life spans do not change, there should always be more

Table 6.1   Saver Ratios in 1990

Country	Saver ratio
Canada	26.8%
United States	27.2%
Japan	36.7%
Eurozone (27)	35.2%
China	16.9%

Ratio of population ages 50–75 vs. population under 50
OECD Statistics as compiled by Morneau Shepell

borrowers than savers and the saver ratio should remain more or less constant at a level below 40 percent. This was true for practically the entire second half of the twentieth century.

The situation started to change, though, thanks to three demographic factors that would have been expected to be fairly stable. Though it would take decades to come to fruition, these factors would eventually tip the balance from borrowers to savers.

The first factor is that people started to live considerably longer, a phenomenon that we describe in some detail in Chapter 8. A longer life span makes the saver group larger than it otherwise would be as fewer savers are dying.

The second factor was a global and long-term decline in fertility rates. This is the rate that measures the average number of children per woman over a lifetime. In some cases, the drop has been dramatic. In the 1960s, the fertility rate in China and Brazil was close to 6, whereas today it is about 1.9 in Brazil and 1.6 in China. The fertility rate has plunged in the United States and Canada as well, from nearly 4 in 1960 to less than 2 today. A lower fertility rate means the borrower group grows more slowly.

The third factor has to do with the baby boomer population, which, as we all know, is aging rapidly. All those baby boomers who, for the most part were in their 30s in the 1980s, and hence big borrowers, are now in their 60s and have become equally big savers.

As a result of these three factors, the saver ratio has climbed steadily. Figure 6.1 shows that the saver ratio in Canada has climbed from 20 percent in 1980 to 42 percent in 2010. The rise in the United States has been a little less steep but is still significant, having gone from 26 percent to 39 percent in the same time frame. It is no coincidence that during the same period, the real yields on long-term government bonds dropped from over 5 percent down to about 1 percent. When we project the ratio for either country into the future, they are both well over 40 percent from 2020 and on.[4]

The same phenomenon is unfolding in Europe as well. In fact, the impact is even more dramatic there because the population is aging faster. We saw that the saver ratio in the Eurozone was 35 percent in 1990. It is now 45 percent, and look at what has happened to interest rates there. In March 2015, the yield on 10-year government bonds in Germany was a mere 0.18 percent, while in Switzerland, the yield actually turned negative for a while, meaning that one had to pay the Swiss banks or the bond issuers to hold their money!

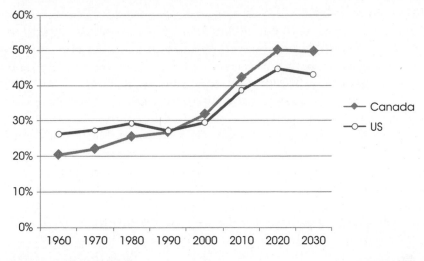

Figure 6.1   Saver Ratio

While this phenomenon has taken most of the developed world by surprise, it is something we could have seen coming. We knew that the demographics were changing, and all we had to do is look at the outcome in Japan, where the demographic changes took place a lot sooner. In hindsight, the Japan experience seems remarkably similar to what Europe is going through now.

The Japan Experience

Japan set the world on fire in the 1980s. Real estate prices and stock prices skyrocketed and Japan became a world leader in automobile production and electronics. The 1980s was also the last decade when Japan still had a reasonably young population. The Saver Ratio in 1980 was 27.2 percent, but it was starting to climb.

Japan's explosive economic growth ended in 1990. While its lacklustre growth in the early 1990s might be blamed on the crippling effect of the bursting of the 1980s asset bubble, another reason eventually had to be found why growth remained anemic for many years to come. That other reason was the aging of the population. The total fertility rate had dropped to 1.4, which is well below replacement level, and life spans had improved to become the longest in the world. The saver ratio had climbed to 36.7 percent by 1990 and breached what now appears to be the very significant 40 percent threshold by 1993. That saver ratio has continued its rise ever since, reaching 51.3 percent by 2000 and 58.1 percent by 2010. During the period 1990 to 2010, Japan flirted with deflation and interest rates on long-term government bonds remained stubbornly below 1 percent.

Contrast this to the period from 1955 to 1975, the time when what has become known as the Japanese "miracle" occurred. The economic boom that took place catapulted Japan from a country that had been devastated by World War II to the second largest economy in the world. In 1960, Japan's saver ratio was a mere 18.8 percent.

More than 20 years after Japan first fell into its economic malaise, there is no sign that it is coming to grips with its problems of low growth, low inflation, and low interest rates. Its saver ratio, by the way, will continue to climb for the foreseeable future.

Applicability to the United States and Canada

One would like to think that Japan is somehow different, and that its economic woes are unrelated to the situation in the Western world. Perhaps it was just a matter of Japan's not having recovered from the 1980s asset bubble. Maybe it protected its local businesses too much from global competition. Or one could argue that Japan did not restructure its banks quickly or meaningfully enough following the losses it incurred when the bubble burst. The idea that the near-zero or below zero inflation rate and interest rates in Japan would eventually seize North America and Europe in its grip seemed inconceivable.

It now seems increasingly clear that the only real difference between the developed economies of the West and Japan is that Japan's demographics had a 20-year head start. This is shown in Figure 6.2 where the saver ratios of Japan and Europe are added onto what we showed in the previous figure. By 2020, both Canada and the United States will have a higher saver ratio than Japan did in 1995.

The good news is that the saver ratio in North America will not be climbing to the extremes seen in Japan. The United States, in particular, is a little better off since it has higher fertility rates and higher mortality rates than Canada or Japan. Unfortunately, that may not be good enough to bring back the boom times of the 1980s and 1990s.

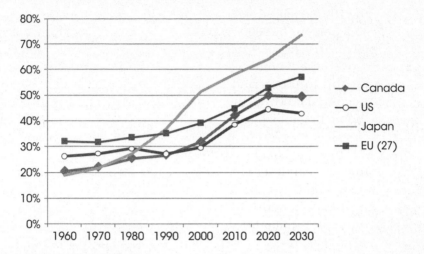

Figure 6.2 Saver Ratio

Possible Remedies

If the demographic shift means that the Western world is going to find itself in the same economic bind as Japan, we should be scrambling for solutions.

One might think that reducing interest rates would help to revive demand for borrowing and stimulate growth in the economy. This mechanism has worked in the past when rates were very high and we were in the midst of a savers' market. In fact, the only problem historically with this sort of monetary stimulus is that it has worked too well at times. When the monetary tap was not turned off quickly enough, the economy has been known to overheat and create even worse problems, such as the 2007 US housing bubble.

Thus, the actions of central banks to reduce interest rates should, in theory, be an effective way to get the economy moving again. The trouble is that it does not work so well in a borrowers' market, as we now find ourselves in. For one thing, interest rates cannot go any lower. For another, the behavior of savers does not follow classical economic theory anymore.

When interest rates are very low, as they are now, the savers (who are now retired or close to retirement) know that it takes a larger block of capital to produce the same income stream. So when interest rates drop further, these savers do not suddenly spend more, as theory suggests they would. Instead, savers actually *increase* their savings rate and spend less. This phenomenon is not just theoretical; it was demonstrated by the IMF in a study of urban savings behavior in China.

It is not clear whether there is any way for Western economies to escape the quagmire of low interest rates, low inflation, and sluggish growth. Demographic trends indicate the advanced economies will continue to age for the next several decades.

If we are expecting China to pull us out of this slow-growth phase, think again. The growth in the Chinese working-age population has slowed since 1980 and is projected to turn negative as soon as 2020. China cannot help the rest of the world if it cannot help itself. The Chinese saver ratio, which has been so much lower than in the West and largely explains China's phenomenal growth, is rising quickly. As shown in Figure 6.3, China's saver ratio will pass the 40 percent tipping point by 2020 and will even reach 50 percent by 2030.

The only other way I can see for the Western world to escape the fate of Japan is if people change their consumption behaviors. When it comes to consumption, could 60 become the new 50, in which case the saver ratios will have to be recalculated? It is perhaps possible that people in their 50s will spend more and save less, but it certainly did not happen in Japan, and what is going on currently in the Western economies indicate it is not going to be much of a factor here, either.

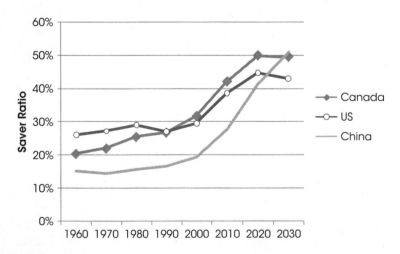

Figure 6.3   China is Next

Implications

So far, we have been talking about how changing demographics affect interest rates. They also have a very direct effect on economic growth, which indirectly affects stock prices. A paper by Arnott and Chaves quantifies a slightly different ratio, the ratio of workers to retirees, and uses it to show the existence of an economic tailwind in previous decades, boosting growth beyond what was otherwise possible. Because of shift in that ratio, that tailwind is now an economic headwind.[5]

The demographic shift can be illustrated by the ratio of the working-age population (ages 20 to 64) to the retiree population (ages 65 and over). This is shown in Figure 6.4 for various countries. By 2030, the United States will have just 2.7 workers per retiree, less than half what it had in 1960.

It is largely this headwind that is responsible for real per capita growth rates in the world's advanced economies having declined to Japan's levels in recent years. European economies have been on the brink of both deflation and recession ever since the Great Recession ended in 2009.

Economic growth is important because without it, most companies cannot be expected to have robust growth in revenues and profit. If Japan is any indication, the stock markets in Western economies will generally languish at some point. There will still

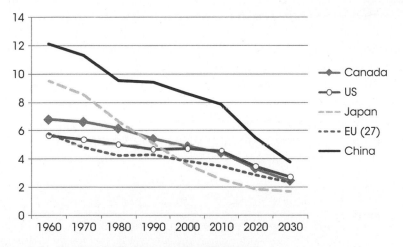

Figure 6.4 Worker to Retiree Ratios Plummet

be an equity premium, but it is hard to see how equity returns can average 6 percent or more a year in real terms as they have historically.

The United States is slightly better off with longer-term bond yields in the 2 to 3 percent range and higher growth than the rest of the developed world. This might be because the saver ratio is a little higher there than in Canada and Europe but the demographic trends are keeping interest rates and economic growth abnormally low in the United States as well and its saver ratio is still headed in the wrong direction.

As a result, interest rates will almost certainly stay low for many years to come, both in real and nominal terms. That is not to say that US government bond yields cannot rise to 4 percent again (in nominal terms), especially during the late stages of an economic cycle, but yields at this level are unlikely to be sustained, much less yields at historic norms of 6 percent or more.

Savers who are nearing retirement and who used to count on real returns on their portfolios of 4 percent or more should expect real returns more in the range of 3 percent, and even then, only if they are investing heavily in equities. Nominal returns will more than likely average less than 6 percent, and maybe even 5 percent will be difficult to achieve.

Skeptics might think this is far too conservative. After all, look what the stock markets have done since 2009. The S&P 500 more than tripled from its low. I would caution that this is not to be taken as an indicator of future market trends. The very impetus for the dramatic rise in the stock markets in developed countries—declining interest rates—is also the reason they will do less well in the years to come. Once rates have stabilized at a low level, the only way for stock prices to go much higher is for dividend growth to accelerate, but this is unlikely to happen if overall economic growth is sluggish.

Finally, annuities, which are closely linked to long-term bond yields, will remain costly for many years to come, though perhaps not as prohibitively expensive as they have been for the past year or two.

Notes

1. Michael Walker, *Why are interest rates so low? A framework for modeling current global financial developments*, The Fraser Institute, January 20, 2015.

2. Walker suggests 75 as the top end of the range since income needs rise once people require long-term care. My analysis of long-term care statistics suggests the top end of the range might be more like 80. I have nevertheless left the 50–75 range intact.
3. Walker calls this the Saver/Borrower ratio.
4. Actually, 42.2 percent in Canada and 38.6 percent in the United States.
5. Robert Arnott and Dennis Chaves, "A New 'New Normal' in Demography and Economic Growth," *Journal of Indexes* (September/October 2013).

CHAPTER 7

How Spending Decreases with Age

In establishing the retirement income target, it is natural to assume that we need to maintain the same level of personal consumption in retirement as we enjoyed in our final years of employment. In fact, this was the basis for how we determined the range of retirement income targets in Chapter 4.

Left unsaid is whether our spending habits continue unabated for the rest of our lives. Do we spend as much in real terms at age 80 as we do at 60? In other words, does our spending really have to keep up with inflation?

I would start by noting that the basket of goods one consumes as a retiree will be very different from the basket that applies to a 35-year-old. The two baskets will be different even if you ignore the portion of spending that relates to children or employment at age 35. With the contents being so different, there is no particular reason to think the two baskets should cost the same. Why should the amounts that retirees spend on lawn bowling, bingo nights, and hearing aids magically add up to what they used to spend on rock-climbing, boys' night out, and designer suits?

In spite of these doubts, the thinking that retirement income needs to keep pace with price inflation continues to be pervasive. It is this implicit belief that underlies the traditional practice in Social Security pensions and public-sector defined benefit pension plans of automatically increasing pensions each year to keep up with inflation. It is fair to say that most of us will not abandon this belief easily; at least not without compelling evidence to the contrary.

If your spending really did increase every year, consumption models say your accumulated retirement savings will slowly decline as you make withdrawals in your retirement years. Indeed, a paper by Moore and Mitchell[1] confirms this presumption when they make the following observation about consumption theories: "About the most precise prediction that can be offered is that virtually no model would predict older people's assets to continue to grow during retirement." But if assets do keep growing, at least after age 70, what does that say about these consumption theories?

Doubts

Just as I had expressed skepticism about the 70 percent retirement income target, my own personal experience led me to doubt that the elderly continue to spend as much money beyond a certain age. My own parents did not buy any new durable goods, like furniture and cars, in the last 10 years, and it was not for lack of money. There is no shortage of anecdotal experience of people in their 80s who no longer drive, rarely go to restaurants, or take few trips, if any, outside of the city. Their doctor visits and prescription drugs are paid for, so the only visible spending is on health-related items that are not covered by Medicare. Provided they remain fit enough to live independently, it is hard to see what else they could be spending their money on.

I suggested this to a friend of mine a while back, and he instantly objected, saying his 85-year-old dad spent a lot of money. I asked him on what, and my friend was temporarily at a loss. He started to mention that his dad paid the rent for a daughter in her 50s, but even as the words came out of his mouth, it dawned on him that he couldn't think of any personal expenditure that his dad made, other than spending a modest amount on food and condo maintenance fees.

On philosophical grounds, there is something vaguely discomfiting about asserting that older people do not need as much money. It is almost like saying we can take some money away from them because they do not need it as much as we (younger people) do. No one is trying to take any money away from anybody, but it is important to understand spending patterns among the elderly since it affects the wealth target.

In *The Real Retirement*, I mentioned the 1992 study by Borsch-Supan[2] of 40,000 German households that found that the households did draw down their assets somewhat in their 60s but then, contrary to all theoretical expectations, assets started rising again after age 70. This is not the only study. Researchers in various countries have made great strides in identifying just how our consumption patterns evolve over the course of our retirement. Overwhelmingly, the results of their research have revealed that consumption in our retirement years is far from steady after all. The higher amount spent on health care as we age is more than offset by reductions in spending in many other areas. The age at which this starts, and the speed of the decline, obviously vary, but in most cases, overall spending starts to diminish just a few years into retirement.

Consider, for example, US census data compiled by HS Dent, a US-based economic forecasting firm. The data show how spending on certain items is very age-dependent. I have condensed the results down to a comparison of spending at age 60 versus age 80. Table 7.1 lists items on which spending declines by at least 50 percent between these two ages and Table 7.2 identifies areas where spending increases.

Spending among the elderly declined significantly in other areas, such as the purchase of new automobiles, but not quite by 50 percent. As an aside, one cannot help but notice just how dreary the items are in Table 7.2 on which we dedicate so much of our spending by the time we reach 80.

Table 7.1   Spending Drops More than 50% on These Items

China and other dinnerware
Admission to movies, theater, opera, and concerts
Airline fares
Alcoholic beverages at restaurants, bars, etc.
Cigarettes
Mattresses
Camping equipment
Men's coats, jackets, and furs
Men's underwear
Women's dresses

Compares spending at age 80 versus age 60
Data Source: HS Dent Foundation

Table 7.2   Spending Increases More than 50% on These Items

Hearing aids
Prescription drugs and medicines
Gardening and lawn-care services
Management fees for security
Nursing or convalescent homes
Funeral, burial, or cremation services

Compares spending at age 80 versus age 60
Data Source: HS Dent Foundation

Quantifying the Decline in Consumption

Obviously, the list of goods and services in Tables 7.1 and 7.2 is meant to be illustrative rather than comprehensive. We already knew that spending on a given item can rise or fall spectacularly with age; the question remains whether aggregate spending rises, falls, or stays the same. There is some rather robust data in both Canada and the United States to answer this question.

Starting with the United States, Michael D. Hurd and Susann Rohwedder analyzed extensive data from various sources, including the Health and Retirement Study (HRS) and the Consumption and Activities Mail Survey (CAMS). The CAMS is longitudinal, which, when combined with data from the HRS, makes the results quite credible.

Longitudinal survey

In a longitudinal survey, the same subjects are observed repeatedly or continuously over a period of time. This is in contrast to cross-sectional surveys, where the subjects being observed will differ from one observation period to the next. Longitudinal studies are very useful in studying how individual behavior changes over time.

Their work[3] confirms that consumption does decline with age, and rather emphatically at that. The rate of decline depends on

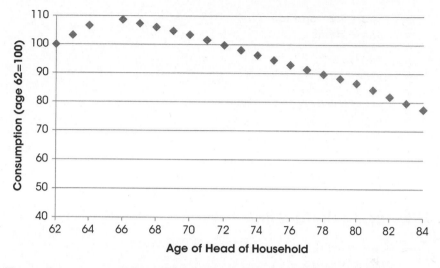

Figure 7.1 Consumption Change for US Married Couples
Data Source: Hurd and Rohwedder, July 2012 EBRI study

whether one is single or married and also by level of education. Consider one of the largest subgroups, married couples where the age gap between partners is less than 5 years. If the couple is college-educated, the rate of decline in consumption is lower than for less well-educated cohorts but is still significant. As Figure 7.1 shows, married retired couples with a college degree will tend to increase spending from age 62 to 64, but then spending in real terms starts to fall rather steadily and continues to do so beyond age 80. By 84, spending in real terms is 23 percent less than it was at age 62.

We find essentially the same results in Canada. Using the results from the Survey of Household Spending that is compiled by Statistics Canada, McKinsey & Company has worked through the data to determine the consumption patterns for Canadians. I have taken a subset of McKinsey's results, specifically the consumption data for households in the third and fourth quintile. I have focused on this segment of the population since it represents the middle income and upper-middle income portions of the population, the 40 percent of the population that is most at risk of retiring with low pensions relative to their final employment income. The results are shown in Figure 7.2.

Compared to a household where the head is age 54, the average Canadian household headed by a 77-year-old spends only 60 percent

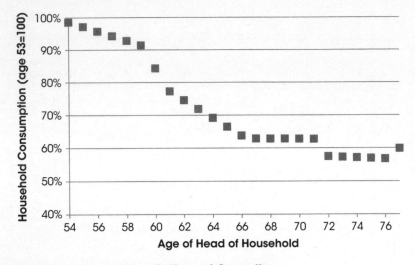

Figure 7.2 Consumption Pattern of Canadians
Data Source: Statistics Canada Family Expenditure Surveys 1982–1992 and Survey of Household Spending 1997 to 2008, with special thanks to McKinsey & Company

as much. The fall in consumption appears to be even more pronounced than in the United States, though much of the difference between countries vanishes when we take into account the differences in starting age, subgroup and methodology. For one thing, the starting age for the Canadian numbers is 54 when households are still supporting children and consumption on children is implicitly included in the result. If we focus on the drop in consumption for Canadians between ages 62 and 77, the percentage decline is almost the same as for US households. What we can glean from all this is that the steady consumption hypothesis is soundly refuted by the data. Consumption falls significantly in real terms throughout one's retirement years.

While we could stop there, why not go further afield to see if researchers in another highly developed and affluent country independently observed similar results? And what more appropriate example than Germany, the land where Otto Von Bismarck established the first formal Social Security system more than a century ago?

The Household Budget Survey of the Statistical Office in Germany compiles highly detailed data on a monthly basis on expenditures by household. The data for 2012 is summarized in Figure 7.3,

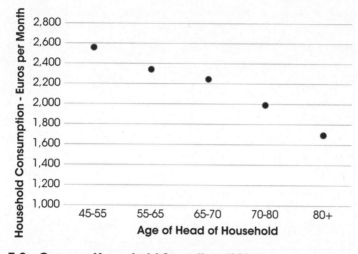

Figure 7.3   German Household Spending (2014)

Data Source: Statistisches Bundesamt (2014) with special thanks to Britta Stöver.

broken down by age of the head of the household. It shows that consumption peaks when the head of the household is between age 45 and 55 and is significantly lower at older ages.

The average monthly consumption level in the 80+ category is 1,694 euros versus 2,341 euros for the 55–65 age group. This represents a drop in consumption of 27 percent, which, if we take into consideration slight differences in the definition of the age groups, is highly consistent with what we have just seen for the United States and Canada.

Given the extensive data from the United States, Canada, and Germany, we can conclude rather definitively that the steady decline in consumption by age during the retirement period is a reality. In Table 7.3, we approximate the rate of decline.

I readily acknowledge that the annual rate of decline in consumption as shown in Table 7.3 was not established with as much

Table 7.3   The Rate of Decline in Consumption (US and Canada)

Age range	Annual rate of decline
65–69	1.25 percent
70–79	1.75 percent
80+	2.75 percent

actuarial rigor as I would have liked. It more or less fits the observed data from all three countries, but there are some variations in the subclassifications of household, such as single versus married or by education level. Table 7.3 is still useful for our purposes since it does three things:

1. It changes the conversation; rather than debating whether compensation declines or not, the question becomes, at what rate does consumption decline, and what are the implications? Tabling some rates puts a stake in the ground by providing a first approximation of the rate of decline.
2. It underscores the fact that the rate of decline accelerates, something most of us have probably witnessed with our own parents or grandparents after a certain age.
3. It allows us to refine our estimates of how much money we will need in retirement, and while the rates might not be precise, nor equally applicable to every household, they are much better than assuming the rate of decline is nil.

Why Does Consumption Decline?

Before we find a practical use for the percentages in Table 7.3, it is important that we understand better why the decline is occurring. It has already been noted that the basket of goods changes and that it would be sheer coincidence if the consumption level in one's later retirement years matched consumption around the time of retirement. Can we somehow rationalize the rather steady rate at which consumption is dropping?

Consider the four most likely reasons for consumption to decrease over time:

1. Not having sufficient money to maintain the same level of spending
2. Wanting to leave money to one's heirs and saving up for it (the *bequest motive*)
3. Concern about healthcare or long-term care costs with advancing age and setting aside some money as a reserve (precautionary savings)
4. Loss of interest in spending or physical ability to spend

These possible reasons were analyzed at some length in the Borsch-Supan study, and the first three were dismissed by the researchers. This is not to say that those reasons carry no weight at all, only that their overall impact is minor and does not go very far in explaining the phenomenon of declining consumption. The only plausible reason that fit the data closely was declining health and/or the loss of loved ones. Declining health impedes mobility, which makes it more difficult to spend money on travel or entertainment, while the loss of loved ones made it less appealing to do so.

What is not addressed in this chapter is what happens at extreme old age, those last few years of life when some of us can no longer live independently. The fear is that expenditures will spike up enormously and offset all of the savings we accumulated by spending less during the middle retirement years. This issue will be analyzed in some depth in Chapters 10 and 11.

Next Steps

End-of-life issues aside, we now have substantial evidence that declining consumption amongst the elderly is a phenomenon that spans countries as well as time. We also have a cogent rationale as to why it happens and will continue to happen.

We now have to decide how we use this information in determining the wealth target. There are three possible approaches:

1. Ignore it on the grounds it builds some conservatism in the wealth target.
2. Incorporate this directly in the wealth target calculations by using the rates of decline in real spending, as set out in Table 7.3.
3. Take this into account indirectly in computing the wealth target by assuming that the retirement income from retirement savings (as opposed to Social Security pension) does not have to be indexed to inflation.

The first approach involves significant but unquantified conservatism that is likely to be forgotten later on when we will be tempted to pad the wealth target further. The second approach would be fine if we were confident that the explicit (downward) adjustments given in Table 7.3 were precise and applied to everyone but that simply is not the case. For these reasons, I opt for the third approach since it tacitly acknowledges that the decline in spending cannot be ignored but nor can it be quantified with any precision.

Notes

1. Olivia S. Mitchell and James F. Moore, "Retirement Wealth Accumulation and Decumulation, New Developments and Outstanding Opportunities," The Wharton Financial Institutions Center, April 1997.
2. Axel Borsch-Supan, "Saving and Consumption Patterns of the Elderly, The German Case," *Journal of Population Economics*, Bonn, Germany, 5(4) (1992).
3. Hurd and Rohwedder, "Economic Preparation for Retirement," National Bureau of Economic Research, July 2012.

CHAPTER 8

Death Takes a Holiday

Everyone knows we are living longer. For retirement planning purposes it is useful to know just how much longer and who is benefiting the most from this phenomenon. My research into the subject was greatly facilitated by Sun Life, one of the leading insurers in the area of managing longevity risk.

It is important to keep in mind that life expectancy is just an average and like all averages, it can be misleading and even dangerous if used too literally. For instance, assume that there are 1,000 men age 60 and the year is 1950. The life expectancy for 60-year-old men in 1950 was 17.7, but that is not to say that all 60-year-olds eventually died between the ages of 77 and 78. In fact, only 40 out of 1,000 would have died in that 1-year interval. The deaths of the other 960 men would have been scattered across all ages from 60 up to 103.

> ## Life expectancy and mortality rates
>
> To express how long we can expect to live, actuaries use the term *life expectancy*. This is an average taken over all future ages up to the end of the mortality table. Life expectancy is measured from a given age, such as 60.
>
> Another way to talk about longevity is in terms of *mortality rates*. The mortality rate at a given age is the probability of dying within the next 12 months. When an actuary says *mortality* is improving, it means that mortality rates are dropping.

Figure 8.1 shows when these 1,000 men from 1950 would have died. For instance, about 16 of them (1.6 percent) would have passed

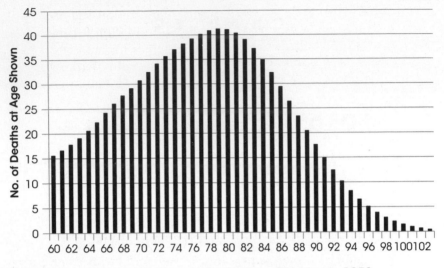

Figure 8.1   When Death Occurs for 60-Year-Old Men in 1950

away between their 60th and 61st birthday. The number of deaths gradually rose in each successive year, peaking at 41 deaths at age 79. The last survivor would have breathed his last in 1993, at age 103.[1]

Since we started with 1,000 men, of which 41 died at age 79, one might think that the mortality rate at age 79 was 4.1 percent. It might also seem that the mortality rate is declining after that because fewer deaths occur in each subsequent year. This interpretation would be totally erroneous. The mortality rate at a specific age is equal to the number of deaths that take place in that year divided by the number of people who had *survived* until that year, not the original number of people. In this case, there would have been only 453 survivors from the original group of 1,000 to reach age 79, which means that 41 deaths represents a mortality rate of 9.1 percent. Mortality rates tend to climb every year until the end of the mortality table. By age 90, the probability of dying within 12 months is 20 percent, and by 95, it is 27 percent.

Even this analysis is not quite accurate, since it assumes that the mortality rates as measured in 1950 would have remained the same 35 years later, when the survivors among the original group of 60-year-olds reached age 95. In fact, mortality rates were dropping steadily after 1950. The mortality rates for 95-year-olds in 1985 would have been lower than it was in 1950.

In 1950, we were almost oblivious to the possibility that mortality rates were constantly improving; the idea of building future reductions in mortality rates into the actuarial tables had not yet caught on. Consider the commentary on recent mortality experience as reported in the 1951 Transactions of the Society of Actuaries:

> The mortality rates for the year 1950 ... are somewhat lower than those for the preceding years. Some of this decrease may be due to statistical fluctuation [i.e., noise] ... but it is quite probable that some of the decrease is also due to the long-range downward trend in mortality rates which has been observed in other studies ...

The description suggests that some actuaries had a suspicion that mortality improvements were part of an ongoing trend, but the profession was not quite ready to accept it yet as a fact.

Present-Day Life Expectancy

As it happened, mortality rates not only dropped further in the ensuing decades, they dropped faster than anyone imagined possible. Today, it is widely accepted that this trend will continue indefinitely. Modern mortality tables routinely build in future reductions in mortality rates on a generational basis. The rates in those tables are a composite of experience to date, modified by expected future improvements.

Figure 8.2 shows the pattern of deaths for 1,000 men who were age 60 in 2015. The chart is based on rates from the 2014 Canadian Pensioners mortality table with adjustment for size and income. With these special adjustments, the remaining life expectancy for a Canadian man is 86.9, which is more than 9 years longer than it was in 1950. As we will describe later on, the US mortality experience has also improved, just not as quickly. Mortality improvements in the United States have lagged behind not only Canada but most other developed countries.

In Figure 8.2, note that the number of deaths at age 60 is now just 6 out of 1,000, versus 16 deaths back in 1950. The mortality rate at age 60 has dropped by more than 60 percent! Other comparisons of 1950 mortality to 2015 mortality are equally impressive:

- A 74-year-old man today has about the same chance of dying as a 60-year-old man did in 1950. In a sense, 74 is the new 60.

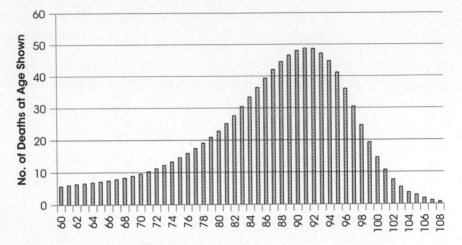

Figure 8.2   When Death Occurs for 60-Year-Old Men in 2015

- For men age 70, the mortality rate has fallen almost 75 percent, from 39 deaths for every 1,000 males in 1950 to just 10 by 2015.
- Among 60-year-old men in 1950, just 24 out of 1,000 could expect to live until 95. By 2015, that number has soared to 199.

Figure 8.3 provides a graphic perspective on how much mortality has improved in the last 65 years as it compares the 1950 mortality curve (i.e., the distribution of deaths) against the 2015 curve. The 2015 mortality curve is shifted well to the right, meaning deaths now tend to occur at later ages.

Dispersion of Deaths

Besides showing that the 2015 mortality curve shifts to the right, Figure 8.3 also shows that deaths are a little less dispersed in 2015 than they were in 1950. By that, I mean that the mountain shape is higher and narrower, which indicates a higher proportion of deaths taking place around the life expectancy age than used to be the case. Nevertheless, deaths are still widely scattered. Table 8.1 shows the current probabilities of death within a given age range.

The fact that deaths are so widely scattered presents quite a challenge for retirement planning purposes. If you are a male, how do you know whether you will have enough money to last a lifetime if there is 1 chance in 3 that you will die before age 77 or after 95? We will address this question in Chapter 12.

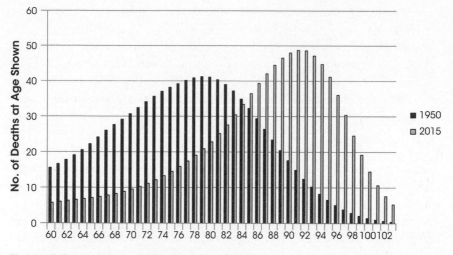

Figure 8.3   Death in 1950 Rates vs. 2015

Table 8.1   Modern Death Probabilities (for a 60-year-old)

	Males	Females
Expected age of death	86.8	89.9
Probability of dying within 5 years of expected age of death	41%	45%
Probability of dying before age 77	16%	10%
Probability of dying after age 95	16%	24%
Probability of dying before age 70	7%	4%

Based on the 2014 Canadian Pensioners Mortality Table with adjustment for size and income

Who Is Benefiting the Most?

While mortality rates have been dropping at virtually all ages, the extent of the drop varies considerably by age, gender, and country. In the first half of the twentieth century, the increases in life expectancy were largely the result of significant reductions in infant mortality as well as better medical care for women in their child-bearing years.

As an aside, the dramatic decline in infant mortality in the early part of the twentieth century is responsible for a major misconception about life expectancy. You will often hear that life expectancy was just 50 in 1900, which might conjure up images of grizzled 48-year-olds sitting in rocking chairs waiting to die. That is not the way it works. If someone made it past 40 back then, they had a good chance of living into their 70s or 80s, and maybe even their 90s. My grandfather was born in 1885 and lived until age 91, and he was not especially unusual in the village he came from. His father was born in the 1840s and lived past 90 as well. If life expectancy was so short in 1900, it was because the people who died at advanced ages were balanced out by the many deaths that occurred in the first 5 years of life. As always, beware of averages.

Getting back to the issue at hand, the main beneficiaries of mortality improvements changed in the second half of the twentieth century and continuing right up to the present day. The greatest reductions in mortality rates have occurred at older ages, especially ages 60 to 90, and as we saw earlier, the mortality improvements for males (especially Canadian males) have been nothing short of sensational.

As for women, the news is also reasonably positive, though the mortality improvements in recent decades have not been nearly as dramatic as for men. In fact, mortality improvements for US women at advanced ages have been nearly at a standstill, a phenomenon that is still not clearly understood.

Women in virtually all developed countries have lived longer than men for as long as actuaries have measured life expectancy, but the gap is shrinking. Based on 1949–1951 data, female life expectancy in the United States as measured from birth was nearly 6 years longer than for males. Today, it is about 5 years longer. In Canada, the gap was always less and currently stands at a little more than 3 years.

Increasing life spans have been a global phenomenon, at least among the world's developed countries. Japan is the world leader in longevity, while Canada is in the middle of the pack among the highly developed countries. While mortality has improved in the United States as well, it is actually quite a laggard when compared to other developed countries.

In summary, when it comes to mortality improvement over the past 65 years, the old have fared better than the young, men have done better than women, and Canadians better than Americans.

Why Is Mortality Improving?

Two of the reasons for the mortality improvements at older ages—better nutrition and medical advances—will come as no surprise. What is a little surprising perhaps is that once a threshold in health care spending is crossed, there is practically no correlation between how much we spend on health care and on how long we live. The United States spends twice as much on health care per capita as almost every other developed country in the world and yet it compares poorly to those same countries in terms of life expectancy.

Another significant reason for mortality improvement is greater affluence, which allows for an easier life and, as we will see, better nutrition, a cleaner environment, and reduced stress all contribute to increased life spans. Even now, mortality studies show that people with higher income live longer. This might help to explain why the US experience has been so lackluster, given that a larger percentage of the US population lives in poverty than is the case for Canada or most European countries. If longevity were the primary goal, one has to wonder whether a portion of the vast amounts being spent on health care in the United States might be more effectively deployed in raising income levels for the poorest segment of society.

The vast majority of the improvement in mortality rates since about 1980 has been due to the reduction in heart disease.[2] In Canada, the number of deaths among males due to diseases of the circulatory system has declined from about 4.4 deaths per 1,000 lives in 1979 to about 1.9 deaths in 2004 (and it would have continued to decline since then). That represents a 57 percent drop in the mortality rate due to heart-related diseases.

On the other hand, the number of deaths from cancers is practically the same. It was 2.1 deaths per 1,000 in 1979 versus 2.0 in 2004. This is not to say that medical intervention has not made any strides at all against cancer. Some of those who were dying of cancer in 2004 would have died of heart disease instead if heart-related deaths had remained at the 1979 level. Still, progress in eliminating cancer-related deaths has been slow. Some experts postulate that this is partly because cancer is a natural outcome of the aging process due to cumulative damage to DNA that occurs over time and so cancer will always be with us.

Another possible reason why US mortality rates are not dropping faster is the obesity epidemic, which, while a global phenomenon, is especially acute in the United States. Based on 2011 statistics,[3] 36.5 percent of the US population is obese. By comparison, the average among OECD countries is just 17.6 percent. A number of life-shortening diseases and conditions are linked to obesity including:

- Cardiovascular and heart diseases
- Cancers
- Type 2 diabetes
- Kidney, liver, and gall bladder diseases
- Musculoskeletal problems

It is hard to overstate the impact of these health conditions on mortality rates. Cardiovascular disease is the leading cause of death, accounting for 32.5 percent of all deaths in the United States as of 2005. Cancer is the second most common cause of death, responsible for another 22.8 percent of all deaths. Diabetes is the sixth leading cause of death as mortality rates for people with diabetes are about twice as high as for people without the condition.

That being said, the link between obesity and mortality is not quite as straightforward as one might think. Clinical studies have uncovered the obesity paradox,[4] in which obese men who were otherwise deemed fit were no more likely to die than nonobese fit men. In this study, subjects were considered fit if they had no known cardiopulmonary disease or diabetes, never smoked, and had a normal exercise test.

The link between smoking and mortality is much more direct as studies have found that cigarette smokers die about 10 years sooner than nonsmokers.[5] Smoking is responsible for much more than lung cancer. It also a major contributing factor in other cancers and neoplasms, chronic obstructive pulmonary disease, ischemic heart disease, cerebrovascular disease and other vascular diseases. As fewer people smoke, it is not surprising that mortality rates are dropping. OECD data[6] show that the percentage of males in Canada who smoke has declined from over 40 percent in 1965 to 16.1 percent in 2012. Smoking prevalence of females is virtually unchanged at about 12 percent, which may explain why the gap in life expectancy between males and females has been narrowing.

The Future

We will almost certainly continue to live ever longer. An approximation of the rate of increase in life expectancy was built into the 2015 mortality table that was charted at the beginning of this chapter. The only question is whether the projected future improvements in mortality embedded in that table are too conservative. If recent history is any guide we could be understating the extent of future improvements in longevity.

Until fairly recently, humans were thought to have a maximum life span and consequently, it was supposed that not much could be done to reduce the probability of death amongst the elderly. This is a very old idea. Consider Psalm 90:10, the King James version: "The days of our years are three score and ten and if by reason of strength they be four score yet is their strength labour and sorrow"; Aristotle likened the life of humans to a log fire. One could throw water on the fire and put it out, a metaphor for premature death. Otherwise, the log would burn, and if it wasn't disturbed it would eventually burn itself out.

Like a log fire, it was assumed that we humans had a maximum life span. This helps to explain the mindset in 1950 that was described earlier and why we were not assuming that mortality rates among the elderly would continue to improve.

Even though demographers and actuaries now take for granted that mortality rates will keep dropping, they continue to be reluctant to assume that the pace of improvement will match what we have witnessed in recent decades. This is in keeping with a long-held tradition among demographers of drawing a line in the sand so to speak by assuming there had to be a natural limit to our life spans and then erasing and redrawing that line repeatedly, as the supposed limit was exceeded time and again.

Indeed, if the factors that will drive further improvement in mortality were the same as what drove progress thus far, it is very likely that the impact would eventually peter out. In the future though, different factors will drive improvement, factors that have had little or no impact so far but have enormous potential to improve mortality further. In fact, the rate of improvement may even accelerate though that may take many years to happen. Figure 8.4 is a chart created by RMS, a company that produces models and software to help insurers, trading companies, and other financial institutions evaluate and manage catastrophe risks. It shows that most of the mortality improvement in the future may come from new sources such as regenerative medicine.

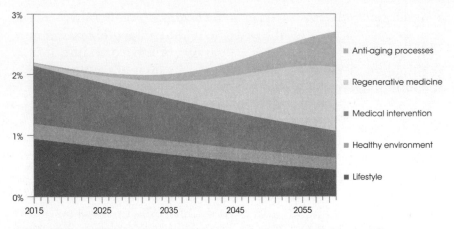

Figure 8.4   Future Drivers of Mortality Improvement (male 80)
Source: Risk Management Solutions, Inc.

One of the pioneers in the field of regenerative medicine, the SENS Foundation, points out that when our medical system treats the diseases that inevitably attack us in old age—heart and stroke disease, cancers, cardiovascular disease, etc.—they are treating the symptoms of aging rather than trying to arrest the process of aging itself. According to SENS and other organizations like the National Institute of Aging, the diseases and disability of aging are caused by the accumulation of damage in our tissues, which, in turn, are caused by the side-effects of essential metabolic processes gone wrong. At the risk of oversimplifying, what they refer to as *metabolic mistakes* affect us but at such low levels that we may not become aware of until our 40s or 50s and then it takes decades more to build up to the point that tissues no longer function properly.

The answer is not to create more drugs that treat the symptoms of disease, since these drugs will have side effects that cause damage of their own. Rather, the future lies in a new class of medicines known as rejuvenation biotechnologies. These are targeted therapies that remove, repair, or replace the damaged cellular or molecular machinery. Instead of simply slowing down the accumulation of damage caused by aging, rejuvenation biotechnologies such as stem cell therapy and individualized gene therapy can reverse it.

Even beyond regenerative medicine, anti-aging processes hold great promise. These involve treatments to extend life by slowing down the natural processes of aging, such as telomere shortening.

Telomeres cap the ends of our DNA and protect them from being destroyed. We are born with a finite telomere length that becomes shortened with age to the point that our cells become inactive and die. It will be decades, however, before the developments in this field lead to practical benefits.

Conclusions

We are living longer and our children will live longer still. The factors that are responsible for this phenomenon will be changing over time as new medical technologies emerge. It is important to understand how this trend affects our retirement planning.

Notes

1. This is a slight simplification from the 1951 GAM Table in that all numbers are rounded to the nearest integer. Hence, the fraction of a person that is left beyond age 103 up to 110 is ignored.
2. Reported by Sun Life using data from Statistics Canada for the period 1979 to 2004.
3. OECD Health Statistics 2013, Table 2.7.1.
4. Paul A. McAuley, Nancy S. Smith et al., "The Obesity Paradox and Cardiorespiratory Fitness", *Journal of Obesity* (2012).
5. Richard Doll, Richard Peto et al., "Mortality in relation to smoking: 50 years' observations on male British doctors," *BMJ*, 2004.
6. I am grateful to Sun Life for pointing this out to me.

Estimating Your Own Life Expectancy

It may be nice to know that people are living longer but how does that affect you? As we learned in the previous chapter, past reductions in mortality rates have varied by age, income level, country, and gender. This chapter gets a little more personal. It helps you to forecast your own life expectancy and the extent to which you can change your so-called fate by making changes in your lifestyle.

Have you ever filled out an insurance company questionnaire to apply for life insurance or critical illness insurance? These are impressively thick documents of up to 50 pages long. They include detailed questions about your use of tobacco and alcohol, driving history, whether you fly a plane or race speedboats, your family history, and your own personal medical history. Insurance companies would not be asking all these questions if they did not think the answers would have a bearing on your longevity.

It should therefore come as no surprise that what you eat, whether you smoke, how much you drink, and how often you exercise all affect how long you will live. You may be surprised, however, to find out by just how much.

Take obesity, for example. A man who is 5 feet 10 inches and weighs 300 pounds will be assigned a life insurance rating of 200 percent or more, even in the absence of any heart disease or other critical illness. What this rating means is that the insurance company will double future mortality rates for this person when calculating insurance premiums. So for each year of his remaining life, the chances of dying are deemed to be twice as high as for someone from the general population. Note that for a 50-year-old male or female, a 200 percent rating translates into a loss of remaining life expectancy of 6 years.

When it comes to life expectancy, smoking is an even bigger risk than obesity. One major study of British doctors[1] showed that excess mortality associated with smoking goes well beyond just lung cancer. It also involves vascular, neoplastic, and respiratory diseases. Male doctors born between 1900 and 1930 who smoked only cigarettes and who continued to smoke died on average 10 years younger than lifetime nonsmokers. Ten years is a long time, especially if you had just 20 to 25 years of retirement in the first place. In the study, the probability of a 70-year-old male smoker surviving to 90 was determined to be about 7 percent. For a nonsmoker, the probability was 33 percent.

The good news from that same study is that quitting smoking can reverse most of the loss in life expectancy, especially if one quits at a young age. If a smoker quits at age 30, he can expect to gain back all 10 years of life expectancy that he had lost. Those who quit at later ages gain back less but they still gain.

An Ontario study[2] showed essentially the same result but with an even greater difference between smokers and nonsmokers. In the case of 20-year-old Ontarians, the difference in life expectancy between a lifelong nonsmoker and a long-term, current smoker was estimated to be 12 years (85 versus 73).

The level of physical activity can also make a big difference. One Dutch study[3] of elderly men showed that exercise helps to prolong life but it was important to maintain that effort. The study found that people who used to be physically active but had become sedentary gradually lost the beneficial effects of past physical activity. If we define men who were physically active continuously over the past 5 years as group A and men who were sedentary over the same 5 years as group B, the mortality rate for group B in the subsequent 5-year period was twice as high. Those who used to be active but have become sedentary ranked somewhere in-between.

A recent US study[4] found that a single measurement of one's fitness level in mid-life was a good predictor of lifetime risk of death due to cardiovascular disease (CVD). Men age 55, who were able to run a mile in under 8 minutes on a treadmill had a 19 percent lower risk of dying due to CVD over the rest of their lifetime compared to men who took more than 10 minutes to run the same distance. This is not to say that running one quick mile at age 55 is enough and you do not have to exercise ever again. Rather, those who ran the mile in under 8 minutes at age 55 could do so only because they had been exercising consistently for years before that and likely continued to do so for many years after because they had made it part of their lifestyle.

If you are a golfer, you will be heartened by a study that was performed by a Swedish medical university.[5] It found that the mortality rates for golfers are about 40 percent lower than for other people of the same sex, age, and socioeconomic status. This corresponds to about 5 years more life expectancy and suggests that regular, lifelong exercise even at a moderate level of intensity is effective.

More generally, five behavioral factors have been identified by medical science as materially affecting our life expectancies:

1. Smoking
2. Alcohol
3. Diet
4. Physical activity
5. Stress

Figure 9.1 shows how many years of life a 20-year-old can expect to gain or lose depending on these factors. Smoking is the most important factor, but all five factors are significant. The overall difference in life expectancy between people who exhibit all five of these behavioral risk factors and people who have none of them is 20 years!

By eliminating unhealthy behaviors early enough, you can restore 7.5 years of lost life expectancy. What is equally noteworthy is that you gain back up to 9.8 years of *healthy* life expectancy. In other words, you not only reclaim some of the years you lost, you also convert some of the years during which you would have been expected to live with some form of disability or illness back into healthy years.

What this all means is that much of the dispersion in remaining life expectancy that we saw in the last chapter represents premature death due to unhealthy lifestyles. Many of the people who died at younger ages smoked, ate or drank too much, or exercised too little. Yes, bad things do happen to good people and one cannot entirely

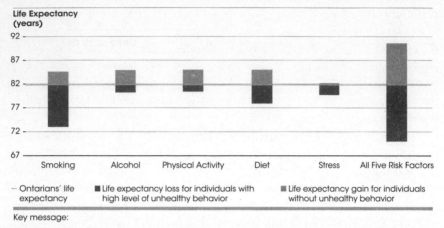

Key message:
· A 20-year difference in life expectancy existed between people who have all five behavioral risks and those with none of the five risks.

Figure 9.1 Gain or Loss in Life Expectancy

Data Source: DG. Manuel, R. Perez, C. Bennett, L. Rosella, M. Taljaard, M. Roberts, R. Sanderson, T. Meltem, P. Tanuseputro, H. Manson, "Seven More Years: The Impact of Smoking, Alcohol, Diet, Physical Activity and Stress on Health and Life Expectancy in Ontario," An ICES/PHO Report. Toronto: Institute for Clinical Evaluative Sciences and Public Health Ontario; 2012, http://www.publichealthontario.ca/en/eRepository/PHO‐ICES&uscore;SevenMoreYears&uscore;Report&uscore;web.pdf.

eliminate the chances of early death but that is no reason to be a fatalist about when death might come. Your life expectancy is more within your control than you probably thought.

If you want to estimate your own life expectancy, I would suggest you try the calculator located at the website: http://www .projectbiglife.ca. This online calculator is essentially a shortened version of the type of application form that the insurance companies would have you fill out. You will be asked a number of questions about your smoking, exercise, and diet habits, as well as some medical history questions. If you want this to be useful, it is important to answer the questions honestly, which may be more difficult than you might think. For instance, it is easy to underestimate the number of drinks you actually average in a typical week. The calculator takes only a few minutes to fill out and it immediately tells you your life expectancy. You can then change some of your responses to reflect lifestyle changes that you would be prepared to make and see how much it affects your life expectancy.

Table 9.1   Estimating Life Expectancy

	Healthy person	Unhealthy person
Age	50	50
Height	5 ft 10 in.	5 ft 10 in.
Weight	170 pounds	230 pounds
Smoking status	Never smoked	Current heavy smoker
Alcohol consumption	1 or more times a month	1 or more times a month
More than 5 drinks once a week?	No	Yes
Fruit servings per week	6	2
Salad servings per week	6	0
Vigorous exercise/week?	3 hours	0 hours
Light exercise/week?	6 hours	2 hours
Stress level	Not much	Quite a bit
Education	University	High school
Existing health conditions	None	Heart disease
Expected age at death	**90.9**	**70.4**

Life expectancy measured from age 50
Project Big Life Health Calculator - http://www.projectbiglife.ca/life/

I completed the Project Big Life calculator for two hypothetical individuals the same age and height. The results are shown side-by-side in Table 9.1. The difference in their life expectancy is a mind-boggling 20 years, and most of that difference is due to lifestyle, which means that change is largely within their control. For example, if the unhealthy person was a *former* heavy smoker, he gains back 5.5 years of life expectancy. He can gain even more if he brings his weight and his drinking under control.

For retirement planning purposes, it obviously helps to know how long you can expect to live. To make the above information useful, let us break down the possibilities for expected age at death into three different intervals (or zones) as defined in Table 9.2. I will assume you use the Project Big Life calculator or some similar tool to estimate your age at death to determine which life expectancy zone you are in.

This information will be useful later on, when we refine the estimate of your wealth target for retirement planning purposes. Remember that if your results indicate a lower-than-average life

Table 9.2   Life Expectancy Zones

Zone	Expected age at death
1	Over 90
2	80 to 90
3	Under 80

expectancy, you might still be able to do something to change the outcome.

Being in life expectancy zone 3 does not mean you will necessarily die before someone who is in zone 1, but the odds are very good that you will. Figure 9.2 shows the distribution of future deaths for 1,000 women who are currently age 50. In one case, they are rated at 250 for insurance purposes, which puts them squarely in zone 3, and in the other they are rated at 50 (zone 1). You can see that the entire distribution of deaths shifts sharply to the right, and the peak number of deaths occurs at age 84 for zone 3 versus 96 for zone 1. Nevertheless, there is still some overlap, which is fodder for anecdotes about how lifestyle does not make a difference. Don't believe it.

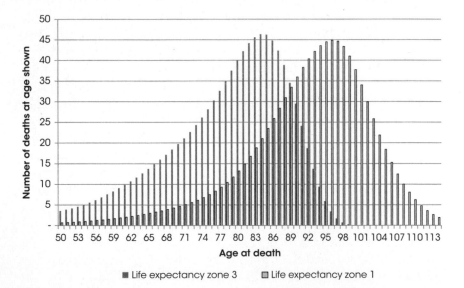

■ Life expectancy zone 3   ☐ Life expectancy zone 1

Figure 9.2   Distribution of Future Deaths for Women Age 50

Conclusions

You will never know for sure when you are going to die, but your own life expectancy is not as random a variable as you might have thought. Lifestyle can make a big difference, so you need to decide what type of lifestyle changes you are prepared to make for a healthier and longer life.

Notes

1. Richard Doll and Richard Peto et al., "Mortality in relation to smoking: 50 years' observations on male British doctors," *BMJ Online* (2004).
2. D.G. Manuel, R. Perez, C. Bennett et al., "Seven More Years: The Impact of Smoking, Alcohol, Diet, Physical Activity, and Stress on Healthy Life Expectancy in Ontario," An ICES/PHO Report, 2012.
3. Fransje Bijnen, Edith Feskens et al., "Baseline and Previous Physical Activity in Relation to Mortality in Elderly Men," *American Journal of Epidemiology* (1999).
4. J. D. Berry et al., The Cooper Center Longitudinal Study, "Lifetime Risks for Cardiovascular Disease Mortality by Cardiorespiratory Fitness Levels Measured at Ages 45, 55, and 65 Years in Men," *Journal of the American College of Cardiology*, 57 (15) (April 12, 2011), 1604–1610.
5. B. Fahramand et al., "Golf, a Game of Life and Death—Reduced Mortality in Swedish Golf Players," *Scandinavian Journal of Medicine in Sports* (May 2008).

CHAPTER **10**

Is Long-Term Care in Your Future?

In Greek mythology, Eos, the goddess of the dawn, fell in love with Tithonus, a mortal. Eos asked Zeus to make Tithonus immortal but neglected to specify under what conditions. Being mischievous, Zeus did grant Tithonus immortality, but not eternal youth. The unfortunate Tithonus did not die but instead lived on countless years, growing ever frailer. Homer expressed this dismal state of deterioration particularly well:

> ... but when loathsome old age pressed full upon him [Tithonus], and he could not move nor lift his limbs, ... she [Eos] laid him in a room and put to the shining doors. There he babbles endlessly, and no more has strength at all, such as once he had in his supple limbs.

Homer's words hit painfully close to home for those of us who have seen an aged parent descend slowly into ill health to the point they need long-term care. We are living longer lives but not necessarily healthier ones. Is our health care system the new Zeus, and are most of us destined to become like Tithonus?

Long-Term Care (LTC)

Whenever I tell people that their retirement income target is not as daunting as they feared, the most common response is, "Yeah, well what about long-term care?" These three frightening words (which we will abbreviate to LTC) constitute the clinching argument to every debate about our financial needs in retirement, conclusive proof that we must have underestimated how much money we will truly require.

Perhaps this is because LTC conjures up a Citizen Kane type of image in which you find yourself dying slowly in your own bed, surrounded by prohibitively expensive doctors who are keeping you alive in a Tithonus-like state for years. In extreme cases, the truth is only a little less dramatic, as we have all heard stories of the elderly (or the people who are charged with their care) burning through hundreds of thousands of dollars a year in their last years of life at home as a coterie of caregivers and private nurses tends to their needs.

The problem is that LTC needs vary widely from one person to the next. The LTC solutions also vary widely in terms of cost, and it is only in a small percentage of situations that the costs become astronomical. The potentially ruinous but highly nebulous cost of LTC may inhibit us from spending as much as we otherwise would during our healthy retirement years, and maybe that is a good thing. We just need to quantify it better to be able to differentiate what is prudent from what is unduly conservative. Otherwise, the outcome at the end of our lives is bound to be financially suboptimal, as we either end up with much more in unspent savings than was necessary or else exhaust our financial resources too soon. In this chapter and the next, we will try to wrestle this problem to the ground, or at a minimum, try to isolate the aspects of the problem that are amenable to a solution and deal with them as best as we can.

What Does LTC Entail?

The term *LTC* is reserved for situations where one is unable to live independently and there is no reasonable hope of recovery. The cause may be a disability due to a critical illness or it may stem from other health conditions that may have started off as minor nuisances but became progressively worse, such as arthritis or osteoporosis.

LTC is defined rather stringently by the insurance companies for both tax purposes and adjudication purposes. By definition, LTC is needed when a person can no longer perform two or more basic activities of daily life (ADLs) without substantial assistance (e.g., adjustable beds, canes, walkers, wheelchairs). The list of ADLs includes:

- Bathing
- Dressing
- Toileting

- Transferring (moving into or out of a bed or wheelchair without assistive devices)
- Continence (ability to control both bladder and bowel functions or to maintain an acceptable level of personal hygiene if not able to control them)
- Feeding (being able to eat without assistive devices)

LTC is also needed in the event of a cognitive impairment that involves loss of intellectual capacity to such an extent that continual supervision is required to protect the individual. Cognitive impairment can be measured by standardized tests (see sidebar) to assess impairment relating to (1) short or long-term memory, (2) orientation as to person, place, and time, or (3) deductive or abstract reasoning.

Cognitive impairment—Questionnaire

One is deemed cognitively impaired, and hence disabled, if one makes three or more errors in answering a questionnaire such as the following:

1. What is the date today?
2. What day of the week is it?
3. What is the name of this place?
4. What is your telephone number?
5. What is your street address?
6. How old are you?
7. When were you born?
8. Who is the president of the United States now?
9. Who was president just before him?
10. What was your mother's maiden name?
11. Subtract 3 from 20 and keep subtracting 3 all the way down.

Note that people may suffer from long-term illnesses—for example, Alzheimer's or Parkinson's disease—and need some degree of assistance long before they qualify for LTC. That middle period can put a strain on family members who are providing most of the caregiving, but the out-of-pocket costs at that stage tend to be fairly minimal.

It is when one's needs grow beyond the ability of the family to manage on their own that outside assistance is required and the high costs of LTC might come into play. Starting with the most expensive, the basic LTC options available are as follows:

1. Private home care provided round-the-clock by a team of personal support workers (PSWs) and private nursing. Based on a cost of $20 to $35 an hour for paid caregivers and home-makers plus upwards of $100 an hour for private nursing care, the annual cost can top $200,000 and can easily persist for 5 years or longer. It is numbers like these that inspire most of the fear in the general public about the cost of LTC. Only the wealthiest households are able to afford this option on a long-term basis.

2. Privately run assisted living retirement homes where the care that is provided in the retirement home may be supplemented by outside PSWs coming in on a regular basis. This type of facility is not subsidized by government. Assuming accommodation in a one-bedroom suite plus 4 hours a day of outside personal care being provided, this care option would cost between $40,000 and $100,000 a year in most states and provinces, though it could still top $100,000.

3. Government-run, or at least government-subsidized, nursing homes where the LTC residents pay for better accommodation but the government essentially pays for everything else. The annual cost assuming a better level of accommodation is in the vicinity of $30,000 to $40,000.

4. Government-run nursing homes involving basic (ward) accommodation. No one will be turned away from such a facility for lack of money so the cost under this option is basically nil.

5. Remaining at home with basic care provided by family members and visits to the hospital for medical attention as needed; in addition, paid caregivers might provide some home care for several hours a day. At about $35,000 or less, the out-of-pocket costs are more affordable, but this option can put a tremendous strain on the family.

Government subsidies are sometimes available to pay for some of the outside care that is received, but such resources are chronically strained and go to the neediest first. Given the growing proportion of the population over age 65, the demand for these resources will likely continue to grow more quickly than the supply. As a result, it is safer not to rely on these subsidies when assessing the potential costs of LTC.

If you are the one who is deciding on an LTC option for a loved one, you might be inclined to choose option 1 (intensive care provided at home) and fund it with the patient's own money as long as it lasts, but cost may eventually become a factor, if it is not already a factor at the outset. At the other end of the spectrum, you probably dread the prospects of option 4 (ward accommodation in a public facility), and option 5 is simply not feasible or not a burden that you will want to impose on your family.

That leaves most readers with options 2 and 3 as the most realistic choices. For the most part, you will prefer option 2 (a more upscale private facility) over option 3 (private accommodation in a public facility) just the same as you prefer to stay in a five-star resort rather than a three-star. It then becomes a question of cost, which will depend largely on how long LTC will be needed and at what age the need arises.

Which options are viable might also depend on whether you bought LTC insurance, which we will explore in the next chapter.

What Are the Chances You Will Need LTC?

The US Congressional Budget Office estimates that 33 percent of individuals turning 65 will need nursing home care at some point in their lives for 3 months or more (which makes them LTC-eligible). Statistics compiled by the Society of Actuaries (SOA) using insurance company data indicate that an even higher percentage will need LTC of some sort, whether in a nursing home or in another facility. Based on the SOA's statistics, Table 10.1 shows the probability at various ages of requiring LTC for the first time.

As Table 10.1 shows, the risk of requiring LTC at any given age between 50 and 70 is tiny, ranging from less than one-tenth of 1 percent in the early years to less than 1 percent at age 70. Most of the LTC claims in this age range are due to early-onset Alzheimer's disease rather than an inability to perform two ADLs. The likelihood of a claim climbs steeply with age; by age 85, there is an estimated 7.2 percent chance that a woman will need LTC assistance for the first time and a slightly smaller probability for a man.

Table 10.1   Probability of Needing LTC for First Time

Age	Females	Males
50	0.09%	0.05%
60	0.16%	0.11%
70	0.83%	0.54%
75	2.0%	1.4%
80	4.1%	3.1%
85	7.2%	6.2%
90	10.3%	9.8%

Annual rates of incidence. Claims are based on being unable to per-form at least 2 ADLs or severe cognitive impairment and a 90-day elimi-nation period; rates have been adjusted upwards by 6% to approximate the experience in the general population.
From the 2000–2011 SOA LTC Aggregated Databases

We can use the incidence rates in Table 10.1 to calculate the cumulative risk that a 55-year-old will require LTC by a given age. You might find the cumulative probabilities more useful for assessing risk than the incidence rates. The results are given in Table 10.2.

The SOA data did not extend beyond age 90 and in reality it is less important because (a) most of us will not live past 90 and (b) even if we do and need LTC at that point, the length of time in an LTC facility will tend to be fairly short. Overall then, the probabilities of requiring LTC for any meaningful length of time are about 50 percent for women and 40 percent for men (after rounding up).

These probabilities are, of course, averages over the entire pop-ulation. The chances that you will need LTC will be higher or lower depending on your genes and lifestyle. If you have a genetic disposi-tion for Alzheimer's, for example, the chance of requiring LTC will be higher. The various probabilities are given in Chapter 21.

Table 10.2   Cumulative Probability that a 55-Year-Old Will Need LTC

By age:	Female	Male
60	0.60%	0.44%
70	4.2%	2.7%
80	20.3%	13.7%
85	35.3%	25.5%
90	49.5%	37.4%

Extension of Table 10.1

How Long Is LTC Usually Required?

Not surprisingly, LTC situations can last a long time, which is why LTC is a cause for concern. A major study,[1] however, indicates that only a small fraction of cases last a very long time. That study reported that about one-third of cases will persist for 2 years or more and just one-fourth will continue for 3 years or more. The duration does tend to vary by the age at which the disability was incurred. Table 10.3 shows the percentage of LTC cases that last 5 years or more, broken down by age at the time the LTC claim was first incurred.

To be clear, Table 10.3 is not saying that 15.05 percent of people age 55–64 will need LTC. Instead, it shows that the tiny fraction of people that age who will need LTC have a 15.05 percent chance of still requiring LTC 5 years later.

While an LTC situation is much more likely to arise at the very advanced ages, it is a less daunting problem financially at those ages since the period of LTC tends to be shorter. Moreover, there is less reluctance to spend the person's remaining assets on LTC since they are unlikely to need the money for any other purpose, assuming there is no surviving spouse. From a financial standpoint, then, the primary concern is that LTC will be needed from a fairly young age and last many years. When assessing the risk, we need to be careful not to combine a high probability of an LTC situation with the expectation of a long duration, because it tends to be one or the other, not both.

Besides age, the other major factor in determining the length of time one will spend in LTC is the type of illness. Situations involving Alzheimer's and other cognitive impairments tend to last about twice as long as situations where a cognitive impairment is not involved. About 10 percent of LTC cases that are due to Alzheimer's will persist for 6 years or longer. Cancer claims, on the other hand, tend to be fairly short.

Table 10.3   Likelihood that LTC Will Persist for 5 Years

Age when LTC started	Still on LTC 5 years later
55–64	15.05%
75–84	10.30%
90+	3.80%

Society of Actuaries, Intercompany experience 1984–2007

Finally, LTC claims are not only more likely to arise in the case of women, they will tend to last longer than for men. The percentage of men who are still on LTC after 6 years is only about two-thirds the percentage in the case of women.

Conclusions

Cost aside, the most attractive LTC option to most people is to remain in their home in their final years, with round-the-clock care provided by outside caregivers and with family members checking in regularly. On a long-term basis, however, this will be too costly and cause too much of a strain for all but the wealthiest of families.

Assuming one does not wish to impose on family, the next best option is a privately run retirement home. This will involve a total cost of up to $100,000 a year, and one has to keep in mind the possibility that care may be needed for 5 years or longer.

Publicly funded options will be much less expensive, and while they can be quite adequate, the impression is that they are suboptimal and likely to become more so as an aging population imposes a greater strain on publicly funded LTC facilities. Judging from my visits to such LTC facilities, this impression may be a little unfair, since the private accommodation that I have seen in these facilities looked quite comfortable.

Over the long term, the probability of requiring LTC is about 50 percent for women and 40 percent for men. The chances of requiring LTC that lasts for more than 5 years—perhaps the situation that frightens us the most—are quite small.

Note

1. Society of Actuaries, "Long-Term Care Experience," committee inter-company study report 6, 1984–2008 (June 2011).

11

Paying for Long-Term Care

In the previous chapter, we learned that there is roughly a chance in two that you will eventually require long-term care (LTC) for 3 months or more. If you do, the overall costs of LTC can vary widely, from nearly nothing if it is a short duration at home with the family providing most of the care to over a million dollars in the case of home care with outside caregivers providing round-the-clock assistance for many years.

The potentially ruinous costs of LTC and the uncertainty of whether it will even be incurred makes for a highly uneasy financial situation. Unless you have very significant financial resources, how do you incorporate the possible need to pay for LTC in your retirement planning?

Normally, when there is a chance of an event with significant and potentially catastrophic financial consequences, you want to insure against that event. Hence, if you have a young family, you buy life insurance to protect them if you die prematurely. If you own a home, you buy home insurance against calamities such as fire. Why not consider buying LTC insurance then? We will explore the pros and cons in this chapter.

Typical LTC Insurance Contract

When you hear the term *long-term care (LTC) insurance*, you might be thinking of a contract that covers all your costs in the event that LTC is ever required. The reality is a little different.

Here are the features of a typical LTC insurance contract:

- Level annual premiums are paid for life or up until a very high age such as 100. The later you start, the higher the premiums. For example, in one typical LTC insurance policy, the annual premiums for a female are $3,740 if payments and coverage starts at age 55 versus $12,887 if payments start at age 70.
- Coverage is subject to the applicant meeting strict underwriting requirements. You cannot wait until you are on the verge of making a claim to apply for LTC insurance because your application will be declined. In fact, you will usually be ineligible for LTC insurance if you suffer any of the following conditions at the time you apply: AIDS, Alzheimer's, ALS, asthma, emphysema, COPD, congestive heart failure, cystic fibrosis, diabetes requiring insulin, Huntington's disease, cirrhosis of the liver, dementia, MS, muscular dystrophy, renal failure, Parkinson's, peripheral vascular disease, sleep apnea, or lupus.
- Premiums are guaranteed not to increase in the first 5 years. Most policies do enable the insurer to raise premiums unilaterally after the initial 5 years.
- If you discontinue premium payments, you lose your coverage and forfeit whatever premiums you paid to date.
- Further premiums are waived if a valid claim is made against the policy.
- Premiums are refunded if death occurs while the policy is in force (less whatever amounts may have already been paid out under the policy).
- Benefits are generally paid out only if the person needs constant supervision because of a severe cognitive impairment (e.g., dementia) or because they cannot perform at least two activities of daily living without substantial assistance.
- When a claim is approved, benefit payments start after a waiting period, which is usually 90 days.

The benefit takes the form of a fixed-dollar payment such as $1,200 a week, payable for anywhere between 100 and 250 weeks in most cases, though an unlimited package is also available at a higher premium. While reimbursement contracts also exist that cover specific expenses incurred rather than providing a flat weekly amount, some insurers will tell you that a fixed weekly benefit is better; weekly benefits are tax-free, they give you flexibility in choosing the type of care you want, and one does not have to submit bills for reimbursement. From the insurer's viewpoint, a fixed weekly benefit is also easier to underwrite and to adjudicate.

Sometimes the policy allows for the weekly benefit to increase at an annual rate such as 2 or 3 percent. This type of indexed coverage will provide some protection against inflation but it will also be considerably more expensive than a nonindexed policy. No policy I am aware of provides unlimited protection against higher inflation.

Does the Math Work?

Let us consider some typical situations to try to assess how effective LTC insurance would be in protecting us financially.

Example 1: Insurance Bought at Age 54

The first example is based on an illustration of an actual LTC insurance contract. Let us say that Aldo, a single person, buys LTC insurance coverage at age 54 under this contract. Annual premiums (after rounding) are $4,500 starting immediately and continuing until age 100 or until death if earlier. If Aldo eventually needs LTC and his condition meets the terms of the contract, the benefit is a weekly payment of $1,200 payable for up to 250 weeks (5 years).

Assume, for example, that Aldo first claims LTC benefits at age 90. Premiums would stop as a result of the claim but he would have paid in a total of $162,000 up to that point. Had Aldo invested the same amounts in a portfolio that earned an annual return of 4 percent after tax (not a certainty, I admit), that money would have grown to $356,000 by age 90. By comparison, the maximum benefit under that particular policy consists of 250 weekly payments totaling $300,000. The weekly payments in this case are not indexed to inflation, so the maximum payout would have been $300,000 whether the claim occurred tomorrow or in 35 years' time. So if Aldo's main concern is needing LTC at age 90, this particular policy is not for him.

What if LTC is needed a lot sooner than age 90? For instance, if a claim occurs at age 70 and weekly payments were made for the maximum 250 weeks, then Aldo would have paid $72,000 in premiums and received benefits totaling $300,000. Even if we adjust the premiums for interest at 4 percent, the value of the premiums paid equals $100,000 (rounded) or just one third of the value of the maximum payout. The LTC insurance would have paid off handsomely in the case of an early and substantial claim.

As we learned in the last chapter, however, the probability of LTC occurring between ages 55 and 70 is rather small, being in the range of 3 to 4 percent, and even then only a fraction of those claims will last more than 2 or 3 years. The probability of a significant claim occurring before age 70 is under 1 percent.

Remember as well that the LTC benefits do not necessarily cover all your costs in the case of an early claim. You would be on the hook for a considerable portion of the LTC costs if the situation continues beyond 5 years or if the weekly cost is more than the $1,200 provided by the insurance. Hence, the LTC insurance money would have been helpful but it would not have eliminated your risk.

Table 11.1 summarizes the value of the premiums that would have been paid in this example versus the maximum insurance payout at various ages. Whether the LTC benefits cover all costs incurred or not, the value of benefits received looks attractive compared to the premiums paid in up until age 80, even when we adjust the premiums for the investment income they would have earned in Aldo's hands. Keep in mind, though, that the maximum benefits are not always paid out. In fact, the average length of time in an LTC facility is closer to 3 years than 5 years. If we replaced the $300,000 in Table 11.1 with $180,000, the case for the insurance is less compelling even in the case of a claim occurring at earlier ages.

Table 11.1   LTC Insurance Premiums versus Payouts

Age at time of claim	Value of premiums paid (rounded)	Maximum value of benefits received
60	$30,500	$300,000
70	$100,000	$300,000
80	$203,000	$300,000
90	$356,000	$300,000

Based on premiums of $4,500 starting at age 54 and payouts of 250 weeks or 150 weeks at $1,200 a week. Value of premiums is accumulated with after-tax interest at 4% a year.

Example 2: Insurance Bought by Steve and Ashley at Age 61

This second example involves an upper-middle income couple that is on the verge of retirement and contemplating whether to buy the LTC insurance. The LTC policy they are considering would cover them both and would pay a weekly benefit of $1,000 for an unlimited period in the case of a claim. The details of their financial circumstances are set out in Table 11.2.

Let us now consider the need for LTC occurring at two possible times.

In the first case, Ashley needs LTC at age 71 and stays in a facility for 7 years. The annual LTC cost, all in, is $100,000 a year at that point in time. Given that the couple was spending just $65,000 a year (in today's dollars) just before the LTC claim, one might wonder whether a $100,000-a-year LTC solution is excessive but let us assume this is what they want. A claim of this size is not quite the worst-case scenario but it would rank quite high among all LTC claims in terms of total cost. The LTC insurance coverage they bought pays $50,000 of that annual cost (I am rounding), which means that the other $50,000 a year has to be covered by the couple's other finances.

The results are shown in Table 11.3. The couple is on the hook for some significant expenses whether they insure or not, though obviously the proceeds of the LTC insurance defray a good portion of the cost. If the remaining spouse was willing to downsize the home in the event of an LTC claim, it could unlock enough equity to fund the total LTC expenses even if they did not insure against LTC.

In the second case, Ashley incurs an LTC claim at age 86, which lasts until her death, 4 years later. This is a more typical LTC situation in terms of the age when the LTC claim occurs and also the duration. Because of inflation, we will assume that the annual LTC cost would

Table 11.2   Couple's Financial Situation

Age (same for both)	61
Savings (in a tax-sheltered fund)	$800,000
Estimated retirement income needs for both*	$65,000 a year
Income needs for 1 spouse if the other is in LTC	$43,000
Cost of LTC insurance for the couple (until 100)	$9,000 a year (at 61)

*Income needs excluding the cost of LTC insurance or comparable self-insurance.

Table 11.3   Claim Occurs at Age 71

	Insured Scenario	Not Insured
LTC cost each year	$100,000	$100,000
Number of years	7	7
Total LTC cost	$700,000	$700,000
Less portion paid by insurer	($350,000)	(Nil)
Less reduced normal spending*	($175,000)	($175,000)
Plus cost of insurance**	$112,000	Nil
Total amount paid by couple	$287,000	$525,000

*See Appendix D for details
**Adjusted for interest at 4% per annum

Table 11.4   Claim Occurs at Age 86

	Insured scenario	Not insured
LTC cost each year*	$140,000	$140,000
Number of years	4	4
Total LTC cost	$560,000	$560,000
Less portion paid by insurer	($200,000)	(Nil)
Less reduced normal spending*	($124,000)	($124,000)
Plus cost of insurance**	$389,000	Nil
Total amount paid by couple	$715,000	$436,000

*Figures are derived in Appendix D
**Adjusted for interest at 4% per annum

have climbed to $140,000 a year by that time. The analysis, which is summarized in Table 11.4, shows that Steve and Ashley are much better off not to be insured, even though a claim of reasonably lengthy duration occurred. Incidentally, they might have difficulty in securing LTC coverage at age 61 as only half of the applicants that age meet the underwriting requirements. One might think that age 61 is early to be worrying about LTC insurance, but in fact, it may already be too late.

The Verdict

Insurance, whether it be on your life, your home, or for LTC, is most effective when (a) the potential loss from which you are seeking protection is easily understood and quantifiable, (b) any losses over a given threshold would be fully reimbursed by the insurance so you get peace of mind, and (c) the cost of the insurance seems reasonable relative to the coverage. Does LTC insurance meet these criteria? The foregoing examples suggest the answer is no. There are many other reasons you might want to pass on LTC insurance.

First, the premiums seem rather high relative to the benefit provided in the event of a claim. If your home is worth $1 million, the annual insurance premiums might be in the vicinity of $4,000 and possibly less, but you get $1 million toward rebuilding the home if it burns down. The premiums in the first sample LTC policy above were $4,000 a year but the maximum lifetime benefit provided is only $300,000. The insurers would argue that the probability of a claim being made is higher in the case of LTC, but the size of the premiums still makes LTC insurance *seem* unattractive.

Second, making LTC insurance premiums is a long-term commitment. Once you start to pay premiums, you practically have no choice but to continue. If you stop, there is no cash value, so you lose whatever you paid in. Of course, you will want to continue your home insurance as well, but you have the flexibility to change insurance companies, an option that is not viable for LTC insurance.

Third, there is no guarantee that LTC insurance premiums will not be unilaterally increased at some point. The premiums are supposed to be level for life but if the insurer's experience is particularly bad, it often reserves the right to raise your premiums after 5 years. Insurance companies have in fact exercised that right in recent years. In 2010, John Hancock raised premiums for most LTC policyholders by 40 percent. AIG, MetLife, and Lincoln National also requested premium increases of between 10 and 40 percent. If you do not like it, you cannot easily walk away—not only because premiums elsewhere would be even higher given the later starting age but because you might have become uninsurable in the meantime.

Fourth, the size of an LTC claim is essentially amorphous. Maybe you will need LTC for only a few months, with most of that care being provided by family members in your own home, so that out-of-pocket costs are almost nil. Or maybe the publicly funded LTC facilities (with private accommodation) in your area are decent so you do not have to avail yourself of a more expensive privately funded retirement home. The thing is, when it comes to LTC, the liability is not as tangible as it is in the case of a claim against your home insurance policy. You might incur seven-figure costs in both cases but in the case of LTC, you do not have to incur that cost if you choose not to.

Fifth, buying LTC insurance does not give you the complete peace of mind you really want. If your house burns down, the cost of rebuilding is fully covered (assuming you insured for replacement cost). In the case of most LTC insurance policies, including the one just described, there is no guarantee that the entire cost of LTC will be covered. In fact, there is no *likelihood* that the entire cost will be covered in the type of situations that you really fear and that induced you to buy the insurance in the first place. The need for LTC can easily continue well beyond the maximum number of weeks of payments that are specified under the LTC policy you elected. And if the LTC costs rise due to unexpectedly high inflation, the promised weekly benefit payments can prove to be woefully inadequate. You can make much of this problem go away by selecting a policy with an unlimited number of payments plus indexing but the insurance premiums will be just that much higher and the overall proposition remains equally unappealing.

Sixth, your LTC premiums do not build up a cash value as whole life insurance would, even though the premiums in the early years exceed the cost of the insurance in those years. This seems a little unfair, even if it is the tax authorities who are making this stipulation rather than the insurers.

Seventh, LTC insurance entails a timing problem. The time when you should be considering buying the insurance is decades before the time when a claim will realistically arise. By contrast, home insurance provides you coverage against a possible event occurring over the 12 months immediately following the payment of premiums. LTC insurance requires you to focus now on an issue that will not be top of mind for many years to come. This might be the biggest stumbling block, since people are simply not inclined to pay out large amounts now for a benefit in the distant future, especially a benefit that may or may not materialize.

Finally, you might just want coverage between ages 55 and 75, rather than lifetime coverage, because that is the period when you feel most financially vulnerable. At very advanced ages, say 85 or 90, the probability of a claim would be higher but the duration should be fairly short and you would have had time to build a side-fund to finance it. Unfortunately, you cannot buy coverage that ends at age 75, and while you could simply stop paying premiums on a life-time policy, you would have overpaid by a significant margin for the coverage you received up to that point.

With all these limitations, you would think the insurance companies must be making a killing on the LTC policies that they do sell, but this is not the case. In the early years of LTC coverage (the 1980s and 1990s), most insurance companies lost money on their LTC insurance product as they had underestimated the number of claims, overestimated the lapse rate (policy lapses would get them off the hook) and also overestimated the investment income they would reap from the premiums. Many insurance companies have decided to abandon the business entirely. It appears that no one has been especially happy with LTC insurance so far.

You can see why LTC insurance is a tough sell. Not only do the LTC insurance policies have some unappealing characteristics, but one would need substantial retirement income to afford to pay annual premiums in the $4,000 to $20,000 range for decades. LTC insurance currently pays for less than 10 percent of all LTC delivered in the United States.[1] The people that can readily afford to pay the premiums also tend to be the same ones who own their home and could tap into the equity in their home if necessary. Also, these same households may very well possess other financial assets that they can liquidate to pay for LTC when the time comes. In summary, LTC insurance is not a particularly effective solution, even for households in the income range that are most likely to benefit from it and even if they incur a claim.

It is unfortunate that LTC insurance is not more appealing. What is really needed is a policy with reasonable premiums and a moderately high deductible that covers all LTC costs for a decent private retirement home in excess of that deductible no matter how long the duration of the stay. It is only in this way that the insured individual would be fully protected from a catastrophic loss.

What we have is almost the exact opposite: LTC insurance policies with high premiums that provide first-dollar coverage but do not protect against catastrophic loss. Nonetheless, the possibility of a large LTC claim occurring when you can ill afford it has not gone away. Before we dismiss LTC insurance out of hand, you should at least scope out your ability to deal with the costs should the need for LTC arise.

The Consequences of Not Insuring LTC

Some households will be more vulnerable than others should the need for LTC arise. Paying large premiums is a nonstarter for households of modest means. They are more apt to rely on family for support or on publicly funded institutions. In the United States, the best strategy for lower-income households is to spend down their assets and apply for Medicaid in order to pay for their LTC. It makes no sense to buy LTC insurance and use the proceeds to pay their LTC claims since most states will reduce dollar for dollar the payments the beneficiary would otherwise receive from Medicaid. In Canada, publicly funded LTC facilities are quite decent if one pays for the upgrade to private room accommodation, and a good part of the relatively modest cost for the room upgrade can be covered with the retirement income that the individual will no longer be needing for any other purpose.

High-wealth households can also do without LTC insurance since they can fund the cost of LTC out of existing assets. The only question for them is whether they take the highest cost solution, which is to remain in their home with outside support provided round-the-clock. If that is too expensive, they still have the fallback option of assisted living in a private retirement home.

It is mainly the upper-middle-income group that is going to feel most exposed without LTC insurance. They will want the type of higher level of care that is available in a private retirement home, supplemented by personal support workers if they have special needs, but where will the money come from?

Households in this income bracket will be able to pay for the quality of LTC they want out of existing financial resources if either one of the following conditions is met:

1. The person who needs LTC is the only person still living in the family home so it can be sold if necessary to meet LTC expenses, or
2. The need for LTC arises at a very late stage in life, for example after age 85, at which time the couple (if both are alive):
   • still have significant financial assets as a result of having underspent their retirement savings in earlier years, and
   • are unlikely to reside more than several years in a LTC facility in any event.

The same household may not have the resources to pay for quality LTC if they are under 80 when the need for LTC arises or if both spouses are still alive, which means selling off the family home may not be an option.

If they have no other assets that could be liquidated to pay for LTC, they could, of course, consider a less expensive LTC option that is within their means. It may be distressing not being able to afford hotel-quality accommodation in the event that one requires LTC, but this is a rather minor issue relative to the more serious problem of dying or incurring a critical illness, a scenario for which there is roughly a 50 percent chance between ages 50 and 70 alone.

The other possibility is to self-insure LTC by building up a special side-fund that is earmarked specifically for potential LTC expenses down the road. Most people will probably not want to establish a separate LTC side-fund because they may believe the odds are on their side. Consider the following statistics:

- More than half of us will never require LTC at all, and as for the rest, most will require LTC only for 2 or 3 years, the cost of which would not be ruinous for an upper-middle income household.
- As for longer (and hence more expensive) stays in an LTC facility, a woman has about a 5 percent chance of eventually requiring LTC for more than 5 years; for men, the probability is about 4 percent.
- If that 5 percent scenario is realized, there is a better than 50 percent chance that the LTC claimant will be the sole surviving spouse by then, which means selling the house to pay for LTC should be feasible.
- The probability of an awkward situation—meaning a long stay in an LTC facility while the other spouse is still living in the family home, which means it cannot be sold—is estimated to be less than 3 percent.

What do we do with all this information? We cannot afford to insure ourselves against every contingency, and if we have enough money to cover at least 97 percent of all situations that might arise, then we might be tempted to ignore the residual LTC risk entirely.

Rather than ignore it, though, you could still decide to put some money aside for the future possibility of long-term care, even if the length of stay ends up being no more than two or three years. By doing

Table 11.5   Provision for Long-Term Care

Confidence that LTC needs will be covered	Addition to wealth target*
Moderate (50%)	$0
Fairly high (75%)	$120,000
Very high (95%)	$240,000

This table applies to upper-middle income households only.
*Increase figures by inflation rate if retirement is not immediate.

so, you end up having enough money to meet expected LTC costs if the stay is moderately long, and if the stay ends up being much longer, you will at least be able to defray the cost of it to a considerable extent.

Table 11.5 shows how much money one should have on hand at the point of retirement to address most LTC situations. I will spare the reader the details of the calculations; a description of the methodology is given in Appendix D.

What Table 11.5 means is that if being 50 percent sure of having enough money is good enough for you, you do not have to put any money aside for LTC. If you want to more certain than that of having enough money to meet your future LTC needs in a better private facility, then I suggest setting aside $120,000 at the point of retirement. To be very sure, it would require setting aside about $240,000 at the point of retirement. By the way, the numbers in this table are in current dollars. If retirement is in a future year, they should be increased by the rate of inflation (as it relates to LTC) during the intervening period.

It is important to keep in mind that once you are in the dependency stage and need LTC, the decisions about your care will be out of your hands. At that point, the decisions may be made by a power of attorney for personal care (POAPC), the person you would have picked many years earlier. It is not uncommon to see that person choose the most expensive option while you still have personal assets remaining to pay for it, after which a less expensive option is chosen by default. If that is not what you want, you should provide written direction to your POAPC while you are still of sound mind. You may prefer a less-expensive LTC option that preserves more of your remaining assets for the next generation.

Note

1. Vickie Bajtelsmit and Anna Rappaport, "The Impact of Long-Term Care Costs on Retirement Wealth Needs," Society of Actuaries, 2014.

CHAPTER

Putting It All Together

If you participated in a defined benefit pension plan for most of your working life, then your retirement planning has essentially been taken care of. The same is true for the bottom 30 percent of the population by income level who will rely mainly on Social Security pensions.

For everyone else, retirement planning consists of putting aside the right amount of money at the right times and in the right investment vehicles so that you accumulate sufficient wealth to meet your income needs for the rest of your life. This wealth target is the key metric, just like a golfer's handicap (if they maintain one) tells you practically everything you need to know about how good they are at playing the game. If you know your wealth target, and you achieve that number by retirement age, it gives you a good deal of confidence that you have achieved your goal of retirement security.

It has taken 11 chapters to reach the point where we can finally attempt a realistic calculation of the wealth target. Chapter 5 offered up a rough estimate but we had not gathered enough information on the risk factors at that point to understand how they affect the target. Now that we have explored longevity, interest rates, spending habits in retirement, and long-term care, we can proceed to refine our earlier estimates.

The first step is to establish the retirement income target. This is illustrated in Table 12.1 for two couples at different income levels.

As the question marks in Table 12.1 show, we need to determine the wealth target that produces the needed retirement income. We will do this in steps, starting with the simplest scenario and progressively building in each of the major risk factors.

115

Table 12.1   Process for Finding the Wealth Target—an Example

	Couple A	Couple B
Final average employment earnings*	$100,000	$200,000
Retirement income target as a percentage of final average employment earnings	50%	50%
Retirement income target in dollar terms	$50,000	$100,000
Subtract Social Security pension**	($30,000/year)	($36,000/yr)
Subtract other defined benefit pension	(nil)	(nil)
Income needed from retirement savings	$20,000/year	$64,000/yr
Convert this to a (lump sum) wealth target	?	?

*Combined household earnings, including spouse's earnings.
**Social Security includes pension of both spouses and is assumed to be payable from 65.

Step 1: Incorporate Investment and Longevity Risk

Let us start by assuming that Couple A and Couple B:

- Have already settled on a retirement age of 65 and do not contemplate retiring sooner, either voluntarily or otherwise,
- Concede that their income needs will eventually diminish in their 70s and 80s (ignoring long-term care needs) and that the modest amount of inflation protection they get on their Social Security pensions will suffice,
- See no possibility of a marriage breakdown, and
- Do not have any specific figure in mind in terms of a bequest.

Under these simplified circumstances, their wealth target is the cost of a life annuity that has an appropriate survivor benefit.[1] Why does the annuity cost represent the right number? You know the wealth target cannot be higher than that number because if it was, then why manage your own monies after retirement and incur the investment and longevity risk?

On the other hand, the wealth target cannot be lower than this number without introducing too much risk. This conclusion is revealed by running a Monte Carlo simulation on a portfolio for Couple A. It is assumed that Couple A wants to draw a steady income of $20,000 a year from retirement at age 63 until age 80. Whatever assets they have left at age 80 will be used to purchase a life annuity. The Monte Carlo simulation shows there is a 10 percent chance that the annuity they can purchase at age 80 will be $64,000 a year or higher, which is more than triple the income they were drawing before 80! While this would be a splendid win, it comes too late in life to be of much use other than to pay for long-term care or to pass along to the next generation.

The real problem, though, is that they have exposed themselves to investment risk that leaves them with a 20 percent chance they will not have enough assets left to buy $20,000 of annuity at 80. In fact there is a 10 percent chance they will not be able to buy even $10,000 of annuity. I am suggesting that this is too much risk to take at age 80 though I admit it depends on one's risk tolerance. They can mitigate the risk by being cautious and spending less before 80 if their investments do badly but then it begs the question of why not just annuitize and make the problem go away?

It is for these reasons that the wealth target in the simplest scenario is equal to the cost of the annuity. If the annuity is to start at age 65, the cost according to Cannex Financial Exchanges, is about $350,000 for Couple A to secure $20,000 of annual income. For Couple B, the cost is about $1,120,000 to secure $64,000 of income. These numbers will change over time if (a) the amount of annuity changes, (b) the insurance companies change their mortality rates to reflect future improvements in mortality and (c) if the age of the spouses is different.

There are two situations under which the wealth target in this simple scenario will be less than the cost of an annuity. The first is if the retirees are prepared to take a chance and manage their own investments, hoping that their investment returns will be better than average and they will not outlive their assets but being prepared to live with the consequences if investment returns are poor. The other situation is if one's life expectancy is lower than average. As we saw in Chapter 9, you can make a reasonably good estimate of your own life expectancy using Web-based calculators. If your expected age at death is less than 80, you might be better off taking the chance and managing your own monies after retirement.

Step 2: Add Retirement Age Risk

You might think that the age at which you will retire is something that is firmly under you control and is not really a risk factor. In fact, surveys show that people tend to retire sooner than they planned and maybe sooner than they wanted. This is especially true of employees versus the self-employed.

A 2013 survey by the Society of Actuaries shows that people who are still in the workforce plan to retire a full 7 years later than when current retirees actually did. A part of this gap might be due to an actual trend toward later retirement, but most of it represents the phenomenon of employees being pushed into early retirement. In some cases, the push might have come from the employer or it might be due to health reasons. A gap of 7 years between intentions and reality translates into a significant potential deficit in terms of retirement savings.

I would therefore suggest that if you are at least a few years away from retirement, it would be prudent to build in a cushion into your wealth target just in case you retire earlier than you had planned.

The wealth target is very sensitive to the age of retirement, particularly in the case of lower income households and for single persons versus couples. The reason for that sensitivity is that we are assuming that Social Security is payable only starting at age 65. On early retirement and continuing up until age 65, one also needs to fund the portion that will be provided by Social Security on and after age 65.

For example, Couple A needs $50,000 in annual retirement income, of which $30,000 comes from Social Security starting at 65 and $20,000 from their own retirement savings. If they retire at 63 instead, they need to fund $50,000 a year of income between 63 and 65, not $20,000. They could, of course, start to receive Social Security early, but it would then be reduced for life, and for actuarial purposes that produces the same result as assuming that Social Security is payable only from age 65.

Continuing the previous example, Table 12.2 shows how much the wealth target rises simply by advancing the retirement age from 65 to 63. You will note that the percentage increase in the target depends on the size of Social Security pensions relative to overall retirement income.

By upping the wealth target to reflect the possibility of retiring early, we are raising our confidence level that we will have enough money. We cannot determine the exact confidence level in percentage terms, since the probability of being forced to retire two years earlier will vary so much from one person to the next.

If these couples end up retiring at 65 as they initially planned, the difference between their original and their new wealth target is instantly freed up and can be used as a buffer against other risks or simply to provide more income at the actual retirement date.

Table 12.2   Neutralizing Risk of Premature Retirement

	Couple A	Couple B
Retirement income target*	$50,000	$100,000
Income needed**	$20,000	$64,000
Original wealth target	$350,000	$1,120,000
Increase in wealth target if retirement is taken at 63 instead of 65	22%	13%
New wealth target (rounded)	$430,000	$1,240,000

*50% of final earnings.
**After 65, net of Social Security pension.

Step 3: Add Inflation Risk

The high inflation that characterized the early 1980s is unlikely to return any time soon. The global phenomenon of aging populations in developed countries will probably keep inflation low for many years to come.

In the unlikely event that inflation does rise, say to 3 or 4 percent, I have already built in a margin of safety by assuming an underlying interest rate of 2.5 percent for annuity purchases. If inflation rises, so will interest rates, which means nonindexed annuities will cost less. This windfall can be used to build some indexation into the annuity and so puts us in the same position as if inflation had stayed low.

Still, inflation could be a problem for different reasons. For instance, inflation might jump only after the annuity is bought, which thwarts the purpose of the margin of safety I built in. It might spike higher than 3 or 4 percent, though you should note that over the 92-year period from 1923 to 2014, it has averaged less than 3 percent. The government might renege on fully indexing Security pensions to inflation, which would force you to make up the difference with your own retirement savings. Or perhaps you fear that your own income needs will not decline as much as was suggested in Chapter 7.

These problems can be addressed by incorporating some indexing into one's retirement income. For instance, if you build a 1 percent annual increase in the annuity you buy from the insurance company, the annuity cost rises by about 12 percent. An annuity that increases by 2 percent a year costs about 26 percent more than a nonindexed annuity.

If you are really risk-averse, you might want to buy a fully indexed annuity that protects you against inflation no matter how high. If so,

Table 12.3   Level of Confidence that Inflation Risk Is Covered

Annual increase in annuity	Wealth target for Couple A	Wealth target for Couple B	Confidence level
0%	$350,000	$1,120,000	Moderate
1%	$390,000	$1,260,000	Fairly high
2%	$440,000	$1,430,000	Very high

Risk of retiring early is assumed to be nil.

you will find yourself out of luck. The few insurance companies that are willing to offer annuities that are indexed to inflation (as opposed to annuities that rise by a fixed amount) usually impose a ceiling on the amount of inflation they will recognize, such as 4 or 5 percent, and even then the annuities get expensive very quickly. This is why there are so few takers.

Table 12.3 shows how the wealth target changes if we want to protect ourselves better against the risk of higher inflation. While it is difficult to quantify the confidence levels precisely, I am suggesting that "moderate" means one is about 50 percent sure, while "very high" signifies a confidence level of 90 percent or more. So far, we have dealt with the first two risks separately. They will need to be combined later on.

New Wealth Targets

Apart from the risk of marriage breakdown or requiring long-term care, we have now quantified the major risk factors. All we have to do is to combine the retirement risk and the inflation risk into one number. We do this in Table 12.4 for Couples A and B. I have also added Couple C with $300,000 in final employment earnings.

Here are the other assumptions underlying Table 12.4:

1. The retirement income target is 50 percent of final income employment earnings for Couples A and B and 45 percent for Couple C.
2. Social Security pensions represent 60, 36, and 26 percent of total retirement income needs for Couples A, B, and C, respectively.
3. Retirement is assumed to take place at age 65, but with a risk it might occur as early as 63.
4. Provision for the costs of long-term care is excluded.
5. Provision for the possibility of divorce or to allow for bequests is also excluded.

Table 12.4   Wealth Targets if the Intent Is to Retire at Age 65

Couple (income needed)*	Wealth target (moderate confidence level)	Wealth target (very high confidence level)
A ($20,000)	$350,000	$450,000
B ($64,000)	$1,150,000	$1,400,000
C ($114,000)	$2,000,000	$2,500,000

*Income needed after 65, net of Social Security pension.
Targets are rounded up to nearest $50,000.
Withdrawals from savings in retirement are assumed to be taxable income.

Table 12.5   Wealth Targets if Intent Is to Retire at 60

Couple (income needed)*	Wealth target (moderate confidence level)	Wealth target (very high confidence level)
A ($20,000)	$550,000	$750,000
B ($64,000)	$1,450,000	$2,000,000
C ($114,000)	$2,300,000	$3,000,000

*Income needed after 65, net of Social Security pension.
Targets are rounded up to the nearest $50,000.
Wealth is assumed to accumulate in tax-assisted vehicles.

The wealth targets are very sensitive to the retirement age, as can be seen from Table 12.5, which shows the wealth targets if the intended retirement age is 60 instead of 65.

For single persons at the same pre-retirement income levels, the wealth targets would be higher still because (a) their retirement income target might be higher (no children) and (b) their Social Security pension is smaller, which means the amount of income they need to generate from retirement savings is higher.

Your Own Wealth Target

The foregoing may give you a rough idea of your own wealth target, but there are many reasons why your personal number could be different:

- Your retirement age could be higher or lower.
- The age difference between you and your spouse is unlikely to be zero, as is assumed above, or you may be single.
- The amount of your Social Security pension could vary.
- You might have a higher risk tolerance and decide to invest your own retirement savings rather than buy an annuity; given this higher risk tolerance, you are prepared to adopt a lower

wealth target and live with the consequences if your investments do not pan out.

- You want to build in the cost of long-term care or the risk of a marriage breakdown, neither of which is incorporated in the above figures.
- You might have already paid tax on some of your assets that form part of your wealth target, and to the extent you have, you can reduce your wealth target by 10 percent or more (depending on income level), since the foregoing wealth target estimates assume that savings were accumulated only in tax-assisted retirement vehicles.

To give you a better fix on your personal wealth target, I invite you to go to www.morneaushepell.com/wealthtarget. There, you will find a link to Morneau Shepell's wealth target calculator.

Buffers

The wealth target is the amount of money you are estimated to require to meet your income needs for the rest of your life. The entire amount does not necessarily have to be on hand at the point of retirement in the form of cash or financial assets but if it is in any other form, you should not include it as an asset unless (a) you are prepared to sell it if the need arises and (b) it is reasonable to think there is a secondary market for that asset.

There are a number of nonfinancial assets that you may want to recognize, in whole or in part, in your wealth target.

The main one is the equity in your home. I suggest you include none of that equity in your wealth target if you are not going to be willing to sell. This reflects more than inherent conservatism on my part; to a large extent it also reflects how we tend to behave. Most households do not tap into the equity in their home until they have exhausted all other assets. For a household that has prepared financially for retirement, this is very unlikely to happen unless one enters a long-term care facility. I believe it makes sense to recognize some of the equity in the home as an asset only to the extent that you had selected a more conservative wealth target or if you want to earmark a part of the home equity for future long-term care needs.

The one exception to this advice is that it is quite normal to consider downsizing at retirement and to add whatever capital gain that is realized to one's retirement savings. That capital gain usually ranges from nil to half the equity in one's home depending on what you do. Besides helping you reach your wealth target, this strategy may also reduce ongoing home insurance, maintenance costs, and property taxes to the extent your new home is smaller and less expensive.

The potential decrease in the size of your household is another buffer, though not one that can or should be quantified. I am referring to the death of a spouse. Tragic as this is, it does not have to result in financial disaster provided that the family home was jointly owned, the couple's assets pass to the surviving spouse after death, and the couple had purchased an annuity in joint and survivor form. (With such an annuity, a percentage of the monthly payments, such as two thirds, would continue to be paid to the surviving spouse.) If all of these conditions are met, the surviving spouse might even be a little better off financially than when both spouses were alive.

Another potential asset is a possible inheritance. By triangulating from the various surveys I have seen, I estimate the probability of an inheritance in the general case to be 40 to 50 percent. As for the amount, the broad average is a little over $100,000, but you would know better what you can expect in your own situation. It could be far more or it could be nil. Unless an inheritance is a certainty, it is probably wiser to plan for your retirement as if it will never happen. If it does, add most of it to the savings you are accumulating to meet your wealth target. Do not consider it as "mad" money unless you have exceeded your wealth target.

There is one other strategy to make up for an asset shortfall, which is to continue working part-time, perhaps in a self-employed capacity. This is a growing phenomenon for reasons of personal fulfilment, as well as enhancing retirement security. Once again, you probably do not want to capitalize this income and include it explicitly in your wealth target.

Conclusion

Even if the retirement income target is as low as 40 or 50 percent of final average employment earnings instead of 70 percent, the wealth target can still be a substantial figure at higher income levels. There will always be the desire to eliminate risk completely by choosing a sufficiently high target, but that is never going to be possible, either before retirement or after.

You will want to go through the process of determining your wealth target more than once in your life, starting perhaps in your late 30s or early 40s and repeating the exercise periodically until the point of retirement. That is because your circumstances—income, marital status, health, investment performance —may change in ways you cannot predict. If and when they do change, knowing your new target will give you a better idea of how to modify your retirement planning to ensure you remain on track.

Note

1. Annuity reduces to two-thirds on the first death so the survivor will always have income. I further assume the annuity is based on a 2.5 percent interest rate. If the interest rate is higher when the annuity is purchased, it allows for some indexation.

PART

III

THE ACCUMULATION PHASE

CHAPTER

Picking a Savings Rate

In the first chapter, I suggested that you could not go far wrong if you saved 10 percent of pay each and every year and invested the money in a constant asset mix, such as 60 percent equity funds and 40 percent bond funds. With the benefit of hindsight, even an 8 percent savings rate would have been enough. We will refer to saving a constant percentage as the *simple savings strategy* to distinguish it from other ways of saving that will be described later on.

Historical Performance

It goes without saying that the success of a plan to save for retirement depends on investment returns, interest rates, inflation, and retirement age. Before trying to forecast how all these factors might evolve in the future, let us first reconstruct the past assuming an 8 percent savings rate. Table 13.1 shows the basic assumptions we will be using for this exercise. A more complete summary of assumptions is given in Appendix D.

Using data on the capital markets going back to 1938, I was able to simulate the simple savings strategy over 30-year periods starting with the period from 1938 to 1967 and ending with 1985 to 2014. That makes for 48 overlapping accumulation periods in all.

For illustration purposes, we will assume that the savers are a two-earner couple with a home and that they have household earnings modestly higher than the national average. We will assume their retirement income target is 50 percent of their average pay in their final years of full-time employment. Social Security is estimated to

Table 13.1   Assumptions for the Historical Estimates

When saving starts	Age 35
Retirement age (saving ends)	Age 65
Amount saved each year	8% plus Social Security taxes
Asset mix for portfolio	30% US equity, 30% Canadian equity, 40% bonds
Return on investments	Actual returns on the major indices, less fees
Converting savings into income	Purchase of a non-indexed annuity at age 65

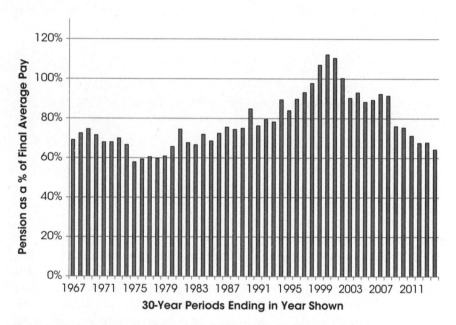

Figure 13.1   Retirement Income if 8% is Saved for 30 Years

provide them with pension equal to 33 percent of their gross earnings, meaning the other 17 percent needs to come from personal
savings.

Figure 13.1 shows the results for all of the 30-year accumulation
periods. There are 48 overlapping periods in total. Each bar in
Figure 13.1 indicates how much retirement income can be purchased at age 65, with the assets that accumulated over the 30 years
ending in the year shown.

The first bar, for instance, is the result for the 1938–1967 period;
total retirement income, including Social Security pension, is 69.2

percent of final average pay. Remember that the target was just 50 percent, so the couple that retired in 1967 would have substantially more income than they needed to maintain their living standards.[1]

For some readers, the results will seem astounding, regardless of which 30-year period they look at. By saving 8 percent a year starting at age 35, the couple in question would have overshot their retirement target by a considerable margin, even in the worst of periods. The worst, by the way, would have been the 1946–1975 period, which was right after the painful bear market of 1973–1974 and the first OPEC-induced oil price shock. Even then, the couple's retirement income would have easily exceeded their income target.

The result is even better for 30-year periods ending around the year 2000. A couple retiring then would have accumulated retirement income over 100 percent of final average pay, which would have provided a vastly better standard of living after retirement. More recent retirees would also be retiring with more income than they needed, in spite of being traumatized by the 2008–2009 financial crisis and the subsequent rise in the cost of annuities to levels we have not seen in nearly a century.

Lessons Learned

Before we move on to consider the prospects for current savers, let us consider what the historical results can teach us. Starting with the obvious, the 8 percent saving rate proved to be excessive, given that the savings needed to generate income of only 17 percent of final average pay. To see how excessive, let us take the very worst result (the period 1946–1975) and the very best result (1971–2000) and bracket the range in savings that would have been required. The process involves subtracting off the portion of total income that comes from Social Security and then normalizing the result to bring the overall income down to the 50 percent target. The results of our calculations are shown in Table 13.2.

At the very worst, it would have taken a savings rate of 5.5 percent of pay to achieve the retirement income target of 50 percent. In the best-case scenario, the required savings rate would have been a mere 1.7 percent.

In spite of this, some people would still be inclined to save at an 8 percent rate, if not higher. Perhaps we can ascribe this to a survival instinct, just like ants storing food for the winter, except that

Table 13.2   Savings Rate Needed to Hit the 50% Target

	Worst 1946–1975	Best 1971–2000
Actual retirement income*	58%	112%
Portion from retirement savings assuming 8% savings rate*	25%	79%
Income needed for a 50% target*	17%	17%
Savings rate needed to achieve the 50% target	5.5%	1.7%

*As a percentage of final average 5 years' employment income

historically they would have been storing a lot more food than they needed. This is not entirely irrational, since we just saw in Chapter 12 how high the wealth target can go if we want to insulate ourselves from adverse contingencies.

The second lesson is that a savings strategy should not be treated like the sorcerer's apprentice: a process we put in place at the outset and then continue without adjustment until retirement, regardless of the excess (or shortfall) that might develop along the way. We need to be able to modulate our savings rate, and perhaps our asset mix, as our circumstances change.

For example, the early 1970s were a particularly brutal time to be saving for retirement. The bear market of 1973–1974 was one of the worst on record, and would have decimated any investment portfolio. If a couple was looking to retire in 1975, they could have compared their savings account balance in 1970 to their wealth target. They would have seen that they were ahead of where they had to be. Armed with this knowledge, they could have reduced their portfolio's equity weighting to reduce market risk in their final few working years. This could have saved them a lot of grief.

On the other hand, the late 1990s was almost the exact opposite scenario. It was a very benign period for investors, whether they chose to invest in equities or bonds. Account balances grew handsomely and high real yields on fixed income investments meant that annuity prices were low. A couple approaching retirement at that time could have considered a number of actions such as reducing their savings rate, buying a deferred annuity to lock in their retirement income, shifting more of their investment portfolio into fixed income securities to minimize market risk or simply retiring sooner.

One potential criticism of the historical calculations underlying Figure 13.1 is that it was assumed the annuity that was purchased with the retirement savings would not have to be indexed to inflation. While this assumption was not entirely valid during periods of high inflation, it is much less of an issue in the low-inflation world we find ourselves in now. Besides, we learned in Chapter 7 that spending needs will eventually decline in real terms.

What the Future Holds

It would be reasonable to think that the capital markets in the next 30 years will behave more or less the same way as they have for the past 75 years. There will be economic boom times and recessions, bull markets and bear markets but surely the overall performance would fall somewhere in the middle of the pack when compared to all the overlapping 30-year historical periods that preceded it.

Given there were 48 such periods represented in Figure 13.1, it seems improbable that the future will be worse than all of them. After all, the capital markets have absorbed the effects of a world war, oil price shocks, extremely high inflation, terrorist attacks and some stock market crashes and yet survived intact. If we assume that the future will not be any more extraordinary than the past, it suggests that a savings rate of 6 percent of pay should be sufficient for a young middle-income couple to achieve their retirement income target in 30 years' time.

Be wary of anyone who tells you, "This time, it's different," especially when that phrase is applied to investments. The tendency we have to conclude that historic norms no longer apply tends to manifest itself just when those norms are on the verge of re-asserting themselves. Yet, this time it just might be different. The prospects for some key variables that affect the success of a savings strategy—expected investment returns, bond yields, and the cost of annuities—might indeed be less auspicious than has been the case at any previous point in our lives, and as I explained in Chapter 6, the situation might not improve for a long time to come.

Another factor working against future retirees is that Social Security will gradually count for less. For Americans, full Social Security pension is currently payable from age 66, but that is gradually increasing to 67 by the year 2027.

It is the same story in Canada, as the portion of Social Security represented by Old Age Security (OAS) pension falls a little further behind every year relative to the average Canadian wage, and moreover, it will become payable only from age 67 as of 2029.

The only significant aspect of the economic environment that is still operating in favor of savers and retirees is low inflation. This is beneficial for retirees, since it means that a nonindexed annuity (which is much cheaper and easier to buy than an indexed annuity) will not lose too much purchasing power. Moreover, low inflation makes it that much easier for savers to reach a retirement income target that is expressed as a percentage of final pay since the contributions made along the way are not dwarfed by higher pay levels at the end of one's career.

Given this background, let us estimate what a 35-year-old couple today can expect if they save 8 percent a year from now until 65. The basic variables in our calculations are summarized in Table 13.3.

Notice that Social Security pension in 30 years' time is assumed to replace just 30 percent of final pay rather than 33 percent, so the retirement savings have to generate income equal to 20 percent of final pay instead of just 17 percent historically.

We will assume that the couple's final earnings in 30 years will be the equivalent of having final earnings today of $96,000 combined. To estimate this, we inflate earnings by general wage inflation for 30 years to arrive at $250,600 in future dollars. Earnings at this level may seem implausible for a couple that is supposed to have just slightly above-average income but remember what you (or your father) were earning 30 years ago and compare that to today's earnings.

Table 13.3   Assumptions for Projecting Pensions 30 Years

Price inflation (CPI)	2.25%
General wage inflation	3.25%
Government long bond yield	3.25%
Annuity purchase rate (not indexed)	2.50%
Return on retirement savings net of fees	5.25%
Social Security pension in 30 years as a percent of final average 5 years' pay	30%
Retirement income target (including Social Security) as a percent of final average 5 years' pay	50%

When we do the calculations based on an 8 percent savings rate, this couple would accumulate an account balance in 30 years of $828,000 which they could use to buy about $47,000 in annual pension. When combined with their Social Security pensions in 30 years, total retirement income represents 49 percent of final average 5 years' pay. Since the retirement income target was 50 percent, it suggests that an 8 percent savings rate is just about right.

Given that our future forecast is more pessimistic than any prior 30-year period, it is likely that most of the downside risk has already been captured. Nevertheless, it is conceivable that a savings rate of more than 8 percent will be needed. This could happen if interest rates dip below even the low rates we are assuming or if we live even longer than we are currently projected to live. Both of these eventualities would make annuities more expensive to purchase. Another way we could end up falling short with an 8 percent savings rate is if investment returns average less than 5.25 percent before retirement.

In conclusion, even though the longer-term prospects for the capital markets do not appear to be particularly auspicious, an 8 percent savings rate (in addition to Social Security contributions) is probably adequate for a couple with slightly above-average earnings that is looking to retire at 65. As usual, though, there are no guarantees.

Generalizing the Results

We have just seen that in any historic period, a savings rate of 1.7 to 5.5 percent of pay for 30 years would have been enough to generate retirement income of 17 percent of final pay. Looking into the future, where it is easier to envision the downside than the upside, the required savings rate could be closer to 8 percent. How do you apply these disparate findings to your own situation?

Let us first recalibrate those results. Historically, 1 percent of savings produced annual retirement income of between 3 percent and 9 percent of final pay depending on which 30-year period one lived through. In the future, 1 percent of savings might produce less retirement income but let us assume that some good news will emerge eventually—such as a technological breakthrough—that will brighten our future investment prospects at least a little. On that basis, let us assume that 1 percent of savings will generate retirement income equal to $3\frac{1}{3}$ percent of final pay. This is equivalent to

3 percent of savings generating income of 10 percent, so let us call it a "30 percent ratio."

If you are worried about the downside, it should provide some comfort that this would be tied for the worst economic scenario we have seen in the past 75 years. Let us now apply this new rule of thumb to determine a savings rate. That rate will depend on income level because Social Security pensions meet most income needs for the lowest income-earners but just a small fraction of the needs of the highest earners. We will break down all households into five equal-sized groups by income level, what I will refer to as income quintiles. Using information gained in Chapter 4 about the overall retirement income target, we can now determine what the target should be for retirement income one derives from savings. This is summarized in Table 13.4.

Now that we have targets expressed as a percentage of final average pay, we can apply the 30 percent ratio to determine what the savings rate needs to be to reach the target. For instance, in the upper income group, the net retirement savings target shown in Table 13.4 is 33 percent of final average pay, which means that households in this income category should be saving 10 percent of pay for 30 years. Upper-middle-income households should be saving about 8 percent of pay.

These numbers are by no means precise. They are based on estimated investment returns, which may not be realized and on a constant saving rate that is maintained for 30 years, which is unlikely. The numbers also vary greatly by retirement age and also depend on how fast your pay climbs throughout your working career.

Table 13.4   Savings Target* for Homeowners with Children

Income quintile	Retirement income target	Less Social Security plus tax breaks	Net retirement income target
Low income group	90%	90%	0%
Low-middle income	70%	60%	10%
Middle income	54%	30%	24%
Upper-middle income	50%	23%	27%
Upper income	45%	12%	33%

Assuming a 30-year savings period and retirement at 65.
*All figures are percentages of final average pay

The point being made here is that as far as a simple rule goes, regularly saving 7 to 10 percent a year is not a bad starting point for households with above-average income. This assumes you will save at that rate for 30 years. If the period is shorter, you need to save at higher rates. If you want to hit your wealth target, you may have to adjust your savings rate further from time to time, depending on your investment returns.

Note

1. The ratio of 78 percent to 50 percent.

CHAPTER

14

Optimizing Your Savings Strategy

In the last chapter we learned that middle to upper-income households will probably be retirement-ready if they save 7 to 10 percent of pay on a regular basis over the long term (assuming retirement around age 65). The calculation was based on what we referred to as a simple savings strategy.

It is possible to improve on this strategy if you make one or both of the following modifications:

- Varying the savings rate when circumstances dictate, and
- Adopting a more aggressive asset mix for the savings you have accumulated to date if you are falling behind your wealth target.

There is actually a third modification, though it may not be triggered until retirement age; it relates to how you convert the accumulated assets into an income stream. The default assumption in this chapter is that an annuity will be purchased from a life insurance company.

Given that the future is unknowable, does having a more sophisticated savings strategy really make a difference? That is what we need to find out. A number of savings strategies exist, some of them will be familiar to you already while others may seem rather novel. These approaches will be described in this chapter, along with an analysis of their effectiveness.

One way to define effectiveness is whether an approach is easy to follow. There is no point in adopting a strategy that is too arduous to maintain over the long term, the same as I would not attempt to stay in shape by adopting an exercise regimen that involves me getting up every morning at 6:00, rain or shine. It might work if I could stick to it but I know I won't.

The Goal

Perhaps the most important test for the effectiveness of a savings strategy is whether it maximizes one's chances of reaching one's retirement income target. In this chapter, I will assume the target is 27 percent of final average pay (plus Social Security) which, based on the previous chapter, would be about right for a household with modestly above average income. The savings period will be 30 years, consistent with previous calculations.

With that as background, we will analyze five strategies. The analysis involves running Monte Carlo simulations, a process that is described at the end of this chapter.

Strategy 1: Simple

Strategy 1 involves making a fixed contribution of 8 percent of pay each year and then investing it with a constant asset mix of 60 percent equities and 40 percent bonds. Nothing is varied over the 30-year savings period.

Based on the Monte Carlo simulations, the probability of achieving the stated goal with this strategy was 49.1 percent. In the simulations, the ultimate outcome could be much better or much worse.

If we ignore the most extreme outcomes, we found this strategy would generate retirement income anywhere between 17 percent and 41 percent of final earnings. Remember, the target was 27 percent. As wide as this range of results is, there was still a 10 percent chance that the result would fall outside the range. These findings are summarized in Table 14.1.

This result is by no means perfect. In fact, some would say it is not even very good. One would have hoped to achieve the desired retirement income target 100 percent of the time rather than just under half the time. The historical simulations in the last chapter underscored the fact that complete certainty is not possible with any approach given that investment returns and interest rates vary widely over 30-year periods.

Table 14.1 Constant Asset Mix, Constant Contribution Rate Approach

Median savings rate	8.0%
Range of savings rate	NA, always 8.0%
Probability of reaching the 27% income target	49.1%
Range of retirement income (90% of the time)	17% to 41% of final average pay

Data Source: Morneau Shepell Retirement Solutions practice

In spite of these drawbacks, Strategy 1 has two saving graces. First, it is very simple to put into place and to maintain. Second, the degree of variability in the overall retirement income does not seem so bad when one combines the retirement income from savings with the income from Social Security. The latter source will always provide a predictable replacement rate and will stabilize the overall pension amount.

Strategy 2: Simple Lifecycle Approach

Under Strategy 2, we continue to assume a fixed contribution rate of 8 percent a year but now we will attempt to improve on the outcome by varying the asset mix throughout the accumulation period.

The term *lifecycle* is used in this context to refer to the idea that your asset mix should vary depending on where you stand on the path to retirement. With a lifecycle approach to investing, the equity weighting in the asset mix will tend to be reduced gradually as we get closer to retirement. The lifecycle approach is becoming the norm in employer-sponsored defined contribution arrangements and is accomplished by the use of *target date funds (TDFs)*.

> ### Target date funds (TDFs)
>
> TDFs are a series of balanced investment funds in which the equity weighting decreases the closer one gets to the target date. The target date in question would be the individual's approximate retirement date. The purpose of TDFs is to put the individual onto a path of progressively less risk the closer the retirement date looms and to do so without requiring any action on the part of the individual to keep adjusting the asset mix with advancing age.

TDFs can be offered by insurance companies, banks, or independent institutional investment managers. Each institution tends to

Table 14.2　Asset Mix in Target Date Funds (in 2015)

Target date	Equity weighting	Fixed income including cash
2013–2017	40%	60%
2018–2022	44%	56%
2023–2027	56%	44%
2028–2032	66%	34%
2033–2037	73%	27%
2038–2042	81%	19%

Based on BlackRock LifePath Model; other TDFs will vary

Table 14.3　Strategy 2 (Simple Lifecycle)

Median contribution rate	8.0%
Range in contribution rate	NA, always 8.0%
Probability of meeting the target	52%
Range of retirement income (90% of the time)	17.2% to 43% of final average pay

Data Source: Morneau Shepell Retirement Solutions practice

define the asset mix for a given target date fund a little differently. An example of how the asset mix varies in TDFs is given in Table 14.2. The equity weightings shown will change as the target date draws nearer.

As with Strategy 1, Strategy 2 assumes that you adhere to the fixed contribution rate of 8 percent and the prescribed target date fund, regardless of how far you might be deviating from your retirement income goal. Table 14.3 shows the results under Strategy 2.

Strategy 2 proves to be a little better than Strategy 1. The probability of meeting the target has increased from 49 percent to 52 percent and the 90-percent range of possible retirement income is a little higher under Strategy 2. It would therefore appear to be better to use TDFs than staying with a fixed asset mix, though frankly, Strategy 2 is still suboptimal, since there is still a 48 percent chance we will not reach our stated retirement income target.

Strategy 3: Modified Lifecycle

In our quest to improve on our retirement saving strategy, the next step is to vary the asset mix. You can do this by checking every 5 years to see whether you are still on course to reach your retirement income goal. If it appears that you are going to fall short of the target,

Table 14.4   Strategy 3 (Modified Lifecycle)

Median contribution rate	8.0%
Range in contribution rate	NA, always 8.0%
Probability of meeting the target	58.3%
Range of retirement income (90% of the time)	17.1% to 44.6% of final average pay

Data Source: Morneau Shepell Retirement Solutions practice

then you use a more aggressive asset mix than the lifecycle approach would normally dictate (meaning a higher equity weighting). That more aggressive asset mix would be the TDF from the previous 5-year period. The hope is that the higher equity weighting will allow us to catch up to our retirement income target. This is a one-way strategy in that we do not use a less risky asset mix if we are ahead of target. Table 14.4 shows the results of the Monte Carlo simulations for Strategy 3.

On balance, Strategy 3 is superior to Strategies 1 or 2. The probability of achieving the retirement income target has jumped from 52 percent to 58 percent. While the 90-percent range of possible retirement income is wider (meaning it is more variable), it is mainly because the top end of that range is higher, which is a good thing. The bottom end is virtually the same as in Strategy 2.

I must caution that Strategy 3 is counting on the superior returns from equities eventually materializing, which is what equities have always done since the Great Depression. The only concern is that the future could be substantively different, as was suggested in Chapter 6, and that the odds of a prolonged downturn in the equity markets may be greater than has been the case for the past 75 years. This possibility cannot be dismissed, but it should be noted that investing heavily in fixed income instead will not improve your chances of meeting the retirement income target.

Strategy 4: Variable Contribution

In Strategy 4, you would vary both the investment strategy and the savings rate as needed to improve your chances of reaching your goal. As with Strategy 3, each simulation assumes we assess our status every 5 years in the 30-year accumulation period. In Strategy 4, though, we are prepared to use both a more aggressive asset mix and a higher contribution rate if we are not on track to reach our goal. The savings

Table 14.5   Strategy 4 (Variable Contribution)

Median contribution rate	7.9%
Range in contribution rate	5.3% to 11.2%, 98% of the time
Probability of meeting the target	62.0%
Range of retirement income (90% of the time)	20.4% to 41.7% of final average pay

Data Source: Morneau Shepell Retirement Solutions practice

rate for a given year can now be as high as 16 percent if we are behind our target, or as low as 4 percent if we are ahead.

To ensure an apples-to-apples comparison with the previous strategies, we imposed the constraint that the median contribution rate under Strategy 4 must be very close to 8.0 percent. As Table 14.5 shows, that condition has been met.

Strategy 4 is appreciably better than any other strategy we have tried so far. Not only is the probability of meeting the target higher, so is the 90-percent range. Most importantly, the bottom end of the 90-percent range is much higher than under Strategy 3, so we have significantly reduced the downside risk.

Strategy 5: The SMART Approach

In the context of Strategy 5, *SMART* is an acronym that was coined by the Morneau Shepell Retirement Solutions practice; it stands for Self-Management After Retirement Tool.

During the accumulation period, Strategy 5 is the same as Strategy 4. It has the potential to vary from Strategy 4 only at the point of retirement. If the account balance is sufficient to purchase an annuity that provides retirement income of 27 percent, then the annuity is purchased and the SMART approach would end up being identical to Strategy 4. As we learned from Table 14.5, this will happen 62 percent of the time.

If, however, the account balance is not enough to purchase the 27 percent annuity, then an algorithm determines how much of an annuity will be purchased and how much of the account balance will be left intact and used to draw a stream of retirement income to make up the balance of the 27 percent retirement income target.

The idea behind SMART is that if the goal is not reached at the point of retirement, the retiree has a chance to catch up to it after retirement by staying invested and giving the portfolio a chance to outperform annuities.

Table 14.6   Strategy 5 (SMART Approach)

Median contribution rate	7.9%
Range in contribution rate	5.3% to 11.2%, 98% of the time
Probability of meeting the target	76.0%
Range of retirement income (90% of the time)	20.0% to 41.7% of final average pay

Data Source: Morneau Shepell Retirement Solutions practice

Strategy 5 might seem risky versus Strategy 4. To use the casino metaphor, it is like we decided to keep on gambling to make up our losses. The prudent action, one would think, is simply to accept our losses and settle for whatever retirement income we can derive from an annuity. The Monte Carlo simulations, however, tell us a different story. The results are given in Table 14.6.

Strategy 5 is far and away the best of the strategies we have explored. You have to put up with slightly higher downside risk but you now have a 76 percent chance of meeting the target. In investment circles, that is about as good as it gets.

Conclusion

The results for all the strategies are summarized in Table 14.7.

The progression from Strategy 1 to Strategy 5 shows that an active retirement savings strategy makes a difference. At any time during the accumulation period, you should be prepared to change both the asset mix and the contribution rate if it appears that your retirement savings account balance is not where it should be. Doing so significantly improves the probability of a favorable outcome, even in the face of an essentially unknowable future. The only question, which we explore later, is if your other spending obligations permit this degree of flexibility in how much you contribute in a given year.

It is at retirement when one reaps the greatest benefit of active management. If you have not accumulated enough assets to purchase an annuity that achieves your goal, you take a chance and continue to invest some or all of those assets into retirement. As the analysis shows, the risk you take—that the investments will do even worse—proves to be worth taking.

To be clear, Strategy 5 does expose the retiree to the risk of outliving one's assets, since the assets might have to be self-managed instead of annuitized. The simulations minimized this risk by

Table 14.7   Summary of Results

Strategy	Median contribution rate	Range of contributions	Probability of meeting 27% target	90% range of retirement income
1 - Simple	8.0%	NA (fixed)	49.1%	17% to 41%
2 - Simple Lifecycle	8.0%	NA	52%	17.2% to 43%
3 - Modified Lifecycle	8.0%	NA	53%	17.1% to 46%
4 - Variable contribution	7.9%	5.3%–11.2%	62%	20.2% to 41.7%
5 - SMART approach	7.9%	5.3%–11.2%	76%	20.0% to 41.7%

adding a margin of safety and assuming that the average life span in self-managed situations would be 93 years.

The Third Lever

The various savings strategies presented here assume there are two levers you can pull if you find that you are not on track to meet your retirement goal. One is adopting a more aggressive asset mix while the other is changing your contribution rate.

There is a third lever as well and it happens to be used more frequently than either of the first two. It involves retiring later. While the prospect of doing so may not appeal to everyone, and is not always even possible, deferring retirement has become a common way of augmenting one's savings to achieve retirement security. The average retirement age in recent years has been climbing and, judging from the many surveys conducted by various banks, the need to save more for retirement is the main reason.

Methodology

The analysis in this chapter was carried out within the Retirement Solutions practice at Morneau Shepell using 1,000 *Monte Carlo simulations* over 30-year periods (65 years in the case of Strategy 5). This is a standard way to predict the probability distributions of a variable within a complicated system.

Monte Carlo simulations

Monte Carlo simulations involve running a given scenario hundreds of times with one key assumption changing with each scenario. After enough simulations are performed, a pattern emerges, which is the probability distribution that we are seeking.

For instance, we might want to determine the account balance we would accumulate if we saved 6 percent of pay each year and invested it in an equity fund. The variable would be the return on equities, which we know might vary between –30 percent and +30 percent in any given year. In running the projections on the account balance, the computer would "randomly" select the return on equities. Strictly speaking, the selection of return is not quite random, since certain possibilities are more likely than others, based on past equity returns. For example, if a return of 10 percent in a year is twice as likely as a return of 0 percent, then the computer would be twice as likely to choose 10 percent in the simulation.

The purpose of stochastic projections is to find the likelihood of achieving a given result as well as the potential variability of results.

Each simulation involves carrying out the following steps for each year in the simulation period:

1. Assume the required contribution is made to the retirement account.
2. Determine the investment income earned for that particular year as dictated by the simulation model and use it to update past contributions to produce a current account balance.
3. Estimate the retirement income replacement rate based on the status of the account and annuity purchase rates that are dictated by the simulation model for that year.

A Gentler Approach to Saving

The last chapter described various savings strategies you can pursue in order to improve the odds of hitting your retirement income target. All those strategies were implicitly based on a premise that is probably not true—that you can always make retirement saving your highest priority. While this might be the surest way to achieve retirement security, it can wreak havoc with your disposable income at certain times in your life.

There is another path to saving for retirement that might work better for you. It involves saving when it fits in best with your other spending priorities. Under this alternate path, saving for retirement would sometimes give way to other financial commitments but would nonetheless remain important.

To decide which path is right for you, you have to ask yourself which of the following statements sounds more appealing:

Path 1: For the first half of my working career, I am prepared to tolerate a lower standard of living than my income would allow, in return for a much higher standard of living closer to retirement (as well as after retirement).

Path 2: I prefer a standard of living that increases slowly but steadily throughout my working career so I can avoid any periods of undue hardship; I still want my highest standard of living to occur just before I retire (and continuing after retirement).

When phrased in this way, Path 2 will sound the more rational of the two, assuming you can still achieve retirement security. A rigid adherence to the regimen implied by Path 1 could even cause you to fall below the poverty line for a while, which may seem a high price to pay to have excess cash at age 60.

Whether it is totally rational or not, we are constantly told to save in a way that more closely resembles Path 1. Even I suggested as much myself in the very first chapter when I said you could not go far wrong by saving 10 percent of your pay every year. If you take a retirement-centric approach to spending during your working years, Path 1 makes sense. On the other hand, there is a certain appeal to the more holistic approach to lifetime consumption that underlies Path 2.

Let us take a closer look at these two paths.

Path 1: Pain Now, Gain Later

The well-trod path to retirement security is to put money aside for retirement every year, come hell or high water. This is what many of us, the hard-core "ants," are inclined to do in any case because we would not feel comfortable otherwise. Under Path 1, retirement saving is a more or less steady percentage of pay each year and personal consumption is the balancing item. Remember that personal consumption is what remains after taking care of mortgage payments, child-raising costs, employment expenses, Social Security taxes, income tax, and retirement saving. Since some of these expenses can be quite volatile from one year to the next, personal consumption can fluctuate significantly under Path 1. This is what makes Path 1 hard to follow.

You can learn to get by without expensive vacations but what about daycare or making mortgage payments? To make Path 1 a little easier to follow, you could pretend that your gross income is 5 or 10 percent less than it actually is. If your employer offers a voluntary savings plan, have the money deducted from payroll so it never gets deposited into your bank account. You would then re-calibrate all of your other expenditures accordingly. Hence, you might buy a slightly less expensive home than the bank manager says you can afford or a less expensive car.

Even though this is more or less the path I chose myself, I have to say that following Path 1 will be painful from time to time. The example from Chapter 3 of Steve and Ashley 1.0 gave us a glimpse of why it is sometimes necessary to stray from Path 1. By age 34, they had

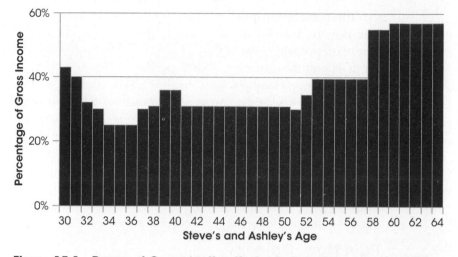

Figure 15.1   Personal Consumption Under Path 1 (Steve and Ashley)

bought their first house and just had their second child. After adding daycare expenses to what they were already spending on the mortgage, they had only 25 percent of their gross income left to spend on themselves. This is illustrated in Figure 15.1, which is the same as Figure 3.3 except that it strips away all the other expenditure items such as income tax, mortgage payments, and child-raising costs in order to highlight the percentage of gross income that Steve and Ashley had available for personal consumption over the course of their working lives.

As volatile as personal consumption looks in Figure 15.1, note that Steve and Ashley did not follow Path 1 to the letter; they saved less for retirement up until age 58 and more after that, when the mortgage was paid off. Under a pure Path 1 approach, their income available for consumption in their 30s would have been closer to 20 percent instead of 25 percent.

Even at higher income levels, it is not easy to follow Path 1 because the temptation to spend money on something you can barely afford is ever-present; it is just that the threshold is higher and the items that are tempting you are more expensive. If the object of your spending is not an indulgence but something that may improve your life or the lives of loved ones, it will be even more difficult to stay on the path. For instance, you might be able to convince yourself to settle for a week in Myrtle Beach rather than two weeks in the Turks & Caicos but do your children do without summer camp or ballet lessons?

Another hurdle to pursuing Path 1 is that your income or your expenditures might not be stable enough. You might be self-employed or working on a commission basis with highly variable pay in either case. Or you might incur extraordinary expenditures that just cannot be put off, like installing a new roof or dealing with some major dental work. Then there are the really major crises that will throw off your retirement planning, such as a business setback, a prolonged period of unemployment or disability, or divorce. When a crisis occurs, you might not be able to save at all for an extended period of time. Skipping a year of saving means having to double up the following year and the more you skip the harder it is to get back on the path.

You might be thinking, what about the participants in the large public sector pension plans who are required to contribute 9 percent of pay or more every year? Isn't this like Path 1? If millions of civil servants can do it, then why not you?

There are two reasons why it works in their case but may not work for you. The first is that a public sector job tends to be safer. Apart from the odd high-profile pay freeze that might be imposed on them from time to time, civil servants can expect reasonably steady pay increases with no interruptions in income. The second reason is that they are better protected than most private-sector workers or the self-employed from certain financial challenges, such as unexpected healthcare expenditures or long-term disability. Hence, both their income and their spending needs will be more stable than for most people.

To sum up, Path 1 can work if your ethos, income level, and job situation permit you to do so, and if life does not put too many road-blocks in your way.

Path 2: Smooth and Steady Improvement

The purpose of Path 2 is to enjoy a level of personal consumption that increases gradually over your working life and in the process avoid excessive hardship, especially in your 30s. This represents more than just an approach to retirement planning—it is a lifetime consumption philosophy.

In the pure version of Path 2, you would postpone retirement saving as well as any other expenditure that can be postponed until the time when you have the income to pay for them. This is more easily said than done, especially since some types of expenditure cannot be avoided or deferred. This includes the cost of raising children, Social Security contributions, employment expenses, and income taxes. In fact, the only major expenditures (other than personal consumption) that can be accelerated or delayed are retirement saving and, to a certain extent, mortgage payments. The objective is to time these more flexible expenditures in such a way that we accomplish the following:

- Smooth out personal consumption as a percentage of gross income (but build in a very gradual increase).
- Ultimately still pay the same amount toward the mortgage on the house (adjusted for interest).
- Still save enough for retirement to maintain the level of personal consumption in effect just before retirement.

When we do all this, we end up with Figure 15.2. This is the same Steve and Ashley as in Figure 15.1, except that they have now

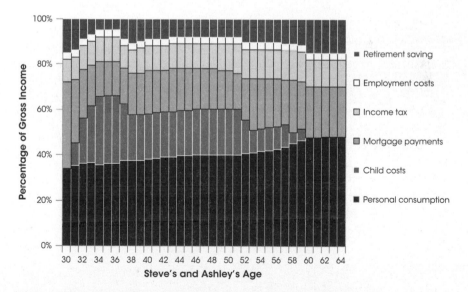

Figure 15.2   Smoothing Personal Consumption (Path 2)

stretched their mortgage payments out until age 65 and are saving less before age 50. The reward for doing all this is that their personal consumption as a percentage of pay never falls below 35 percent of gross income and they are much better off in most years between ages 32 and 52.

Path 2 represents a paradigm change for most people. It is more evocative of an enlightened grasshopper than a hard-saving but inflexible ant. We tend to assume there are times in life when financial struggle is unavoidable, but we live through those times in the hopes that better days will follow. For those with spotty earnings records or health issues, times of financial struggle may indeed be unavoidable, but for others, Path 2 should look quite appealing.

While I like Path 2 in principle, it does present some significant risks. First and foremost, you need to be able to trust yourself. If saving for retirement is no longer your highest priority, there will be the temptation to overspend on other aspects of your life on the grounds that delayed saving has been "officially" sanctioned. Once that genie is out of the bottle, it is hard to control.

Certain ways of overspending may seem unobjectionable but are nevertheless subtly dangerous, such as buying a slightly more expensive house than you should. And after a number of years of overspending and not saving, can you really find your way back to any path that leads to retirement security? The irony is that it takes more discipline to follow Path 2 than Path 1.

Another shortcoming of Path 2 is that you can no longer follow the savings strategies that were described in the last chapter. All those strategies put retirement saving first, unimpeded by any other spending priorities such as trying to regulate your personal consumption. To some extent, you can modify the various strategies to fit Path 2; it will just be more complicated than under Path 1 and it will be harder to gauge whether you are on track at any point in time.

The final problem is that Path 2 requires a certain number of years of high disposable income toward the end of your career so you can ramp up your retirement saving and mortgage payments to make up for lost time. If you are forced into early retirement by your employer or by ill health, both of which happen with alarming frequency, you will not be able to do that. Of course, unexpected early retirement is a problem under Path 1 as well, just not as big a problem.

Ultimately, you are unlikely to choose either Path 1 or Path 2 in their purest form, since both extremes present challenges. The question is, which of the two paths will you tend to favor? This depends heavily on your personal preferences about when you want to concentrate your consumption and on your risk tolerance. What is important is that you make an informed choice.

A Comparison in Dollar Terms

The foregoing charts compared personal consumption under versions of Path 1 and 2 with consumption expressed as a percentage of gross income. It is useful to make the comparison in dollar terms as well since percentages can mask the true effect. In particular, percentages hide the effect of real increases in earnings during one's working life.

Over a career, your pay tends to rise for three reasons:

1. General price inflation as measured by the consumer price index (CPI)
2. General productivity increases, which is why national average wages usually rise a little faster than CPI
3. Individual merit and promotions, which reflect your own performance

Even if we strip out general price inflation (CPI), your earnings will tend to be significantly higher toward the end of your career than at the beginning. By backing out the CPI portion of the increases, year-over-year earnings are more directly comparable.

I therefore show one more chart, which tracks personal consumption for Steve and Ashley in constant dollar terms. I have backed out the effects of general price inflation, but left in the impact of productivity increases as well as individual merit and promotions. I have been conservative in assuming that their wages rose by only 1.25 percent per annum over and above general price inflation. This is less than what most people experience over a career.

With all that, Figure 15.3 takes the percentages from the two previous charts and shows the personal consumption for Steve and Ashley under Path 1 and Path 2 in constant dollars.

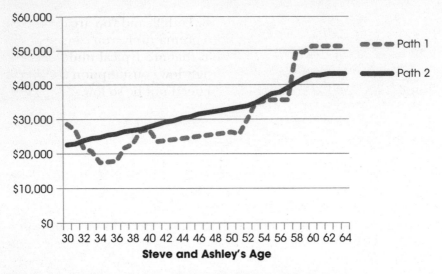

Figure 15.3 Personal Consumption (Constant Dollars)

In real terms, personal consumption for Steve and Ashley under Path 2 rises throughout their working lifetime and allows them to spend nearly twice as much in real terms by the time they retire. By the way, they also saved enough to enable themselves to carry on at this level of consumption after retirement.

Under Path 1, personal consumption is significantly lower than under Path 2 for nearly two thirds of their working life. Steve and Ashley's early 30s is a particularly challenging time as personal consumption in real terms actually declines for a few years. The reward, and it is significant one, is they have a higher level of personal income from age 58 and on.

Conclusions

Both paths to retirement security can make sense under the right conditions, but both of them could be hard to follow when a financial crisis arises, a threat that is ever-present and rarely foreseeable. Perhaps the best way to minimize the problem of saving enough in the event that a crisis arises is to overfund your retirement slightly in good times. This may mean saving an extra 2 or 3 percent of pay each year than the savings strategy and the path you are on would otherwise dictate so that you can expect to reach your wealth target a little sooner.

If you have the discipline to follow Path 2, and you are confident you will not be forced out of your job prematurely, you can avoid the wild swings in personal consumption that are typical under Path 1. In particular, the periods of exceedingly low consumption that many households face in their 20s and 30s need not be so low.

PART

IV

THE DECUMULATION PHASE

CHAPTER

16

Rational Roulette

We know that aging takes its toll on us physically. For a while, we can almost delude ourselves into thinking the effect is minimal but that illusion is shattered the moment we use an objective yardstick to measure our performance. The office worker at age 50 might think she feels as fit as she did at 30, but the former athlete with a stopwatch knows differently.

Is it possible that our mental abilities also diminish sooner and faster than we like to believe? If we look around us, we can find some objective benchmarks that suggest this is indeed the case.

Take chess, for example, which seems like a purely mental pursuit. Surely players keep on improving with experience and practice. One would think a wily 60-year-old with 10,000 lifetime games under his belt should be able to trounce a 20-year-old of equal talent. Yet the world chess rankings tell a different story. Among the top 30, no one is older than 47, and only 6 of them are over 40. On the other hand, 16 of the top 30 players are under age 30. The number one and two ranked players are just 25 and 23, and they are probably looking over their shoulder as the young upstarts gain ground.

Or consider the world of science. Einstein was 25 when he formulated the special theory of relativity and 35 when he published the general theory of relativity. Great as he was, Einstein made no significant contribution to science after 40. Indeed, it is hard to find any Nobel Prize winner for physics or chemistry who produced his or her seminal work after 50.

When a specific intellectual capability can be measured objectively, the inescapable conclusion is that it declines with age. But maybe the decline is insignificant in the case of the more mundane activities of life? When it comes to managing our investments, for example, or choosing appropriate insurance coverage, perhaps we are just as capable at 80 as we were at 40?

The answer is, apparently not. A recent study of the link between age and financial literacy[1] (Fink, Howe, and Huston) tested older Americans and their ability to answer standard questions relating to investments, insurance, and borrowing. As the authors of the study put it, the test measures *crystallized intelligence* that requires both memory and problem-solving skills.

In the study, a standard multiple-choice test was given to 1,725 people age 60 to 88 with varying education levels. To give an idea of the difficulty of the test, one of the questions asks, "If your assets increase by $5,000 and your liabilities decrease by $3,000, your net worth would increase by (1) $2,000, (2) $8,000, or (3) $3,000." Another question: "Savings accounts and money market accounts are most appropriate for: (1) long-term investments like retirement, (2) emergency funds and short-term goals, or (3) earning a high rate of return." So the questions were not dead easy, but really, anyone overseeing a six-figure investment portfolio should be able to answer them.

The test proved to be more of a challenge than it should have been. The average score for 60-year-olds was about 60 percent correct, which is barely a pass, and remember the test was multiple choice. Test scores actually rose a little up to age 65 but after that, they fell rather steadily. By age 73, the average score was less than 50 percent and subjects in their 80s did not even reach 40 percent. For the very oldest subjects, the test results were worse than if one answered the questions randomly.

The foregoing may confirm what you already thought to be true—but here is where it gets interesting. While older test subjects scored quite poorly by any absolute or relative measure, their confidence in their financial abilities was actually higher than that of their younger counterparts. People in their 80s were generally more confident than those in their 60s, even though the older group scored barely half as high.

The knee-jerk reaction is to find fault with the study. Maybe the test was somehow biased against older test subjects. For instance, the older cohort might not have been as highly educated or age might have correlated with lower income, which was the real reason for the lower scores. The researchers were well aware of these possibilities and tested rigorously for any such bias. Moreover, the results of this study merely corroborated similar findings reported by others.

Another important finding in the study was that the test scores were dropping at a fairly steady rate. This eliminated the possibility that the deterioration was caused by the sudden onset of a stroke, dementia, or other condition, which is significant for two reasons. First, staying physically healthy is no guarantee that your cognitive abilities will remain intact. Second, there is no clear line of demarcation that signifies when you are no longer mentally competent; the process is gradual.

Call to Action

The reader might be thinking that the polite thing to do is to turn a blind eye to this deterioration, but that would be doing the elderly a disservice. The results of the study suggest preemptive measures need to be taken. This issue is important to all of us, regardless of age, since we will grow old eventually (if we are lucky) and we need to use whatever insights we have at our disposal to protect ourselves.

Seniors need to grapple with a variety of important financial decisions at various stages of retirement, such as deciding when to start Social Security benefits, choosing between purchasing an annuity versus managing their own portfolios, picking service-providers for financial planning and investments, changing the manage the asset mix of any savings they maintain in retirement, selling off nonfinancial assets, writing or revising their wills, deciding whether to co-sign loans for their grown-up children, assessing long-term care and critical illness insurance, and deciding on what type of long-term care facility they would want, should it ever come to that.

I am not suggesting that we delegate all these decisions to our grown-up children once we reach a certain age. All the older people I know are fiercely determined to hold onto their independence and to control their own affairs as long as they can; we will be no different when it is our turn. My point, rather, is that we should get our affairs in order as much as possible while we are still young enough to be confident of our abilities and our judgment. If we take the right steps in our 60s, we can operate more or less on autopilot after age 75. You may still be eminently competent in your 70s, or perhaps not; the trouble is that you may not know for sure.

For example, if you continue to manage a portfolio of investments, set up a long-term investment policy that dictates how the asset mix will change as you age. Better yet, convert at least a part of your life savings to an annuity by the time you reach age 75. If you are a US citizen, you can make the arrangements in advance—say, at age 50 or 60—by buying a deferred annuity to commence at 75 or 80. The cost of a deferred annuity will be considerably lower than an immediate pension because it will be discounted for both interest and survivorship. In Canada, it is generally not possible due to tax reasons to buy a deferred annuity where payments commence after age 71, so you may need to wait until age 75 and buy an immediate annuity instead. But make it a part of your plan to do so now.

If you have your own business, succession planning is something else you need to settle while you are still capable. I know of situations very close to home where the business-owner waited too long to do this and then simply was incapable of making the necessary decisions when the need for it became obvious (to others).

It seems to be common practice for the people who make arrangements on behalf of the elderly, once they are no longer capable of doing so themselves, to pick the most expensive long-term care solution available—ostensibly because they are trying to do the right thing—and thus run that person's finances into the ground. If the person receiving the care is still alive when their money runs out, they then have to be moved to a less expensive long-term care facility. If you have any strong views on how your own long-term care should be arranged, make those views known, preferably in writing, before you need it. You might very well decide not to waste your legacy on an ultra-high level of care if you would be satisfied with a less expensive option.

If any new and significant financial matter arises in your 70s or later that requires a decision, take counsel from a younger person whom you trust and who does not have a vested interest. If at 80 you are bent on doing something that everyone around you is saying is a mistake, they are probably right.

You might think, "Why bother setting this decision delegation process up so early? I can wait until I see signs that managing my affairs is becoming too much for me to handle and I will act then." You know yourself that will not work. As the study pointed out, our confidence in our mental abilities grows with age, even as that ability is deteriorating.

By trying to maintain complete independence in your financial matters as long as possible, you are essentially playing a sort of Russian roulette, or what we might more appropriately name *rational roulette*. How long is it safe to make all the decisions, and how will you know when it is no longer safe?

Watch Out for Your Children

Financial planner Rona Birenbaum points out that most of her older clients "hold onto every expression of their independence for as long as they possibly can," sometimes to their detriment. If you are eventually going to be forced to relinquish control, you will no doubt prefer to have the conduct of your ongoing financial affairs reflect your own preferences from a time when you were still of sound mind and body rather than the preferences of others who take over from you, no matter how competent they might be.

It is exceedingly common for the grown-up children of elderly parents to start to feel a sense of ownership of their parents' assets while one or both parents are still alive. Sometimes, the children of elderly clients slowly bleed their parents dry with ongoing requests for financial support. I know of one case myself, and Rona tells me it is not atypical.

The elderly parents reach a point when they become especially vulnerable to requests for money, but they could have protected themselves better by taking appropriate action earlier on. As already mentioned, such action might include buying an annuity. By the time you really need it, it may well be too late to do it, either because you are no longer capable of making that choice or because your own adult children block you from proceeding. You will therefore want to plan ahead for that dreaded time when you need to cede control to your children or other guardians.

This brings up the issue of the power of attorney document (POA). I asked Kimberly A. Whaley, certified specialist in estates and trust law, for her thoughts on the POA. She said that this document has long been viewed as a means to legally protect one's financial and personal care interests by planning in advance for illness, infirmity, or decisional incapacity respecting property and personal care. The POA also can be useful in minimizing future family conflict and perhaps preventing expensive and avoidable litigation. In certain circumstances, however, POA documents may cause rather than prevent conflict, and as such they must be drafted to reflect the specific needs of the individual and that individual's family dynamics.

In essence, a POA is a legal instrument that grants an individual (known as the attorney) the right to making financial decisions and conducting certain transactions on behalf of the grantor. In the case of property transactions it is known as a power of attorney for property (POAP). A POAP can be limited to a specific time or task and is often used in business or for a short-term purpose. Also, if the grantor of a POAP becomes mentally incapable, his or her attorney can no longer act for them. However, a POAP can also be cast in "continuing" or "enduring" form (a CPOAP), in which case it permits an attorney to continue to act even after the grantor becomes incapacitated.

The powers to act on your behalf under a POAP/CPOAP are effective *immediately* upon signing, unless there is a triggering mechanism in the document stating that it will come into effect at a specific future date or event, such as the incapacity of the grantor as determined by a recognized third party. This can make a POA both a desirable and a dangerous document. Many older adults use a POA so that an adult child can assist with banking, not realizing the extent of the power they have granted. A POAP is an extremely powerful document that enables an attorney (the person appointed to make financial decision on your behalf) to do virtually anything on the grantor's behalf in respect of property that the grantor could do if capable, except make a will.

An unscrupulous child could see this as an opportunity to access an inheritance early, or misuse the power in a self-interested manner. In one real-life case, an only child of an elderly widow used a POA that his mother granted him to deplete her of all her assets, leaving her penniless and reduced to living in a homeless shelter. The mother had over $1 million in assets, including several properties. The son used the powers under the CPOAP to mortgage all of her properties for his own benefit and then defaulted on all of the mortgages. He also drained her bank account and investment accounts. At trial, the judge noted, "In jail, [the son] would be better off physically than his own mother. He will be sheltered, fed regularly and kept warm." The son was sentenced to 10 years in prison though this was reduced to 8 years on appeal.

Another real-life story involves an older adult who was duped into granting a POA for property to her caregiver. The older adult was a frail elderly woman who suffered a number of physical challenges that left her vulnerable and dependent upon her caregiver. The caregiver used the POA to obtain a bank card for the older adult's savings account and drained the bank account of over $100,000. The caregiver was sentenced to 21 months in prison.

POAs are a practical, flexible, and convenient way to plan for your potential decisional incapacity or illness. However, they can make older adults vulnerable to financial abuse. Obviously, the choice of an attorney is very important. While children may be an obvious choice, they may not be your best or wisest option. Regardless, you will want to settle these matters long before the need for a POA arises.

You may never lose your ability to handle your financial affairs, but you do not want to rely on dumb luck that you can somehow avoid the infirmities that afflict most of us in our later years. My advice is to take action sooner rather than later.

Note

1. Michael S. Fink, John Howe, and Sandra J. Huston, "Old Age and the Decline in Financial Literacy," Social Science Research Network, 2012.

Revisiting the 4 Percent Rule

Hard as it is to save for retirement and to invest those savings wisely, it is harder yet to watch the pile of savings that you nurtured for so long start to shrink. It has to happen eventually, of course, but it will likely cause some quiet anxiety in the early days of retirement. After all, you do not really know whether you are spending your hoard down too quickly. What you do know is that you will never again have employment income to augment your savings in case you miscalculated on your retirement needs.

On the other hand, you do not want to shortchange yourself by spending less than you could. As my friend Borden would say, you do not want to be the richest person in the cemetery.

There is a quick fix for this dilemma, which is to buy an annuity with your life savings. An annuity will furnish a steady stream of retirement income for the rest of your life and, if you wish, also for the life of your spouse if he or she survives you. Annuities are not popular, however, for reasons which we will review in the next chapter, so let us assume for the time being that you will not buy one. If instead you decide to maintain control of your savings, you will need to establish some guidelines to regulate how much of your account balance you can safely spend each year.

The 4 Percent Rule

A long-standing rule of thumb is that one should limit annual withdrawals from savings to 4 percent a year. If your savings total $500,000, for example, the 4 percent rule allows you to withdraw

Table 17.1   How the 4 Percent Rule Works

Year	Account balance	Withdrawal of 4% at end of year	Investment return
1	$500,000	$20,000	$30,000
2	$510,000	$20,400	$30,600
3	$520,200	$20,808	$31,212
4	$530,604	$21,224	$31,836

Assume inflation is 2% and real return is 4%

$20,000 in the first year. If all goes according to plan, the remaining $480,000 would earn enough investment income to recover the $20,000 you withdrew plus a little more to make up for lost purchasing power due to inflation. In theory, this enables you to keep spending $20,000 plus inflation every year into perpetuity.

In the ideal situation, the 4 percent rule is intended to accomplish three goals:

1. Provide a retirement income stream that grows over time to keep pace with inflation.
2. Allow you to maintain control of your money in case of an emergency.
3. Leave a substantial bequest to loved ones.

The implicit assumption is that your portfolio will generate a high enough real return (close to 4 percent) to achieve these three goals. Table 17.1 gives an illustration of the rule in action, using an initial account balance of $500,000 and a real return on the portfolio of 4 percent. I simplified the math by assuming withdrawals are made once a year, at year-end.

As Table 17.1 shows, the 4 percent withdrawals grow every year in step with inflation, but thanks to a real investment return of 4 percent, so does the account balance. This sounds like a tidy arrangement in theory. Let us see how it would have worked in real life.

Figure 17.1 shows the income that a retiree could have withdrawn under the 4 percent rule from 1988 to 2012, with a starting balance of $200,000. It is assumed that the account balance was invested 50 percent in equities and 50 percent in bonds the entire time and that annual investment management fees were 1 percent of assets.

If anything, the chart seems to confirm that the 4 percent rule works admirably in practice. The initial income of about $8,000

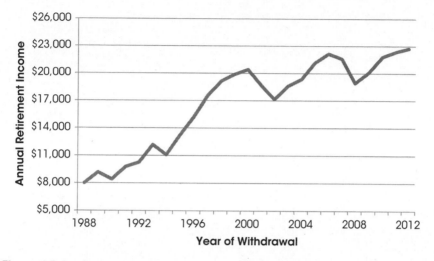

Figure 17.1 **Historical Income from 4 Percent Rule**

almost triples in nominal terms and also rises substantially in real terms (with a couple of hiccups between 2000 and 2009 during the bear markets). What could possibly be wrong with this?

Problems with the 4 Percent Rule

The 4 percent rule contains at least four major flaws, though the first two flaws, as described next, at least offset each other to some extent.

Unrealistic Returns

The 4 percent rule is contingent on achieving a real return of close to 4 percent per annum. As Figure 17.1 showed, a market-based portfolio easily did that and more in the past 25 or so years. In the 1990s, even a boring portfolio of super-safe government bonds would have delivered real returns in the vicinity of 4 percent. As we learned in Chapter 6, however, the capital markets are not what they used to be. In this era of low interest rates, a 4 percent real return would be a stretch, even in a professionally managed portfolio. You will be doing well to earn a little more than 3 percent, and even then you will need to assume some risk to do so.

Part of the problem is that we cannot expect as high of a return from equity investments as we used to. Equities have done an admirable job in producing high returns over the long run,

Table 17.2   High Returns on Equities

Period	Average real return per annum
1934–1943	4.63%
1944–1953	9.87%
1954–1963	10.66%
1964–1973	4.67%
1974–1983	3.42%
1984–1993	4.99%
1994–2003	6.64%
2004–2013	6.12%

Geometric averages of returns on Canadian stocks, including dividends and capital gains
2013 Canadian economic statistics, Canadian Institute of Actuaries

assuming one averages returns over long enough periods to smooth out the volatility. Table 17.2 shows the real returns on Canadian equities in each 10-year period since 1934 (US equities would have performed similarly well).

Over a 75-year period, the real return on both US and Canadian equities averaged over 6 percent a year, compounded annually. If one combined equities with long-term government bonds and 91-day T-bills and maintained an asset mix of 60/35/5, the average real return from the late 1930s until now would have exceeded 4 percent. The problem, however, is that an aging population means there are many more savers around who are seeking places to invest their money and fewer borrowers who are requesting loans. As we learned in Chapter 6, this demographic phenomenon is depressing investment yields in a very obvious way in the case of bonds, and more subtly in the case of equities.

Even if demographics were not rewriting the investment story, the real return on bonds will almost certainly be less than the long-term average of 2.25 percent. Returns on bonds are composed of regular interest, as expressed by the bond yield, plus irregular capital gains or losses when bonds are sold before maturity. Right now, we are at or near the bottom of a long-term cycle that saw long-term bond yields fall from over 15 percent down to less than 3 percent over the past 30-some-odd years. Nominal yields on government bonds can either stay in the 2 to 3 percent range where they are today, in which case the real return will be close to nil, or yields can rise, in which case bonds will produce capital losses. Given where we are today, the only scenario under which bonds will produce good returns is outright deflation and that is not a scenario to wish for.

It is not obvious that any asset class will do well over the next 20 years but assuming equities are the place to be, it will be difficult to persuade retirees of that. The stock market crash in 2008 and early 2009 scared many investors out of the market for good. One survey taken shortly after the 2008–2009 financial crisis indicated that 6 people out of 10 thought they could save for retirement without having to invest in equities at all. It is unlikely then, that many, if not most, retirees will be comfortable allocating more than 50 percent of their portfolio in equities in the years to come. They should be even less comfortable doing so now that the stock market indices have more than tripled from their 2009 lows. The upside potential has diminished and the downside risk is starting to look increasingly ominous.

At best, if we apply the same principles that underlie the original 4 percent rule, it would now become the 3 percent rule, or maybe even the $2\frac{1}{2}$ percent rule.

Leaving Too Much on the Table

Historically, a 4 percent rule would have been a bit of a disaster in terms of money management in retirement. Although Figure 17.1 might look good because the income stream is trending strongly upward over time, the retiree in the example could have comfortably drawn much more income in the early years of retirement, which is the time when she could really have used the money. Fully 25 years after retirement and after all the withdrawals that were made, she would still have $608,000 left in her account, more than triple the starting value!

If you really did earn a real return of 4 percent in the future, and withdrew 4 percent a year in accordance with the rule, think of what that would leave in your estate at the end of your life. If that life was lived frugally, the amount of unspent money borders on the tragic.

Once again, let us say your account balance at the point of retirement is $500,000 and you withdraw 4 percent each year for 25 years and then die. If you actually earned a 4 percent real return the entire time, you would have $500,000 (in present-day dollars) left in your account when you die. In nominal terms, assuming inflation averaged 2 percent a year, your account balance upon death would be

$820,000. The scenario sounds like an article one might find on page 17 of the local newspaper: "Miser dies at 90 leaving behind 15 cats and $820,000 in his mattress." Is this why you saved so diligently?

So when investments actually produced a real return of 4 percent, the 4 percent rule historically would have left too much money on the table. By extension, if the best estimate of the real return from this point on is 3 percent, it would be too conservative to withdraw just 3 percent of your account balance each year. Does that mean the 4 percent rule used to be wrong but now that rates have fallen, it has redeemed itself? We will see.

Investment Returns Are Volatile

The average annual return that a market-based portfolio will produce in the long run, whether it is 3 percent or 4 percent in real terms, is not the return you will necessarily achieve over shorter periods. It should come as no surprise that market-based returns are volatile, even if we average them out over longer periods, such as 5 years. Figure 17.2 shows the average annual real returns achieved by the median Canadian pension fund (which is usually invested 60 percent in equities and 40 percent in bonds) in every 5-year period since 1964.

The real return over 5-year periods varied from negative 2.9 percent to a positive 10.3 percent. To put that into perspective, on a starting balance of $500,000 with no withdrawals, the balance after 5 years would have ranged from $430,000 to $816,000. The real return in any 1-year period would have varied even more, from negative 17 percent to 19 percent. If you decide to spend a constant percentage of your remaining savings, do not expect it to equate to a stable number of dollars.

Withdrawals Do Not Match Spending Patterns

The final problem with the 4 percent rule is that the withdrawals do not mirror your spending needs. The assumption underlying the rule is that your spending will rise in lock-step with inflation; in other words, spending will remain constant in real terms. As we saw in Chapter 7, this is not usually the case. If you are like most retirees, you will tend to spend a little more each year until about age 70, and then you will gradually spend less (in real terms) throughout your 70s and 80s. You would be better off spending more in the early part

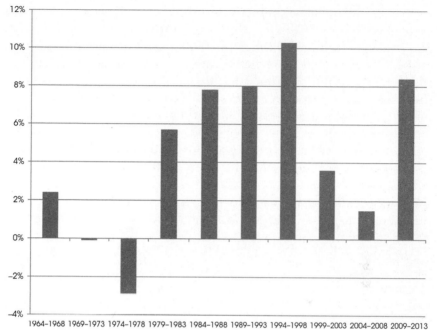

Figure 17.2   Average Real Return on a Balanced Portfolio

of your retirement and less later on, which is the opposite of what the 4 percent rule tends to do.

A More Rational Spending Rule

The foregoing suggests we need a better set of guidelines for drawing down our retirement savings. The first step is deciding what size of estate you would like to pass on. Consider three scenarios:

- Scenario A: Leaving an account balance at age 90 that is worth as much in real terms as when you were 65.
- Scenario B: Leaving an account balance at 90 that is worth as much as at 65 but only in nominal terms at 90.
- Scenario C: Having barely enough left to pay your funeral expenses.

Scenario A

Note that Scenario A is consistent with the original 4 percent rule. As I have already indicated, it is highly doubtful that you really want to leave that much behind in unspent savings. If you are still not convinced, look at it this way. Say that your parents retired 25 years ago at age 65 with a final salary of $60,000. After diligently saving in an RRSP their entire working life, they had accumulated $200,000, which was a sizable amount back then but more or less realistic if they had saved 8 percent or 9 percent a year and invested it well. As a prospective heir, would you be expecting your parents to hold back from spending their money so they could leave you $340,000 on their death, which is what the original account balance would have grown to with inflation? I will assume the answer is no. You can safely assume your children or other heirs will feel the same way when it is your time to go, and if they feel otherwise, they probably do not deserve the inheritance anyway. Either way, you should not feel morally compelled to make a large bequest.

On this point, it is interesting to note the disconnect between what elderly parents intend to leave their adult children and what the children themselves expect. Consider a survey that was conducted by Kyungmin Kim of the Population Research Center at the University of Texas. They polled the parents, who were age 59 to 96, as well their adult children, who were age 40 to 60. Among the parents, 86.2 percent indicated they planned to leave a bequest. Among the children, however, just 44.6 thought they would receive an inheritance. Most tellingly, in only 2.4 percent of the situations did the parents indicate they did not intend to grant an inheritance but the child was expecting one.

Scenario B

Under Scenario B, you spend the nominal return each year, not the real return. If the nominal return was 6 percent, the same as in Scenario A, and you had $500,000 when you retired, you would earn investment income of $30,000. If you spend all of it, the account balance would remain at $500,000 year after year, as is illustrated in Table 17.3.

You will note that under this scenario, your withdrawals would remain static at $30,000 a year, which means that their purchasing power is slowly eroding. Conventional thinking is that this is a problem, but if inflation is low and spending declines in real terms after age 70, the problem essentially goes away. In any event, you will receive a modest amount of inflation protection from Social Security pensions.

Table 17.3   Scenario B: Spending the Nominal Return

Year	Account balance	Withdrawal of 6% at end of year	Investment return
1	$500,000	$30,000	$30,000
2	$500,000	$30,000	$30,000
3	$500,000	$30,000	$30,000
4	$500,000	$30,000	$30,000

Assume inflation is 2% and the real return is 4%.

Under Scenario B, you still have $500,000 left in your account at death. In present-day dollars (assuming 2 percent annual inflation), this would be worth $305,000 if you die in 25 years. Most people would agree this is a more appropriate amount to leave behind than under Scenario A.

Scenario C

Under Scenario C, you would be withdrawing not just the 6 percent of your account balance each year, which would leave the $500,000 of principal intact, you would also be slowly drawing down the principal so that the amount of savings left at the end of your life is minimal. Assume that your initial payout is 6.5 percent of the account balance and that you increase it each year by 80 percent of the change in CPI.

Because the initial withdrawal is large and it is increasing in subsequent years, it means you are withdrawing an increasing percentage of your account balance each year. This is shown in Table 17.4.

Scenario C has a certain appeal to it. Unlike Scenario A, the initial withdrawal is quite sizable, and unlike Scenario B, the withdrawals increase every year. The resulting income is quite attractive, assuming it is sustainable. As long as the fund earns a 6 percent annual return,

Table 17.4   Scenario C: Accelerated Withdrawals

Year	Account balance	Withdrawal at end of each year	Investment return
1	$500,000	$32,500	$30,000
2	$497,500	$32,825	$29,850
3	$494,925	$33,153	$29,672
4	$491,043	$33,485	$29,463

Scenario C allows increasing withdrawals to be made until age 95, at which time there would be about $54,000 left in the account.

To summarize, spending only the real return (Scenario A) is what some experts will tell you to do, but you should know that the 4 percent rule used to leave a lot of money on the table when real returns actually were 4 percent. Spending the nominal return (Scenario B) will seem a lot more reasonable to most people. Spending a little more than the nominal return and then increasing that each year (Scenario C) can be even more appealing, assuming you did not intend to make a large bequest.

How does all this jibe with real-life situations? I asked Franco Barbiero, investment counselor at RBC Phillips, Hager & North Investment Counsel. Here is what Franco sees among his clientele:

> The 4% rule continues to appeal to investors who are determined to either preserve or grow their capital over their entire lifetime; however, I have found that this life-long capital accumulation and preservation approach is far less common than it was 20 years ago. I am increasingly encountering clients who ask, "How much can I comfortably spend without running out of money?" The answer is almost always more than 4%.
>
> For retiring or retired clients who are more concerned about maximizing cash flow than in preserving capital, I am typically able to show via cash flow forecasting that annual withdrawal rates of 5–7%, and sometimes higher, are safe and reasonable under a variety of investment return and life expectancy assumptions. As one can imagine, clients delight in the outcome and waste little time in finding uses for this "new-found" cash flow.

The same conclusions apply whether the real return in the future is 4 percent or 3 percent. It seems reasonably safe to spend the expected long-term nominal return on your savings with the proviso that you might revisit that spending rate every 5 years to assess whether you can be spending more or should be spending less.

A Monte Carlo Simulation

When I say it seems to be *reasonably safe* to be spending the nominal return on the fund each year, I would be the first to agree that such a statement needs to be supported by some hard analysis. Admittedly,

Scenario C does seem a little dangerous. To test it more rigorously, I had the Morneau Shepell Retirement Solutions team run a Monte Carlo simulation for me.

This involved starting with an account balance of $500,000, which is invested conservatively, and running it through hundreds of simulations in which the investment returns vary the way we would expect in a real-life situation. The assets were assumed to be invested 30 percent in equities and 70 percent in bonds. After running hundreds of simulations, the (nominal) median long-term return on this portfolio turned out to be about 4.5 percent after investment fees.

In the simulation, it was assumed that the amount withdrawn each year is 5 percent until age 80 and that whatever assets remain are used to purchase an annuity for life. In effect, this is a blend of Scenarios B and C above.

The withdrawal assumption appears to be inviting trouble, since it is higher than the median return. Moreover, we know that under some of the simulations, the return will be nil or even negative in some years. You would think that there is a good chance the retiree might run out of money by age 80. That is why the results are surprising.

With a withdrawal rate fixed at 5 percent, the maximum amount that was withdrawn in any year in all the simulations was $46,381, or almost twice the initial withdrawal of $25,000 (being 5 percent of $500,000). More important, the minimum withdrawal in any simulation was $12,003, and in more than half the simulations, the minimum withdrawal was over $20,000. As for the amount of annuity that could be purchased with the remaining account balance at age 80, the median amount was $40,737 and the lowest amount was $21,856.

The bottom line is that if we believe in the assumptions used in the Monte Carlo simulations, withdrawing 5 percent a year is conservatively low, even though the fund is expected to earn only 4.5 percent a year. Alternate scenarios such as investing the portfolio less conservatively and/or withdrawing more than 5 percent a year, produced even better results in terms of cash flow and the downside risk continued to be minimal. It seems Franco's clients are on the right track.

Conclusions

Withdrawing 5 percent a year is still relatively safe these days assuming your investment portfolio is expected to earn 4.5 percent a year or more.

In fact, withdrawing 6 or even 7 percent might not be outlandish, depending on the asset mix.

You can reduce the chances of running out of money and also reduce the volatility in the amounts you withdraw by purchasing an annuity at age 80, if not earlier. Not only does this give you more certainty at a stage in life when you are better off not making complicated financial decisions, it also tends to result in higher income if you live an embarrassingly long time.

Remember that the higher the percentage payout, the less you will have left to spend at more advanced ages. This might seem like a negative, but it might actually dovetail nicely with your natural spending habits as you move to a less-active phase of your retirement. You will probably want spending to keep up with inflation when you are in your 60s, but the odds are that you will eventually start spending less.

18

Why People Hate Annuities (But Should Still Buy One)

Let's face it: almost no one likes annuities. After saving diligently your whole life to build up a six-figure or seven-figure nest egg, are you really going to surrender all that money to an insurance company in return for a seemingly paltry stipend? If that is not bad enough, the insurance company keeps your money if you die early.

The general apathy, if not downright antipathy, toward annuities dates from long before the current era of low interest rates that has made this insurance product so much more expensive than it used to be. People were not buying traditional annuities even back in the day when interest rates were over 10 percent.

To put a number to it, Thomas Reid (senior VP of Group Retirement Services at Sun Life Financial) confirms that fewer than 5 percent of participants in capital accumulation plans use their account balances to buy an annuity at retirement, a figure that is based on data on about 1 million participants. The vast majority of participants in such plans continue to manage their own monies after they retire.

And if you think annuities are a product that only an actuary can love, think again. Even actuaries (with some notable exceptions) tend to avoid annuities in their own personal retirement planning. This tendency does not stem from a careful analysis of the pros and cons but more from a general feeling that actuaries have that they can do better managing their own investments after retirement. To be clear, this general feeling does not usually hold up to hard scrutiny, even in the case of actuaries.

In spite of all the resentment we might harbor against insurance companies or insurance products, I strongly suggest that the reader give serious consideration to the purchase of an annuity. Before we go into the reasons, let me make it clear that I work for a human resources consulting firm (Morneau Shepell), not an insurance company. I own no shares in any insurance company stock and have no pecuniary or other interest in whether insurers sell annuities or not, other than one of purely professional curiosity.

Why Annuities Should Be Popular

Surveys have consistently shown that, health aside, the biggest worry amongst retirees is outliving their money. Dying penniless might seem a romantic way to go if you are a starving nineteenth-century artist, but it does not hold much allure in the modern world. Annuities are the only product specifically designed to guarantee that this unfortunate outcome will not come to pass. When the insurance company accepts your money, they are committing to making monthly payments to you for the rest of your life, regardless of whether you live to 64 or 104.

Cases of insurance companies not fulfilling their obligations to make the promised annuity payments are exceedingly rare. No one in Canada has ever lost a penny as a result of an insurance company failing to its contractual commitment. There have been a very few high-profile failures in the United States, specifically Executive Life in 1991 and Baldwin United in 1983, but even then, the damage was limited and no failures have occurred since then, in spite of the 2008–2009 global financial crisis. Moreover, Assuris in Canada and an array of state-run Life and Health Guaranty Associations in the United States reduce even further the possibility of not receiving the promised annuity payments, if a failure does occur. This is not to say there is no chance that an insurer will default on annuity payments, just that the odds of it happening are exceedingly slim.

Even if we agree that annuities are safer than most investments, you might still balk at buying an annuity since the payouts seem rather meager. Why not manage your own portfolio into retirement, you might ask, since it enables you to draw a monthly income and continue to maintain control of your money well into retirement? I will call this the *portfolio* option.

This is a question that demands a good answer. To that end, let us consider the case of a 65-year-old retiree who is deciding between the portfolio option or buying an annuity. We will break this down into two examples. In the first, we will compare annuities to investing in a market-based portfolio of stocks and bonds that achieves a level of return that one can derive only by taking risks. In the second example, we make an adjustment for the investment risk in such a portfolio. The adjustment involves assuming a lower return from the portfolio option, in line with what risk-free investments yield these days.

Example 1: Market-Based Portfolio vs. Annuity

In this first example, the portfolio option involves drawing income from a market-based investment portfolio that is invested 50 percent in stocks and 50 percent in bonds (50/50 mix). You should note this first example is skewed in favor of the portfolio option, since we ignore the risk that is inherent with such an asset mix. The assumptions we use for the example are set out in Table 18.1.

Given that the portfolio contains equities, the portfolio option *should* do better than the annuity option because it is riskier. While higher risk usually goes hand in hand with higher returns, at least in the long run, it also gives rise to the possibility of doing worse. As history has shown, the stock market might perform badly for more than a decade.

Based on the assumptions in Table 18.1, a comparison of the annuity versus the 50/50 portfolio option is given in Table 18.2. I assumed that the annual income under the portfolio option would be dictated by the amount of annuity that could be purchased. In

Table 18.1   Long-Term Economic Assumptions

Age of individual (male)	65
Lump sum at that age	$500,000
Price Inflation (CPI)	2.25%
Annuity purchase rate (not indexed)	2.75%
Type of annuity	For life, with 66.7% continuing to surviving spouse after death of first spouse
Return on (50/50) investment portfolio net of fees	5.00%

Data Source: Morneau Shepell Retirement Solutions Practice

Table 18.2   Annuity vs. Drawing Income from an Investment Portfolio

	Annuity	Portfolio option
Annual amount paid	$30,000	$30,000
Age when money runs out	Never	98 (on average)
Residual value for spouse if annuity holder dies at 70	$268,000	$466,000
Residual value for spouse if annuity holder dies at 90	$95,000	$211,000

Based on the assumptions in Table 18.1.

other words, I estimate the amount of the annuity payments first and then set the voluntary withdrawals under the portfolio option at the same level. From the perspective of the retiree, the scenarios differ only in how long the annual income can be paid out and the residual value at the time the annuity holder dies.

As Table 18.2 shows, the portfolio option looks pretty good, which it should since we assumed it would achieve a decent return and ignored the potential downside risk. Even so, the annuity did not fare too badly in the comparison. The value of the death benefit for the spouse is still substantial, and only the annuity option guarantees a steady income for life.

Example 2: A Risk-Adjusted Example

The second example is similar except that we assume the assets under the portfolio option are invested entirely in GICs. The GIC yield will be assumed to be 2.5 percent, which is actually a little higher than is available at the time of writing.

As Table 18.3 shows, the annuity option under this set of circumstances is practically a no-brainer. You cannot afford to have your money run out at 86 when there is a better than 50 percent chance that either you or your spouse will survive that long. The only point in favor of the portfolio option is that it provides a better death benefit in the event of early death (age 70). The annuity option, however, is better from age 80 and on and, moreover, it eliminates any need to worry about what the stock market is doing or what happens if you live beyond age 86.

One caveat is that the death benefit under the annuity option in this example is payable only to the surviving spouse. If there is none, then there is no residual value.

Table 18.3   Annuity vs. Drawing Income

	Annuity	Drawing income from a 50/50 investment portfolio
Annual amount paid	$30,000	$30,000
Age when money runs out	Never	86
Residual value for spouse if annuity holder dies at 70	$268,000	$404,000
Residual value for spouse if annuity holder dies at 80	$176,000	$174,000

Based on the assumptions in Table 18.1

This example is still a little biased against annuities because 5-year GICs are yielding less than 2.5 percent at the time of writing. When one has to reinvest the GICs in 5 years, the concern is that rates might fall further, whereas one does not have any reinvestment risk under the annuity option.

The foregoing gives the financial justification for buying an annuity with one's retirement savings. As we learned in Chapter 16, another important reason to annuitize is to protect yourself in your later retirement years from bad financial decisions, either of your own making or made by someone who exercises power of attorney over your affairs.

The Psychology Behind the Unpopularity

Some of the reasons we steer away from annuities are a little irrational or at least irrelevant. For instance, many of us dislike insurance companies themselves, a feeling that might stem from an unpleasant experience in dealing with a claim. If you get into a minor car accident, you usually pay for the repairs out of your own pocket, even though the insurance could cover it. You do so because you are afraid your premiums will go up if you file a claim, a perception that is likely to cause you some resentment. Or you might have filed a claim after incurring damage to your home, only to be told of some obscure clause in your home insurance contract that excludes that particular type of incident from coverage.

The insurance companies that provide automobile and home insurance coverage are different from the ones that provide annuities or life insurance, but frustrated people are unlikely to make that distinction. As far as they are concerned, all insurance companies are faceless monoliths that take care of their own interests first.

Let us put aside the emotional reasons for rejecting annuities and consider the psychology behind our investment decisions. Science tells us that annuities are unpopular because our brains are wired to dislike them. It will come as no surprise that people do not make financial decisions based on purely rational factors. When there is a wide array of possible outcomes, it is human nature to focus on the extreme outcomes[1] and ignore the others, even if the latter are much more likely to occur.

Thus, people will unconsciously make their assessment of annuities by looking at what happens under extreme situations. The extreme of living too long, of course, is adequately covered. The other extreme, however—that of dying prematurely—is not as well protected, at least not with a typical annuity. (Later on, we will see that even this problem can sometimes be remedied.)

Another reason that we perceive annuities so negatively is their opaqueness. As wary consumers, we prefer transparency, but annuities are the ultimate black box. You cannot see how the premium is calculated, or how much the insurance company has loaded in for expenses and profits.

This suggests that annuities would be a lot more popular if the insurance companies could create a product that did a better job of covering you in extreme situations and that was more transparent. Such a product once existed in the United States and Europe.

Tontines

Over a century ago, tontines used to be wildly popular in the United States, so much so that enormous amounts of money were accumulated and eventually misused, which led to them being outlawed in the United States by 1905.

Within a tontine, the insured paid an annual premium for a number of years. These premiums were split into two parts, one part providing life insurance in the case of early death and the other part going into an investment fund that would be shared by the participants who survived for a specified period, usually 20 years.

Unlike regular annuities, tontines gave a payout that was not only fair, it was *perceived* to be fair in the event of dying early. If one died before the end of the specified period, the beneficiary received the life insurance payout while the participants who were still alive at the end of the specified period shared in the proceeds of the investment fund.

The reason for the resounding success of tontines can be attributed to the fact that the two main objections to annuities described above were both addressed. People were covered against the extreme outcomes and the arrangement was reasonably transparent.

The trouble is we do not have tontines anymore. But can we approximate the benefits of a tontine with existing life insurance products?

The Insured Annuity Strategy

It is possible to pursue an insured annuity strategy that bears a strong resemblance to a tontine. It involves the back-to-back purchase of both life insurance and a regular annuity. The life insurance provides a tidy sum for one's heirs while the annuity furnishes a good level of after-tax income for as long as one lives. Thus, both the eventualities of dying too young and living too long are covered off, one of the prerequisites for an annuity product to be viewed favorably. Since this is a life insurance product, additional benefits include creditor protection and avoidance of probate fees.

Any actuary knows this type of arrangement is possible in theory, but can it be put into practice? To find out, I asked financial planner Rona Birenbaum. Rona confirmed that this insured annuity strategy is in fact used in real-life situations, though she did stress that there are some conditions and caveats, as are described below.

The strategy works best if one uses after-tax savings to purchase the annuity. The resulting annuity will largely be free from income tax and will produce much more income than one can obtain from a GIC. The fact that the annuity income is so high will prove to be useful, since we need to use a part of it to pay for the death benefit in this "back-to-back" arrangement. That death benefit comes from a life insurance contract that requires annual premiums, which are paid out of the annuity income. The proceeds of the life insurance are tax-free when they are eventually paid out upon death.

I will use an example to illustrate the concept. Say a 65-year-old retiree has $500,000 of after-tax savings, which he uses to purchase a prescribed life annuity from a life insurance company. Based on one annuity quote, the amount of income that can be purchased with $500,000 is $30,952 and because most of it is non-taxable, the annual income after tax is very nearly the same, being $30,199. By comparison, a 2.5 percent GIC produces only $12,500 of interest income each year which nets out to just $7,500 after tax (a 40 percent marginal tax rate is assumed in both options).

A portion of the annuity income is used to purchase a life insurance policy that would be paid to the estate or a named beneficiary upon the death of the annuitant. If the death benefit is $500,000, the annual insurance premium is $15,026, based on an actual quote. This is deducted from the $30,199 of annuity income leaving $15,174 available for the retiree to spend. Of course, a lower death benefit could be selected with a correspondingly lower premium.

To summarize, if the $500,000 in assets is used to deploy the insured annuity strategy, it produces $15,174 of after-tax income plus a tax-free life insurance benefit of $500,000. If the same $500,000 is used to invest in GICs, the annual after-tax income is just $7,500 with the same $500,000 death benefit. All of this is illustrated in Figure 18.1.

What makes the strategy effective is the preferred tax treatment of prescribed annuities and the tax-free nature of life insurance death benefits. The example assumed a male annuitant but the strategy works for a female retiree as well, though it would be a little less effective since women live longer, which means the insurance company would provide less annuity income.

The foregoing example assumes that the annuity that is purchased provides no death benefit. This same strategy can also be implemented on a joint basis where the annuity income continues to the surviving spouse for life. In that case, the life insurance benefit is paid only when the second spouse passes away.

While this insured annuity strategy can be effective, there are various considerations to keep in mind when buying:

1. One needs to use monies that are not tax-sheltered to make this strategy work.
2. The effectiveness of the strategy depends in part on the gap between interest rates on GICs versus the underlying interest rate on the annuity. This will vary over time (though we did assume a rather small gap in our example). The effectiveness

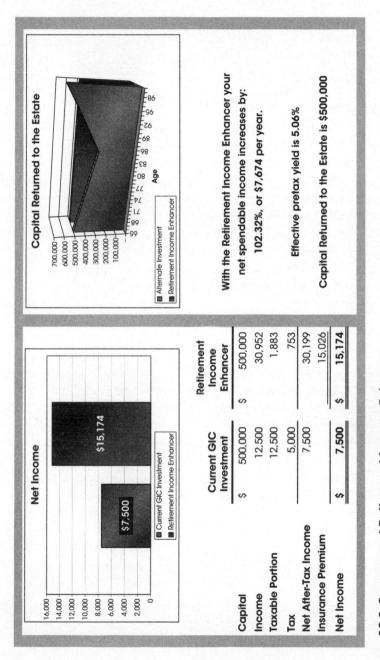

Figure 18.1 Summary of Retirement Income Enhancer

Source: Rona Birenbaum, "Caring for Clients"

of the strategy also depends on changes to mortality tables, and tax legislation.

3. Once it is put into effect, it cannot be undone, with the exception of canceling the life insurance, in which case the premiums that were already paid are forfeited.

4. If this is the retiree's only source of nongovernment retirement income, they will not have a source of capital to draw on in the event of an emergency or change of circumstances that requires a lump sum withdrawal of assets. (Some people may see this as a drawback and others as an advantage!)

5. You must be in sufficiently good health to obtain the life insurance. Before committing to the annuity purchase, it makes sense to apply for the life insurance first and ensure that the policy is approved at the expected premium level.

6. The annuity and the life insurance contracts should be purchased from different insurance companies. If purchased from the same insurer, the tax authorities could consider them "one contract," which would have negative tax implications.

Indexed Annuities? Forget It

Most scholarly papers that estimate the retirement income one can generate from savings assume that the annuity the saver buys at retirement is indexed to inflation. This seems to imply that purchasing an indexed annuity would be routine but in fact, few if any insurers will grant one, and few savers would want one when they see the price attached to it.

The problem from the insurance company perspective is the open-ended risk. Inflation might take off again and the reserves that they use to back-stop the annuity do not accommodate such a situation very easily. Insurers will, however, provide a fixed annual increase such as 1 or 2 percent a year though even this may prove problematic if inflation falls below that level since the tax authorities permit increases in pension income only to the extent warranted by inflation.

The main problem with a fully indexed annuity from the retiree's point of view is the cost, which will seem absolutely prohibitive. If regular, nonindexed annuities are unpopular, indexed annuities (to the extent they are available) are much more so. Fortunately, Chapter 7 tells us there is not much of a need for full inflation protection after retirement.

Conclusions

Buying an annuity is usually a better bet than managing your own investment portfolio after retirement and drawing an income from it (the portfolio option). You lose a little upside potential but you also eliminate some major risks.

There are, however, two possible situations when annuitizing might not be for you. First, if you want to make the largest possible bequest in the event of early death, the portfolio option provides a better benefit, though you can attach a fairly substantial death benefit to an annuity as well. The other situation when you should pass on an annuity is if you have good reason to believe that your life expectancy is shorter than average.

Assuming neither of these circumstances applies to you, the questions you should be asking are (a) whether you convert all of your retirement savings into an annuity or just a portion, and (b) when is it best to annuitize.

Annuitizing All or Some

You no doubt are investing some of your retirement savings in fixed income investments, such as a bond fund. If you are close to retirement, the fixed income portion of your savings is probably 40 or 50 percent of your total portfolio and possibly more. It makes sense to liquidate these fixed income investments and buy an annuity, provided that the amount of assets is large enough to make this worthwhile—say, $100,000 or more. There are several reasons why you would buy an annuity instead of holding bonds.

First, the implicit yield underlying the annuity is better than the yield from regular fixed-income investments in your portfolio, once you adjust for differences in level of risk. Second, the annuity provides a steady income stream and eliminates the chances you will outlive your money. Third, to the extent that you annuitize, you are avoiding the problem described in Chapter 16—that you might do something foolish with your investments when you reach an advanced age.

Why stop at annuitizing just the fixed-income portion of your portfolio? Why not apply all your retirement savings toward buying an annuity and get rid of the headache of investing your own monies after retirement? There is something to be said for pursuing this strategy, especially if you are risk-averse, but most people will want to hedge their bets. If all their income is in the form of an annuity, they no longer have a rainy-day fund in case of ill health, a desire to provide a one-time cash gift to their children, or unexpected inflation. Having no degrees of freedom can create an uneasy feeling. Even if you do not want to derive all of your income from an annuity when you are 65, you might change your mind later on for the reasons given below.

When to Annuitize

Just as there are good and bad times to buy stocks, there are also better times and worse times to buy an annuity. The trick is to identify the best possible time. One of the signs will be when the gap between the yields on long-term government bonds and inflation is relatively high—that is to say, when the real yield on long-term bonds is high.

You might wonder what long-term bonds have to do with annuities. The interest rate that determines the cost of annuities is never advertised by the insurer but it happens to be closely tied to the yield on long-term government bonds, which is readily available. The gap between long-term bond yields and inflation is currently rather small, even though inflation is low which means that now might not be the best time to buy an annuity. Note that the nominal yield on bonds is not important, just the real yield. Hence, you are better off buying an annuity when long-term bond yields are 4 percent and inflation is 2 percent than when long-term bond yields and inflation are both 5 percent.

A second reason why now may not be the best time to buy an annuity is you are competing with the big defined benefit plan sponsors. Many of them have closed their pension plans to new entrants in recent years and are currently in the process of *derisking* those plans. This process could involve buying a group annuity to cover all of their retirees so that the company can get the risk off their books. Another de-risking strategy is loading up on long-term bonds to emulate the effect of buying an annuity within the pension fund. The upshot of all this activity is that it seems everyone wants to buy long-term bonds these days and this has depressed the yields that those bonds offer. This unusually strong demand should eventually taper off since there are only so many defined benefit plans out there and once they have derisked, the buying pressure on the bond market will ease. I would give this process 5 years.

Another factor in the timing of an annuity purchase is to know how the insurance companies are currently pricing their product. At certain times, some insurers will price their annuities more aggressively, thereby giving the consumer a better deal. This is essentially like taking advantage of a sale on annuities. This type of situation might occur toward the end of a year when the insurance company has not yet met its sales quota (not unlike a car dealership), or it might happen when the insurer has access to an especially favorable private fixed income investment, which they want to pass along to the consumer in the form of an annuity purchase to lock in their own profit. Your insurance broker might have some insights as to whether certain insurers are motivated to provide a better price on annuities at a given point in time.

In spite of this, you can never know for sure whether you bought an annuity at a good time, except in hindsight. This is not unlike purchasing a house. If you are retiring and know that you can buy an annuity big enough to meet your income needs, you might decide to proceed with the purchase immediately without worrying if the price might be better 6 months from now.

One reason you cannot afford to wait too long to make your annuity purchase is that you never know when you might become cognitively impaired. Waiting too long to close the deal is a phenomenon that I referred to in Chapter 16 as *rational roulette*. While you should obviously annuitize before your ability to make sound financial decisions starts to fail, you may not realize it when it starts to happen. Prudence suggests acting sooner rather than later. One approach may be to decide in advance to annuitize at age 75.

Note

1. Goldstein, Johnson, and Sharpe, "Choosing Outcomes vs. Choosing Products," Consumer-Focused Retirement Investment Advice, *Journal of Consumer Research* (2008).

PART V

RANDOM REFLECTIONS

CHAPTER

19

How Workplace Pension Plans Fit In

Implicit in the previous chapters is that you are saving for retirement on your own. In fact, there is a good chance that your employer maintains some sort of retirement arrangement that you as an employee can (or must) join. This is especially likely if you work for a large organization. We will refer to these arrangements as *workplace pension plans.*

The good news is that participating in almost any workplace pension plan is a good thing. This might sound obvious but pension plans existed back in the 1970s in which employees received little or no interest on the contributions they were required to make and got only their money back if they left the company before meeting stringent vesting requirements. Thanks to various pension reforms regarding disclosure, the crediting of interest on contributions and vesting, this is no longer the case. The only situations in which participating in the workplace plan is still questionable are (a) where the only investment option is the company shares and (b) if the annual management fees that are charged within the plan are at retail levels, meaning 2 percent or more. Apart from those exceptions, a workplace plan not only enhances your retirement security, it can also improve your standard of living while you are still working.

While the following comments are directed at you as a plan participant, employers may also find this chapter of interest, since this can have a bearing on how workplace plans should be designed, administered, and communicated.

Why Employers Offer Workplace Plans

Unless it was established under a collective bargaining agreement, a workplace pension plan is not something your employer is forced to offer. Many employers, especially smaller ones and those in certain industries, do not offer any pension plan at all. If your employer does sponsor a plan, it may help you to understand why they bother.

Conventional wisdom suggests that employers maintain pension plans in order to attract and retain employees. You can judge from your personal experience when you were seeking your first job whether that reasoning seems valid. If you were like most prospective hires, you accepted an offer of employment because the cash compensation was attractive or you liked the prospects for advancement. Other factors that might have affected your decision include location, the chance to do interesting or challenging work and good health and dental benefits. In surveys, employees will indicate that a pension plan is "very important," but it nonetheless ranks fairly low on the list of employee priorities. When participation in a pension plan is made optional, it is not unusual to see only half the employee population join.

If the existence of a pension plan is barely a positive factor in attracting employees to a given company, the *type* of plan is even less important. Prospective employees may be glad to learn that the company they are looking to join has a pension plan, but they seldom ask whether it is a defined benefit or a defined contribution plan or how substantial the pension benefits are. To the extent they have any questions about the plan at all, they relate to how much they have to contribute, not so much because retirement security is top of mind but because required contributions reduce their take-home pay.

We can conclude that pensions are rarely a show-stopper in the decision to join a company, although there will be exceptions. For instance, working for a company with a defined-benefit pension plan may be critically important for mid-career hires who participated in a similar plan in their previous place of employment. This is less of a factor for people who were covered by a defined contribution pension plan in their previous workplace.

As to whether a pension plan helps an employer retain employees, this is rarely true either, especially for the under-45 age group, where turnover tends to be high. By and large, employees leave one job for another not because of the existence or nonexistence of a pension plan, but because they may not get along with their supervisor, they do not enjoy the work or the hours, or because the money or prospects for advancement are better elsewhere.

Once again, at least one exception exists. An employee who is on the verge of qualifying for an immediate pension under a defined benefit pension plan will tend to stay with that employer because of the pension plan alone. A 53-year-old employee will not leave her company voluntarily if she becomes eligible for an immediate defined benefit pension starting at age 55.

That particular set of circumstances is becoming rare, at least in the private sector, because defined benefit pension plans are an endangered species. Outside of the public sector and collectively bargained pension plans in the private sector, most employees participate in a defined contribution (DC) plan instead, assuming they have pension coverage at all. In a DC plan, their pension entitlement is not affected by their age and so once they satisfy the vesting requirements (usually a nominal length of service), they are free to take their money as well the employer's contributions on their behalf, plus interest, when they leave.

Another theoretical reason for sponsoring a pension plan is that employers should be able to pay less in cash compensation as a result. If so, this strategy seems to be neither very effective nor used very often. Employees tend to be cash-oriented, and when asked how much they earn, will usually offer an answer that reflects basic salary only. Very few employees are willing to accept lower cash compensation because the employer is making contributions on their behalf to a pension plan. In companies where plan participation is optional, there is rarely a difference in cash compensation between employees who participate in the plan and employees who do not. The same is true in organizations where some employees participate in expensive defined benefit plans while others participate in less expensive defined contribution plans. While more and more employers say they are trying to communicate total compensation (cash plus the value of various benefits), they still administer cash compensation in isolation of other components of the compensation package.

So why would an employer maintain a pension plan? The best reason, perhaps, is that some employers really do care about the welfare of their employees. No one wants to send a 65-year-old employee packing if that person has no retirement income. A situation like that imposes a moral obligation on the employer to help ease the employee into retirement with some money, such as one or two times annual salary. If that happens often enough, why not formalize the promise and set up a pension plan to be fair to everyone, especially since the benefits can be pre-funded on a tax-assisted basis?

Another way to look at it is that having employees retire penniless would be detrimental to a company's image in the community and could also be harmful to the morale of employees who remain. While employees will readily join an organization without a pension plan, they might not respect such an employer as much or work as hard if they perceive that their employer does not really care about their welfare.

An important side-benefit that emerges from sponsoring a pension plan is that employees can benefit from the economies of scale that a group arrangement entails. Investment and record-keeping fees can be much lower in a workplace plan than what an individual can expect in the retail market. This is especially true in the case of larger organizations where the total cost of maintaining a plan is often less than 50 basis points (.5 percent) compared to 250 basis points in the case of mutual funds that an individual would buy in the retail market. A difference in fees of 200 basis points a year over a lifetime is hugely important; it translates into a difference in retirement income of nearly 40 percent.

Getting the Most out of Your Workplace Plan

If you are covered by a pension plan, and you work in the private sector, the odds are it is DC plan, more commonly known in the United States as a 401 (k) plan, and in Canada as a DC pension plan, or group RRSP. Here is some advice about getting the most out of the plan.

Whether to Join the Plan

Joining the company plan may be optional. If so, you should definitely join as soon as you are able, even if it means being required to make contributions to the plan as a result. This advice might seem to fly in the face of what I was suggesting in a previous chapter, that there may be times in your life when the burden of other expenses is so great you will want to defer saving for retirement. The difference here is that the employer is making contributions on your behalf so passing up on the chance to join the plan is tantamount to saying no to free money.

Before you do join, though, you might just want to confirm that participating in the plan will not affect your cash compensation but as I stated earlier, I have yet to find a situation where this is the case. The people in HR who enroll employees into the pension plan and set up the payroll deductions are rarely the ones who decide on your pay raises.

In some cases, employees opt not to join the company plan because they think they can do better on their own, say by going with a high profile mutual fund company or investing directly in the stock market. There is very, very little chance this is true. First, no one investment manager outperforms the other managers year in or year out and it is hubris to think your manager will be the exception. Second, the contribution that your employer will be making on your behalf swamps any superior investment performance that you might enjoy by investing on your own. Third, remember the comments about fees; fees tend to be much lower in group arrangements than in the retail market, and fees are important.

Another reason you may have for not wanting to join a workplace plan is that you might be worried about what would happen if your employer went out of business; would you somehow lose the monies you contributed to the plan? There is indeed some reason to worry in the case of defined benefit pension plans. A company with a DB plan may go bankrupt when such a plan is underfunded and retirees are sometimes forced to accept a 20 or 30 percent permanent cut in pensions, or even worse. This type of situation is rare, but it does happen.

In a DC plan, however, you have less reason to worry since the pension fund is held in a separate trust or insurance contract that is safe from creditors and cannot be touched by your employer. It may take a while for you to get your money out as the trustees in bankruptcy make alternate arrangements but when you do, you will get 100 cents on the dollar. This may not be true, however, if your investments in the pension plan take the form of shares in the company itself. In the interests of risk diversification, I strongly advise against holding too much of your retirement savings in company shares. It is bad enough that you would lose your job if your company went under; there is no reason you should jeopardize your retirement security as well.

Optional Contributions

In most defined contribution plans, you may be required to contribute a basic amount into the plan, such as 2 or 3 percent of pay or maybe more. In addition, you may be permitted to make optional contributions, which the employer will match in whole or in part. Common matching percentages are 25, 50, and 100 percent of the amount contributed by the employee.

I strongly counsel you to take advantage of any employer matching that is offered. This is free money with no strings attached. It is amazing how many employees pass up on this offer. I recently studied the behavior of participants in some large defined contribution plans and found that about one-third of participants make no optional contribution to the plan even when their optional contribution is 100 percent matched by the employer. This is hard to fathom, especially since at least some of those employees are making contributions to personal retirement vehicles.

In some situations, you might rightly feel you cannot afford to maximize your pension contributions simply to get the maximum company matching. For instance, the company plan might allow you to contribute a maximum of 8 percent (basic and optional combined), but you might feel you cannot afford to put in more than 5 percent given other financial obligations, such as mortgage payments. You might consider working your way up to a higher contribution rate by having contribution rate increases coincide with pay increases.

Investment Choices

Almost all DC plans these days offer investment choices. These choices take the form of being able to direct your contributions, and usually the employer's contributions on your behalf, into various funds such as a domestic or international equity fund, a money market fund, and a fixed-income fund. Sometimes, there are multiple equity fund options and even multiple fixed-income fund options being offered. The most common number of fund options in larger plans is about 20 though, in my opinion, this is more than employees really need. From the employer's point of view, it is difficult to communicate and oversee that many options, while from the employee's perspective, it is hard to make an informed choice with so many options to choose from.

The plethora of choice can be confusing so it pays for you to seek a little professional advice or to attend in-house seminars in order to choose a sensible asset mix. I do not suggest that you take any extreme position such as allocating 100 percent of your monies into either fixed income or equities. As we saw in the section on the accumulation phase, you will do well over the long term simply by picking a constant asset mix such as 60 percent equities and 40 percent bonds. If you are young, you might do better with a 70/30 mix or even an 80/20 mix. We also saw that target date funds are a good idea if your employer makes such funds available.

If you do not make your investment choices when you first join a company plan, a default fund will apply. Even though statistics show that about 80 percent of plan participants simply stay in the default fund out of inertia, you should not do so without checking out what the default option is because some are better than others. The most common default fund used to be a money market fund but this is a terrible choice if you are investing for the long term. In modern defined contribution plan design, the default tends to be a target date or balanced (mix of equities and bonds) fund. Either one of these should be quite acceptable, provided the fees are not too high.

Although it is not always prominently communicated, you should learn about the level of investment fees that apply to your fund options. In most defined contribution plans, the investment fees are deducted from gross investment returns so you may never see them. Sometimes an employer will offer you a choice of higher-cost investment funds as well as low-cost funds. You might think that a higher-cost fund with a prominent name means higher quality and translates into higher returns, but no one in the investment industry seems to be able to demonstrate any significant correlation between fees paid and returns achieved. You are probably better off in low-cost funds over the long term.

Remember that the two most important determinants of investment performance are (a) your asset mix and (b) the cost of the funds. Over the long term, the choice of investment manager is rather unimportant by comparison.

Decumulation

One of the problems with DC plans is that the participants get a good deal of hand-holding during the accumulation period but that ends at the point of retirement. When they retire, they are essentially left to fend for themselves in terms of what they do with their pension monies from that point on. This is fine if they have a good understanding of the capital markets, including annuities, but less than half of DC participants do.

The fact you are reading this book probably means you are more investment savvy than most DC participants. You will be given the option of purchasing an annuity or transferring your money to another retirement vehicle that you can manage on your own (or with the help of an investment manager). The advice in the rest of this book about annuities and drawing an income from your retirement savings applies equally to the monies in your DC plan account.

An emerging and intriguing possibility is being able to keep your savings in your employer's plan and drawing an income from that source. This is not possible yet in most plans, but it is receiving an increasing amount of attention. Rules are being drawn up in various jurisdictions to permit this. Depending on how it is rolled out, this may be better than managing the monies on your own.

How a Workplace Pension Plan Affects Your Dollar Target

In Chapter 4, we established some retirement income targets that varied primarily by the extent of the "investments" you made. In this context, *investments* meant the money you allocated toward paying off your home, raising your children, employment expenses, and saving for retirement.

Note that participating in a workplace pension plan means that your retirement income target will be higher than it otherwise would be. That is because your employer will be contributing to the plan on your behalf so you do not have to set aside as much of your own money. This means you have more disposable income during your working years, which translates into higher personal consumption, and hence higher expectations for personal consumption after retirement.

The impact of participating in a workplace plan on one's retirement income target is shown in Appendix C. Of course, a higher retirement income target translates into a higher wealth target as well.

Online Forecast Tools

A basic purpose of this book is to give you a better idea of what it takes to be retirement-ready and how much to save in order to reach that goal. Your workplace pension plan may offer online tools that can help you do the same. Instead of starting with the retirement income you think you will need and telling you the wealth target, an online tool typically will project your expected retirement savings to the future date when you plan to retire and estimate the retirement income it will generate. They can serve other purposes as well. The online tools offered by Morneau Shepell, for example, in its administrative solutions practice, can do the following:

- Forecast your retirement income at your chosen future retirement date and enable you to test alternative dates.
- Provide what-if results under multiple investment scenarios.
- Estimate the amount of pension from Social Security.
- Incorporate account balances and pensions that you and your spouse have from personal sources in order to produce an integrated picture of your retirement readiness.

Other service providers offer similar services and tools. You should avail yourself of whatever online tools your employer offers.

CHAPTER

20

Bubble Trouble

I recall reading an article in the local newspapers in the early 1980s about a marble bust of Pope Gregory XV. It made enough of an impression on me that I recently decided to look up the details.

Dating back to the early 1600s, this bust had been in the hands of an aristocratic English family until 1978, when they sold it to an antiquarian for £240 (about $600). At that time, its provenance was unknown. A few years later, an art expert attributed it to a student of Bernini and the bust changed hands again, this time for £178,000. Shortly thereafter, the experts finally agreed that it was a genuine work of Bernini himself. The bust was resold at a Sotheby's auction for £2.78 million and subsequently donated to the Art Gallery of Ontario, where it still resides.

This was an early lesson for me in the vagaries of intrinsic value. Authentication alone raised the price more than one thousand-fold! This may not seem extraordinary to an art historian, but to an actuary it is nothing short of astounding. It was the same bust, imbued with the same beauty and craftsmanship whether it was made by Bernini or the work of a less-celebrated sculptor, but in the latter case it had virtually no value.

In much the same way, the price of a financial asset, such as real estate or common shares of a publicly listed company, depends on more than the intrinsic value of the real estate or the company. The whims, greed, or fears of investors figure largely in dictating price movements, and this essentially is what makes a financial bubble possible.

One would think that a financial asset is fundamentally different from a piece of art. After all, art is subjective, whereas the value of future dividends can be quantified with some degree of confidence. How, then, to explain the price level of gold, which will never pay a dividend, has limited commercial application, and yet sells at prices that are high by any measure? Or the share price of a company like General Electric, a solid company with a long history of profitability and paying dividends? Yet, its shares, which were selling at $40.04 on October 19, 2007, fell all the way to $7.06 by March 6, 2009, even though the company and its long-term prospects were virtually unchanged.

Why Worry about Financial Bubbles?

The reader might well ask why a book about retirement planning should dedicate a chapter to financial bubbles. It is because saving for retirement is a long-term proposition and bubbles represent the biggest risk to long-term investors. Indeed, they are about the only risk that should give us pause about following the usual advice and staying fully invested at all times.

When we plan for retirement, our focus should be on achieving our long-term financial goals and ideally we should pay very little attention to short-term gyrations in the capital markets. Hence, we invest in equities even though there will be two to four calendar years in every decade when returns on major stock market indices will be negative. We are comforted by the fact that long-term returns on equities have consistently been high in real terms, at least in the post–World War II era. The need to rely on equities to achieve a decent long-term return has never been as great as it is today with bond yields at record lows.

We invest in equities even knowing there will be the odd stock market crash such as on October 19, 1987, or the more recent financial crisis of 2008–2009 that lopped off half the value of North American equities. We put our faith in the markets bouncing back eventually. In my own case, I managed to achieve a compounded annual rate of return on my own portfolio of 9.6 percent from November 2005 to December 31, 2014, in spite of being heavily invested in equities in 2008–2009. I was no smarter than anyone else, nor did my investment manager achieve significantly better results than other managers. My strategy was simply to hold on for dear life. In the midst of the painful losses of 2008 and early 2009, I grimly stuck it out, having faith that the markets would eventually turn positive again, which they did.

Financial bubbles, however, are fundamentally different from the frequent short-term market downturns that we are accustomed to seeing. When a bubble bursts, the losses can exceed 75 percent and prices might not recover for decades. This type of scenario will obviously wreak havoc with one's retirement planning.

If we need to invest in market-based assets to produce decent returns, it would be tremendously useful to be able to identify a financial bubble in the making so we can take evasive measures. This is going to be a challenge, though, since the best professional investors and policy makers have been caught unawares when past market bubbles have burst. Consider the comment by former Federal Reserve Board Chairman Alan Greenspan in reference to the subprime mortgage and credit crisis of 2007 that led to the collapse of the US housing market and a severe recession, "I really didn't get it until very late in 2005 and 2006."

If ever it was important to predict when markets are getting dangerously overheated, it would be now, when some observers claim we are in the midst of an "everything bubble" that is being fed by low interest rates. Before we examine the current state of financial markets, let us take a look at some of the most famous financial bubbles in recent history to identify their common characteristics.

Examples of Recent Financial Bubbles

Summarized here are the stories behind some of the high-profile bubbles of the past century.

The Stock Market Bubble of the 1920s

The Roaring Twenties really began in 1922, after the severe recession of 1921 ended and the horrors of WWI had finally started to fade. The period 1922 to 1929 was marked by great optimism, and for good reason. It was an era of newfound prosperity that was enabled or accompanied by relatively new concepts such as mass production and consumerism as well as the proliferation of game-changing technologies, including the electrification of urban centers, automobiles, and telephones. This expansion had to be financed, and the US quickly became the dominant global player in financial markets. From 1922 to 1929, GNP grew at an annual pace of 4.7 percent and unemployment averaged just 3.7 percent.[1]

As a result of all this activity, the Dow Jones index rose from 63.9 to over 100 between 1921 and 1923. It was in 1924, however, that stocks really took off, fueled by margin buying by an increasingly affluent, but not particularly sophisticated, general public. Even the banks weighed in by speculating in the market using depositors' reserves.

The Dow Jones index peaked at 381.17 in September 1929. Trading then became more erratic and more active over the next month. Panic selling did not really set in until October 24th of that year, and the bubble finally burst on October 29, a day that will be remembered forever as Black Tuesday, when prices fell 12 percent across the board. The fall in stock prices continued virtually unabated until mid-1932 when the Dow Jones index bottomed out at 41.22, nearly 90 percent below its peak. It did not reach the 381 level again until 1955.

The Japanese Asset Price Bubble of the 1980s

In the early 1980s, Tokyo became an important international finance center thereby increasing demand for office space. Real estate in Tokyo's commercial districts rose by 42 percent in 1985 and by another 122 percent in 1986. Stocks also rose in this period.

Until 1986, the rise could be attributed to improving fundamentals. Besides the real estate phenomenon, Japanese companies took products that were developed in the Western world—automobiles and electronics in particular—and found ways to manufacture similar products both faster and better. The government played an active role too (hence the phrase "Japan Inc.") by providing subsidies to Japanese companies and quietly discriminating against foreign companies that bid on domestic government contracts.

The financial bubble formed between 1987 and 1990, when both real estate and stock prices rose much more steeply. Reasons cited for the emergence of the bubble included financial deregulation, inadequate risk management by financial institutions, protracted monetary easing, and taxation policies that were biased toward accelerating the rise in land prices.[2] All these factors led to mass euphoria. By 1990, Japanese property was estimated to have a value of nearly $20 trillion, which represented 20 percent of the entire wealth of the world and five times the value of all property in the United States.

The Japanese stock market also reflected these developments. From a level of about 11,000 in 1984, the Nikkei 225 Index rose to 38,957.44 on December 29, 1989. In the process, price/earnings ratios on Japanese shares reached levels that were unheard of in North American stock markets (until the dot-com bubble that is). Even this signal that prices had advanced too far and too fast did not faze most professional investors at the time. I recall attending presentations by investment managers in 1988 in which they rationalized that the price/earnings ratios were reasonable when one took considered the different accounting practices in Japan.

As with all bubbles, this one could not inflate forever. An increase in interest rates and a slowdown in the real estate market triggered a sharp decline in stock prices in early 1990 from which Japan has never really recovered. More than 25 years later, the Nikkei 225 Index is still just half of its 1989 peak.

The Dot-Com Bubble of 1995-2000

There were some similarities between the stock market bubble of the Roaring Twenties and the dot-com bubble in the last decade of the twentieth century. In both cases, exciting new technology was transforming the world and bringing with it the promise of increased wealth. In the 1990s, it was the arrival of the Internet that introduced the nearly unlimited potential of online commerce as the new way to conduct business. Investors could not get enough of the new tech companies.

The stocks involved in this new electronic frontier were traded primarily on the NASDAQ. Investors were particularly attracted to companies that exhibited rapid growth, or the potential for growth, and did not worry at first about the lack of profits or even revenues. From a level of about 750 in January 1995, the NASDAQ closed at an all-time high of 5048.62 on March 10, 2000. When profits from these new Internet businesses did not materialize, however, the bubble finally burst. The NASDAQ fell 75 percent between 2000 and 2002. Even by 2007, a full 7 years after its peak, the NASDAQ had got back to only half its all-time high in nominal terms. It was only in March 2015, 15 years later, that the index finally regained its 2000 peak.

Other Financial Bubbles

Table 20.1 summarizes a few other financial bubbles of the past century.

Table 20.1   Other Financial Bubbles

Event	When	What happened
Florida real estate bubble	1922–1926	Tourism in Florida began to boom, which caused the population to grow quickly and raised land prices. Investors fed the rise with speculative buying. In 1925 alone, real estate prices quadrupled. By 1926, prices became prohibitively high for new investors, and early investors wanted to lock in profits by selling. In the panic to sell, many investors who had bought on margin went bankrupt.
The gold price bubble	1976–1980	The gold price was pegged at $35 an ounce until 1971, when Nixon changed US policy regarding private ownership. Gold rose to $125 an ounce in 1976 and then rose more steeply to a peak of $850 an ounce in 1980, mainly due to fear of inflation, at which point it collapsed. That price level was not breached again until 28 years later.
Toronto housing bubble	1985–1989	Over the 4-year period ending in 1989, the average price of a home in Toronto rose by 113% in real terms. Baby boomers and wealthy immigrants triggered the initial rise in prices, but the main driving force ultimately was speculators buying multiple homes to flip for a quick profit. The party ended very abruptly in the middle of 1989. Over the next 7 years, the average price fell by 40 percent in real terms. In nominal terms, prices did not recover to the 1989 peak until the early 2000s.
US housing bubble	1997–2007	Home prices in the United States had been relatively flat in the 1990s but started to escalate quickly in 1997 thanks to artificially low mortgage rates. Prices ultimately rose 132% by the time they peaked in the second quarter of 2006 but then started to fall, first slowly and then more steeply. This led to credit defaults around the globe and triggered the deepest recession the world has seen since the Great Depression. Even 6 years after the market bottomed out, the economies of many developed countries are still fragile, especially in Europe.

Common Characteristics

Actuaries recognize the danger of generalizing based on a limited number of data points. This is especially true with something as amorphous as a financial bubble. That said, the financial bubbles described above, as well as infamous bubbles from prior centuries, all do appear to share a few distinctive characteristics:

- Initially, there are legitimate and compelling reasons to cause a rise in prices. In many cases, it is a major technological advancement (railways in the 1870s, electrification of the United States in the 1920s, Internet commerce in the 1990s).
- For a period of several years, price increases tend to be orderly and grounded by fundamental factors but eventually euphoria sets in. As the bubble starts to inflate, prices rise much more steeply than they did in the early stage.
- The general public eventually wants to get in on the action. Once the bubble expansion is well underway, even the unsophisticated investor becomes aware of rising prices and jumps into the market to make what seems to be a quick and sure profit.
- Adding to the frenzy, there is usually a mechanism that enables speculators to buy "on margin" or with only a small down payment. This was a major factor in the stock market bubble of the 1920s and the US housing bubble of 1997–2007.
- In the late stages of the bubble, experts strain for rational explanations for the high valuations. They muse about being in the midst of a new paradigm in which old norms regarding asset valuation or price/earnings ratios no longer apply. Such reasoning offers hope to latecomers that prices will continue to rise, which allows the bubble to inflate a while longer.
- In the case of stock market bubbles, prices peak at a level that is significantly higher than ever before seen. The peak price tends to be three to five times the previous *local peak* (which might have occurred 4 to 5 years earlier when investors were still behaving rationally) though the dot-com bubble was exceptional in that it rose more than six-fold from its previous local peak.
- In the case of housing bubbles, the ultimate peak might be "only" twice as high as the previous local peak. This can be

rationalized by the fact that most homeowners hold a mortgage and so the equity in their home will rise by a factor of 3 to 5, if not more, as a result of a 100 percent increase in price.

- When prices have defied gravity long enough, roughly 3 to 5 years after the bubble started to inflate, market observers resign themselves to accepting the new normal. Irving Fisher, described by some as the greatest economist the United States has ever produced, famously said three days before the stock market crash of 1929, "Stock prices have reached what looks like a permanently high plateau." This is also the time when elevator operators give stock tips (1929), people line up to buy gold (1980), and even barbers buy one or more condos as an investment (the situation today in Toronto).
- In spite of widespread euphoria, every bubble eventually bursts. When it does, it may not be apparent for some time that it has done so, and can be confirmed only in hindsight. (For that reason, the metaphor of a bubble is less than perfect.)
- More useful to the investor is the observation that the decline following the bursting of a bubble will typically last many years or even decades before it runs its course and prices finally surpass the peak reached just before the bubble had burst.

It is interesting that in the bubbles I have lived through, more sophisticated investors were well aware that they could be in the midst of a bubble, and yet they continued to buy into the market because the opportunity cost seemed too great. Mention of a possible bubble appears with increasing frequency in newspaper articles and in the modern world as hits on the Internet. Even this growing realization tends not to save most investors, however, as talk of a *new paradigm* keeps them in the market.

Ultimately, there is not enough money to sustain the rise, and as with any Ponzi-like scheme, the process inevitably collapses under its own weight as there is not enough new money coming in to produce further gains.

The Everything Bubble

The rise in the stock market since 2009 and in property values around the world in the same period has been described by some as *the everything bubble.* It has been stoked by interest rates that are even lower than what triggered the US housing bubble of 2006 and the need to take ever-greater risk in the search for higher yields.

To my knowledge, no one in the investment industry foresaw that interest rates outside of Japan would ever fall so far. Today, 10-year bonds are below 2 percent in most developed countries. This is one of the factors fuelling the rise in the stock market. The S&P 500 is currently more than triple the low it reached in March 2009, and most European stock indices are recording new highs as well. Is this then a new bubble?

So far, it does not exhibit all the characteristics described above of past bubbles. Some international stock markets have not exceeded previous peaks in real terms and some not even in nominal terms. While the market indices might be three times as high as they were 6 years ago, the price levels then were quite depressed, which is not how bubbles usually start. Similarly, US housing is much more robust than it was several years ago, but has not surpassed its 2006 peak.

This is not to say there will not be some market corrections along the way, but a bubble-like collapse does not appear to be in the offing. I have to conclude that it is relatively safe to invest in global equities for the foreseeable future, though the returns might not be anywhere near as high as what we have enjoyed in the past 6 years. On the other hand, if a new bubble is indeed forming, the returns may be spectacular, at least for a little while.

Notes

1. Alvaro Jimenez Jimenez, "Understanding Economic Bubbles," Programa Universitat-Empresa (2011).
2. Shigenori Shiratsuka, "Asset Price Bubble in Japan in the 1980s: Lessons for Financial and Macro-Economic Stability," Institute for Monetary and Economic Studies (2003).

CHAPTER

Carpe Diem

I am 62, and my guess is that people who know me would say that I am above average in terms of health and fitness, maybe even well above average. I stay physically active, eat salads and vegetables regularly, and drink moderately. I do not have a paunch, never binge, rarely get sick, take no medication, and have never ever spent a night in a hospital, not even at birth.

Outside of golf season, I work out 5 days a week and there is nothing wussy about these workouts. Each session entails 45 minutes to an hour of self-torture; I get my heart rate up to 160 beats a minute and keep it there by running on a treadmill at 6.5 miles an hour or by doing strength training to the limits of my endurance.

This is not the entire picture, however, as a Dorian Gray type of transformation is emerging alongside this wholesome impression of well-being. It is a transformation that my friends do not see (yet), and one that I am powerless to arrest.

To start, I suspect there has been some mental deterioration, but it is so subtle it is hard for me to say how far it has progressed. As a preemptive measure, I start my sentences more often than I used to with, "I don't know if I told you this but . . . ."

My physical mini-ailments are more definitive and the list is long. I have tinnitus, which might clinically be described as a ringing in the ears but comes across in my case more like a dozen tiny, atonal violins constantly playing in my head at a very high pitch. My right wrist is chronically sore, having never quite recovered from a break that occurred 8 years ago. An MRI reveals my shoulder is on the verge of succumbing to years of "wear and tear." (The doctors use that term a lot with me.) I have arthritis in my big toes that makes it painful to do push-ups. I have been told I have a "creeping arthritis," to use the specialist's words, in both my hands. A nerve is dying in the middle finger of my right hand, producing a constant sensation of having just touched nettles. My lower back is permanently stiff and a little sore; at best, it makes it difficult to find a comfortable sleeping position and at worst, it triggers spasms that render me incapable of any type of movement. My left knee locks up every so often, and even when it doesn't, it delivers a sharp pain when I walk down stairs first thing in the morning. My right ankle became quite tender a year ago and, in spite of many months of rest and physiotherapy, simply refuses to heal. Oh, and did I mention the mental deterioration?

What is sobering about this litany of afflictions is that none, absolutely none, of them existed when I blew out the candles on the cake on my 50th birthday, and that was barely a decade ago. If I could not foresee any of these challenges then, it prompts me to wonder what fresh surprises will surface by the time I hit 70.

I am not looking for sympathy. No doubt all my contemporaries suffer stoically from similar physical maladies if not worse, some much worse. In fact, I am one of the lucky ones. By simply having survived my 50s, I have already dodged an uncomfortably high probability of contracting a life-threatening illness, as was described in Chapter 1. We are perennially in transition, and once we pass a certain age, it is rarely for the better. One can never say, "I am," but rather, "I am becoming."

Grim as this sounds, every decade of our lives involves trade-offs of some sort. When I was 40, I might have yearned for the energy and enthusiasm I possessed in my teen years but I would not go through the awkwardness of adolescence again for all the money in the world. Now, I might wish for the physical prowess I had at 40, but job security then was a constant background worry, financial obligations were ever-present, and a demanding career left little time for family and other pursuits.

When I take into account all the positive and negative aspects of my life at various points in time, it occurs to me that my 60s just might be as good as it gets. On the negative side of the balance sheet, there are all the nagging little physical challenges that I have accrued, and the frustrations of not being able to do what I could do 20 years ago. On the positive side, I have more time to enjoy my life than at any time since high school, except now I have more money to spend in that free time. Taking all the pluses and minuses into account, my 60s could be my "glory" decade, so to speak.

I am not there yet, but judging from my growing assortment of physical setbacks, it is a near certainty that 60 will turn out to be better than 70. A decade from now, I will still be financially independent (probably), but I will have started to take my comfortable financial status for granted. I will still have considerable free time, but ongoing physical and mental deterioration will impose new restrictions on how I can use (or want to use) that freedom. And there is an alarmingly high probability that a critical illness may develop.

The words *Carpe diem* are applicable at any age, but never more so than when we turn 60. The guiding principle is simple: Don't wait too long to do the things you really want to do. Take that bicycle trip in Iceland now. Or maybe you always dreamed of learning to scuba-dive. As for the more sedate activities—like scrap-booking, playing Euchre, or gardening—why not put them off until your 70s when you can still do them sufficiently well in spite of the arthritis or some other malady that will have slowed you down by then? You should not have enough time to indulge in those types of pastimes now if you are doing all the things that you may not be able do much longer.

The Numbers

In Chapter 1, I already showed that there is roughly 1 chance in 2 that we will not make it from age 50 to 70 without dying or incurring one of the following 14 critical illnesses:

- Life-threatening cancer
- Benign brain tumor
- Early-stage malignant melanoma
- Early-stage prostate cancer
- Acute myocardial infarction
- Coronary artery bypass graft
- Coronary angioplasty
- Heart valve replacement
- Aorta surgery
- Stroke
- Kidney failure
- Alzheimer's disease
- Parkinson's disease
- Loss of independent existence[1]

Table 21.1 Percentage of Healthy People Who Develop a Critical Illness or Die

Between ages	Males	Females
50 and 60	18%	11%
60 and 70	36%	22%
70 and 80	56%	39%
80 and 90	82%	69%
90 and 100	98.5%	94%

Morneau Shepell calculations, derived from 2008 CANCI Tables

Table 21.1 shows the percentage of healthy people who will experience a critical illness or die in each 10-year span, starting in their 50s. While it should come as no surprise that the risk of death or critical illness rises the older you get, the steepness of the rise may shock you.

Table 21.1 shows for instance that out of 100 healthy 60-year-old males, 36 of them will either suffer a critical illness or die before they turn 70. After age 70, the incidence of disease or death climbs exponentially. The numbers are a little better for females, but ultimately, no one is unscathed.

The foregoing numbers combine both the probability of death and the probability of contracting a serious illness. Up until age 80, it is not so much death that we need to fear but critical illness. This is shown in Table 21.2, which breaks down the numbers for males from the previous table.

Of course, some critical illnesses are more prevalent than others. Between ages 60 and 70, the main threats are heart disease and life-threatening cancer, which combined account for about

Table 21.2 Prevalence of Critical Illness versus Death (Male)

Between ages	Deaths (out of 100)	Critical illness (out of 100)
50 and 60	4	14
60 and 70	8	28
70 and 80	16	40
80 and 90	46	36
90 and 100	90.1	8.4

Assuming 100 healthy males at the start of each decade of life.
Derived from 2008 CANCI tables

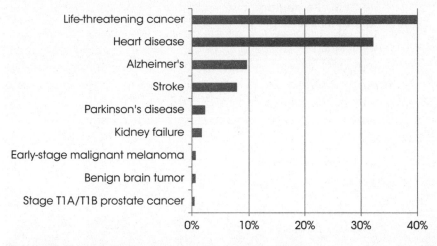

Figure 21.1   Risk Between Ages 50 and 80—Male

90 percent of all critical illnesses in that decade of life. Stroke comes in a distant third, and the chance of getting any of the other critical illnesses listed earlier is really quite remote. In a way, this is rather encouraging, since it means our fate is in our own hands to some extent. Diet and exercise can do much to reduce the chances of heart disease, while not smoking greatly reduces the risk of various types of cancer.

Figure 21.1 gives us a better idea of which critical illness is most likely to bring us down between ages 50 and 80. The figure shows total probabilities, assuming death does not occur first. Not surprisingly, cancer and heart disease dominate.

At later ages, cancer and heart disease remain predominant but Alzheimer's starts to become much more common and displaces stroke as the third most common type of critical illness between ages 80 and 90.

Healthy Life Years

In earlier chapters, I showed that a 60-year-old male today can expect to live to about 87 but also explained that your own life expectancy can vary quite significantly, depending on your lifestyle. Even more important than how many years we have left is how many *healthy* years of life we can expect. Among demographers, this is known as *disability-free life expectancy,* or, alternatively, *healthy life years.* We already know it is not going to be anywhere close to 37 years in the case of the 50-year-old male, but just how much shorter it is may surprise you.

We will start with European data, where they actually try to measure this statistic. I will caution that the Europeans use a less stringent definition of disability, which would include situations that would never qualify for long-term care. Nevertheless, the data are interesting and reinforce the data I will show later for the United States and Canada.

Disability-free life expectancy (DFLE)—Europe

In general, this is the number of years as measured from a given age, such as 65, that one can expect to live without disability. It is highly dependent on the definition of disability. In the European Union, it is based on self-reporting and is defined as a health problem that affected the respondent for at least 6 months and that would have limited the activities that people (not necessarily the respondent) usually do.

The European Union (EU) consists of 27 countries. The length of time that an EU citizen age 65 can expect to be free of disability, mild or severe, is 8.2 years in the case of men and 8.4 years in the case of women.[2]

When measured as a percentage of a 65-year-old male's remaining life span, the disability-free period is just 47.8 percent of total life expectancy. For European women, the news is even worse, as the average 65-year-old woman will be disability-free for just 40.5 percent of her remaining life.

Official statistics measuring disability-free life expectancy do not exist in the United States and Canada, but we can at least approximate it in various ways. One US study breaks down the number of remaining years between healthy and nonhealthy years, as is shown in Table 21.3.[3]

US healthy life expectancy is not very different from what was reported in Europe, and may in fact be shorter if one includes various other health problems that would have been reported by Europeans but do not meet the more stringent definition of disability that underlies Table 21.3.

Using data from the 2008 Canadian Critical Illness tables, we can estimate the disability-free period for Canadians. Assuming that a

Table 21.3   Number of Disease-Free Years Americans Can Expect

	Men age 65	Women age 65
Total life expectancy	17.0 years	19.7 years
Years without disease	8.1	11.3
Years with at least 1 disease	8.9	8.4

Self-reported assessment
2006 data from US National Health Interview Survey

person ceases to be disability-free when he or she suffers any one of the 14 critical illnesses listed earlier in this chapter, I calculate the disability-free life expectancy for males in Canada to be 71.5 when measured from age 50. For Canadian females, the disability-free life expectancy is a little longer, but the lack of good data on Alzheimer's, for example, makes it hard to quantify accurately.

The Canadian numbers will be higher than the disability-free periods measured in Europe because disability in the Canadian case is narrowly defined as having one of the 14 critical illnesses. A number of other serious health conditions, such as arthritis, osteoporosis, Type-2 diabetes, mental illnesses other than Alzheimer's disease, and nonfatal accidents can also lead to severe disability. As a result, the disability-free life expectancy from age 50 for a Canadian male is almost certainly less than 70.

Trends

While medicine is making major strides in extending our life span, it is not clear that the incidence of disease and other health conditions is diminishing. At the risk of oversimplifying, we are still getting very sick, and while modern science is keeping us alive longer, it is not making us healthy again.

For instance, the US National Health Interview Survey mentioned in Table 21.3 tabulated results in both 1998 and 2006, which provided some insight into how our collective health status is changing. Tables 21.4 and 21.5 show the results separately for men and women. The number of years of life expectancy with at least one disease climbed significantly between 1998 and 2006, while the number of disease-free years actually dropped over the 8-year interval. In comparing the 2006 figures in the two tables, note that

Table 21.4   Changes in Health—1998 to 2006

Males	1998	2006
Life expectancy at 65 without disease	8.8 years	8.1 years
Life expectancy at 65 with at least 1 disease	7.2 years	8.9 years
Years after 65 unable to function	2.9	4.5

Mobility function loss means unable to walk 1/4 mile, walk up 10 steps, stand or sit for 2 hours.
Result shown is for 70-79 age group.
National Health Interview Survey

Table 21.5   Changes in Health—1998 to 2006

Females	1998	2006
Life expectancy at 65 without disease	11.8 years	11.3 years
Life expectancy at 65 with at least 1 disease	7.4 years	8.3 years
Years after 65 unable to function	5.8 years	7.3 years

National Health Interview Survey

women can expect to spend considerably more time after age 65 when they are unable to function.

The good news is that a healthy lifestyle can significantly improve mortality. It can also reduce one's risk of contracting certain critical illnesses in a very material way.

Personal Genome Testing

To the extent that disease is the result of our genes, personal genome testing can give us some insight as to what is in store. Such testing has recently become available at a more affordable cost. In Canada, for instance, Medcan will perform a noninvasive saliva test that can screen for about two dozen health conditions, including Alzheimer's, breast cancer, colon cancer, lupus, type-2 diabetes, glaucoma, and rheumatoid arthritis.

Except for certain rare diseases, personal genome testing will never reveal your medical fate with certainty, only your disposition for developing certain diseases. In most cases, environment and lifestyle also play an important part. Still, a personal genome test can provide valuable insights that are not possible otherwise.

To understand the possibilities, I asked Jill Davies, genetic counselor and director at Medcan, to provide some background information. The human genome, which essentially defines who you are, consists of about 20,000 genes. Those genes come in pairs, one from the mother and one from the father. In the entire genome, there are about 6 billion data points (3 billion pairs), about 99.9 percent of which are identical in all humans. To the extent that one person varies from another, it is due to the other 0.1 percent of genes. These are known as *variants* or *genetic markers.*

Having the marker for a given medical condition may increase the chances of incurring that condition anywhere from about 50 percent to 500 percent. A 50 percent increase might sound high, but if the original risk was small, say less than 1 percent, then a 50 percent increase does not make that much of a difference, at least in the short term. The predictive ability of some markers is therefore limited.

Other markers, however, do have significant predictive power, especially if the probability of incurring a certain medical condition is fairly high in the general population. For instance, the presence of the APOE gene means your chances of getting late-onset Alzheimer's at some point in your life are much higher than it would be otherwise. In the case of women, for instance, the lifetime chance of developing Alzheimer's is 17 percent on average, but this becomes 37 percent if 1 copy of the APOE gene is present and 75 percent if both copies are present. If neither copy of the APOE gene is present, the lifetime probability of getting Alzheimer's drops to 9 percent. Hence, the difference between no APOE genes and two of them is an eight-fold increase in the chances of getting Alzheimer's. This can be very useful to know if you are considering long-term care insurance for example, or if Alzheimer's runs in your family and you want to know if you are likely to get it as well.

There are certain very rare diseases—like Huntington's disease or early onset Alzheimer's—where the presence of a certain genetic marker makes it almost a certainty that you will eventually contract that disease. If you have such a mutation, this can obviously be critically important information in terms of how you decide to live the rest of your life.

Using genetic markers to predict disease is complicated by the fact that it is often a combination of many markers that dictate whether you will get a disease, not just one. For instance, most cancers and cardiovascular disease involve a combination of hundreds of genetic variations. Work is still needed to identify all these combinations and to understand exactly what they mean.

For 99 percent of diseases, however, the genetic marker or combination of markers indicates only a predisposition for incurring certain illnesses and is not a death warrant. Environment (including lifestyle) is usually important in determining whether the disease is triggered. For instance, environment is more important than genetics in determining whether you will eventually get cancer. On the other hand, late-onset Alzheimer's is dictated 63 percent by genetics and 37 percent by environment. The weighting of genes versus environment varies from one disease to the next.

Even if the predictive power of a given marker is not especially high, it can be quite useful in prescribing the most effective treatment. The results will give you and your doctor better information about how you would respond to various medications (pharmacogenomics), and they can also prompt you to make changes in your physical activity and diet that can improve future health outcomes.

Personal genome testing will continue to improve over time. We will eventually map all 6 billion data points, and in the process we may even learn that the 99.9 percent of data points that are considered to be identical in all people actually differ in subtle but important ways from person to person.

Notes

1. The state of being disabled, with no reasonable chance of recovery, and unable to perform at least two of the basic activities of daily living such as bathing or going to the toilet unassisted.
2. *Aging and Solidarity between Generations: A Statistical Report of the European Union 2012*, Eurostat Statistical Books (2011).
3. Crimmins and Beltran-Sanchez, "Mortality and Morbidity Trends: Is There Compression of Morbidity?" *Journal of Gerontology* (2010).

CHAPTER

A Life Well Lived

... I am a part of all that I have met;
Yet all experience is an arch wherethro'
Gleams that untravell'd world whose margin fades
For ever and forever when I move.
How dull it is to pause, to make an end,
To rust unburnish'd, not to shine in use!
As tho' to breathe were life! Life piled on life
Were all too little, and of one to me
Little remains: but every hour is saved
From that eternal silence, ...

Ulysses by Alfred, Lord Tennyson

Retirement and Happiness

If you are going to seek retirement planning advice from an actuary, you probably want to keep it within the financial sphere. Ours is not a touchy-feely profession. Nevertheless, it may be useful to reflect on some of the emotional aspects of retirement, if only because they have financial implications.

Statistics Canada used to put out a publication called "A Portrait of Seniors in Canada." It appears that it stopped publication in 2006, which is a shame. Buried in a mountain of somewhat dreary statistics are some fascinating survey results about whether retirees enjoy life. [1]According to the survey, 47 percent responded that they enjoyed retired life more, while 41 percent ranked retired life and working life about the same. Only 11 percent—barely 1 in 9—said they enjoyed life less after retirement.

What makes this last statistic so remarkable is that a significant number of people are compelled to retire before they are financially or mentally ready. If you were forced to leave early because your employer no longer wanted you around or because of ill health, you are hardly going to be in a frame of mind to say you enjoy your retirement; and yet so few retirees express dissatisfaction. Here is how I would explain this rather counterintuitive result:

- The vast majority of people must not really like their jobs, no matter what they tell you. There are exceptions, of course, such as the self-employed, university professors, artists, musicians, and actors—all of whom tend to retire late, or not at all.
- It is interesting to note that none of the aforementioned professions require their adherents to grind out regular "9 to 5" days, week in and week out. These lucky people get to pick their hours and sometimes even the type of work they do. For many of them, continuing to ply their trade after a certain point is no longer about the money, except to the extent that money, as Warren Buffett has observed, is a way of keeping score. Employers who are looking for ways to keep certain older workers around longer would do well to offer flexible hours with commensurately flexible pay.
- The survey results suggest that people are better prepared for retirement than is commonly perceived. Few people who retire in a state of quasi-poverty would be inclined to say they enjoy retired life more.
- On the flip side, people who retire with excessive wealth are not necessarily happier. I personally know many recent retirees who are financially secure but admit privately to being bored and restless. A number of them are keen to find a little part-time work to alleviate the ennui. Maybe they are part of the 11 percent who enjoy retired life less, but there seem to be too many of them. Perhaps we can reconcile this disconnect by noting that the definition of *retirement* is by no means clear-cut. Many people who report themselves as being retired continue to work in some capacity, albeit on a part-time or irregular basis; such people are much more likely to say they enjoy retirement more than working, but strictly speaking, they are not really retired if they are still working for money.

- Whether we end up enjoying our retirement is ultimately not about money. Of course, we need enough money to meet our basic needs but as long as retirement income exceeds a certain financial threshold, the key to happiness lies elsewhere.

Speaking of needs, consider how Mazlow's triangle depicting the hierarchy of human needs applies in the case of seniors (Figure 22.1). The bottom two rows of the triangle represent basic needs. Fulfilling these needs is a prerequisite to making retirement bearable, but doing so is by no means sufficient to ensure enjoyment, much less happiness.

It seems our prospects for happiness hinge on how successful we are in satisfying our emotional needs—in particular, the dual needs of love and belonging. Humans are social creatures, and even the curmudgeons among us need to connect with others on a deeper level. Retirement is a time when we no longer have work to distract us, which makes it that much more important to be surrounded by a network of family and friends if we are going to have a chance at happiness. You will note that love and belonging have little to do with how much money we have or how much we spend.

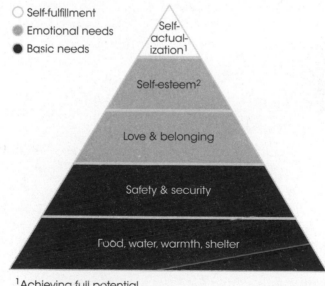

Figure 22.1   Maslow's Hierarchy of Needs

There is no better example of this than my own parents. They lived through World War II in southern Italy. Their hometown, Cassino, was in the middle of one of the most heated and prolonged battles of the entire war. The entire town was leveled in the process. Food was scarce and danger was ever-present. My father and mother (who had not met each other yet) had to keep moving in the nearby mountains to avoid the German soldiers on the ground and the constant bombardment from the air by the Allies. The strange thing is that decades later, when my parents reminisced about their experiences, their eyes would shine with an inner light, a look that I interpreted as betraying a bittersweet nostalgia. In spite of the hardships, they looked back on those difficult years with a quiet yearning in a way that evokes Tennyson's Ulysses.

Many years later, my father became quite wealthy as a result of his success in the construction business and some shrewd investing in the Toronto real estate market. He retired from active construction work at a youngish age with more money than he could ever spend in his new life of leisure. You would have thought this would be the recipe for happiness in retirement, but in the last 20 years of his life I rarely saw him smile. Ultimately, the money brought him no real joy.

As for the top row of Maslow's triangle, self-actualization, if you have not achieved it before retirement when you are at the peak of your mental and physical abilities and fully absorbed in your work, you are unlikely to realize it after you retire. Too many people I know start off retirement with the best of intentions to pursue various ambitious projects, but eventually find themselves moving in slow motion, getting very little done. If we make self-actualization our main goal late in our lives, we are setting ourselves up for failure.

Connecting all this back to the wealth targets I established in Chapter 12, I still stand by my calculations, but if your goal is happiness, you can safely choose a wealth target that is closer to the bottom end of the range rather than the top end. In the worst case, it may mean that you cut back on discretionary spending and expensive hobbies, but probably not until later on in your retirement when you would be inclined to cut back in any event. In the end, it is unlikely to affect your happiness. If you have not accumulated enough money to meet even the bottom end of the wealth target range, postponing retirement by even a year or two goes a long way toward making up the difference.

Final Thoughts

I would like to end by highlighting some of the major ideas described in this book.

A major theme is moderation in both one's saving and spending habits so as to avoid periods of unnecessary financial deprivation either before or after retirement. I advocate emulating neither the lifestyle of the ant or the grasshopper but something in-between. Implicit in this message is the importance of staying out of debt, credit card debt in particular. In a consumerist society, it is in our nature to push the consumption envelope. To paraphrase Robert Browning, our reach (when it comes to the things we want to buy) tends to exceed our grasp. If we give in to the impulse, our lives can turn into a constant tug of war between yearning for instant gratification and anxiety about whether we will attain income security in old age. Perhaps it may help to avoid overspending by managing your money a little differently. Once your income is comfortably above the subsistence level, why not keep a little money off the table at all times? If you make $70,000 a year, pretend it is just $65,000 and save the rest. If you make $150,000, spend as if it were $140,000.

Remember that saving for retirement is a two-dimensional problem. The more you save in a given year, the less you have left over to spend, and the converse is equally true. There is a happy medium that I have tried to identify in the chapters on finding one's retirement income target. Ideally, you want to save in such a way that you avoid extreme highs and lows in your personal consumption. As a priority, saving for retirement falls somewhere between buying Super Bowl tickets and buying shoes for your young children.

When it comes to investing, keep it simple. Maintaining the same asset mix throughout the accumulation period may not be the optimal strategy, but it is a better option than varying the mix for the wrong reasons. No one, including the professionals, times the market highs and lows with any degree of consistency. Do not reduce your equity exposure out of fear during a down market but nor should you increase it out of greed in the midst of a bull market. Invest your money in pooled funds or ETFs, as opposed to picking your own stocks, and do not overpay for investment management. There is no correlation between high fees and good returns.

The main challenge of retirement planning is identifying the risks and then quantifying and dealing with them as best we can. Most risks cannot be eliminated, just managed. When a risk can safely be transferred to a third party (like an insurance company) at reasonable cost, you have to ask yourself why you would not do so. Annuities, in particular, can be useful vehicles for minimizing some significant risks that start to loom large once we retire. Exposing yourself unduly to downside risk is irrational if the only upside is to produce a windfall gain you do not really need.

Keep in mind that we humans are inherently fragile creatures. We may be living longer than we used to, but too many of those extra years are impaired ones. As though to breathe were life! Rather than accepting eventual poor health as your fate, take preventative measures. A healthy lifestyle may not have seemed necessary when you were 40 but it becomes critically important by age 60. If you exercise regularly, eat properly, and do not smoke, you might or might not live longer, but you will almost certainly live a fuller life. As for staying mentally sharp, we have yet to find a cure for Alzheimer's, but in the meantime I would suggest you try doing something outside of your comfort zone on a regular basis.

Finally, try not to worry too much about how you will finance long-term care down the road. If you end up requiring it, you should take comfort in the fact that only a small percentage of situations involve a prolonged stay in a long-term care facility. Although the potential cost is an issue, that is not the real problem. No matter how you finance it, the real problem is finding yourself no longer able to function fully and having no reasonable prospect of recovery. Make some provision for the possible expense, but save most of your money for your living years. That is when it can do the most good.

Note

1. 2002 General Social Survey, conducted by Statistics Canada.

Similarities between the United States and Canada

When it comes to retirement and related tax issues, the similarities between the United States and Canada far outweigh their differences:

- In both countries, it is a matter of ongoing national concern that workers may not be saving enough for retirement.
- The same debate is being carried out about what the retirement income target should be, and in both countries there are stakeholders who are overstating that target.
- Both American and Canadian retirees dread the possibility of outliving their savings.
- Extraordinarily low interest rates and longer life spans are presenting similar challenges to individuals and pension plan sponsors on both sides of the border.
- The income tax rates are broadly comparable.
- The choice of various retirement vehicles and their tax status are similar.
- The type of pension plan that had dominated the landscape for decades—defined benefit—is rapidly on the decline and is being replaced with defined contribution arrangements.
- There is the same anxiety about how to deal with the potentially high cost of long-term care.

As a result, the themes presented in this book should be equally relevant to both Americans and Canadians.

This is not to say there are no significant differences.

- While most Canadians perceive the country has a retirement crisis, an actual crisis has not materialized in Canada. Americans are not as lucky in this respect, as a much higher percentage of seniors in the United States live in poverty.
- The economic group that is most vulnerable to retiring with insufficient income is the low-income group in the United States but the middle-income group in Canada.
- The US Social Security pension is funded on a pay-as-you-go basis, which is more precarious than in Canada, where the Canada Pension Plan funding level has been stabilized (see Appendix B).
- There is no serious talk of improving Social Security pensions in the United States, but it is a subject of ongoing national debate in Canada.
- While the United States took steps decades ago to move up the age of full retirement benefits under OASDI (Social Security pension) to 67, there is practically no discussion of similar steps being contemplated under the Canada Pension Plan.
- The dollar limits for making contributions to tax-assisted retirement savings vehicles for individuals are significantly higher in Canada.

The Social Security programs, tax rules, and various retirement vehicles in the two countries are also different of course but as will be shown below, they are broadly comparable in terms of what they deliver.

Social Security Programs

We start with a comparison of government-sponsored pension programs. The US Social Security pension is known as OASDI. In Canada, "Social Security" (which is more typically referred to as government-sponsored pension programs) includes Old Age Security pension (OAS) and the earnings-related Canada Pension Plan (CPP). Canada also has the income-tested Guaranteed Income Supplement (GIS), which is enormously important for households with below average income but has little or no impact at the earnings levels that we consider in this book. A more detailed description of the government-sponsored programs can be found in Appendix B.

Tables A.1 to A.4 illustrate contributions and pension benefits under Social Security in the two countries at different pay levels. The first two tables compare single persons and the last two compare married couples. Amounts are rounded and pay levels are expressed in local currency in each case.

The contribution to Social Security as shown (what is known as a *tax* in the US rather than a contribution) is just the employee's portion. The employer pays an equal amount (not shown here), and the self-employed pay double the employee's portion.

The ratio of pension to the current Social Security tax is not a perfect way to compare the value received from the program, but it is no worse than using historical contributions, since the contribution rates have increased markedly and in the United States at least, will continue to do so.

The example in Table A.1 is for a single person who earns slightly more than the average national wage. The table shows that Canadians get significantly more pension for their money, but that is partly because the monthly pension includes OAS, which is paid out of general tax revenues.

Even though the Canadian Social Security tax is already significantly lower than in the United States, the gap between the countries is likely to grow rather than shrink in the years to come, assuming the CPP is not enhanced. This relates to the differences in the funding approaches used, as is explained in Appendix B.

Comparing Table A.2 to A.1 shows that a higher-income individual derives much less value from OASDI than a lower-paid person as the ratio of pension earned to tax paid drops from 49 percent at $60,000 of earnings down to 37 percent at $100,000.

Table A.1   Single Person, 5-Year Average Earnings of $60,000*

Provision	United States	Canada
Social Security (SS) tax in 2015**	$3,947	$2,480
Monthly pension if age 65 in 2015	$1,937	$1,629
Ratio of pension to SS tax	49%	66%

*These tables assume pay increases of 3% a year in determining average earnings.
**Also known as a FICA tax in the US. Medicare portion is not shown here. In Canada, the Social Security tax is the employee's CPP contribution.

Table A.2 Single Person, 5-Year Average Earnings of $100,000

Provision	United States	Canada
Social Security tax in 2015	$6,578	$2,480
Monthly pension if age 65 in 2015	$2,404	$1,629
Ratio of pension to SS tax	37%	66%

In Canada, though, the contribution and pension at the higher earnings level are identical to the middle-income individual in Table A.1. This underscores the low earnings ceiling for benefit coverage under the CPP and the fact that Canada's Social Security program is geared to the middle-income—or perhaps even the lower middle-income—worker, whereas OASDI covers earnings up to more than double the average national wage.

There is a good chance that Social Security contributions and pension benefits in Canada might soon start to resemble those in the United States. That is because the CPP is likely to be enhanced in the next few years, and that enhancement will almost certainly increase the earnings ceiling as well as the benefit rate.

The next two examples deal with married couples. In Table A.3, the primary wage-earner is assumed to have average earnings in the last 5 years of $60,000 and the secondary wage-earner averages $30,000. Table A.4 is the same, except the earnings levels for the couple are $100,000 and $60,000, respectively.

When comparing the ratio of pension to Social Security tax in Table A.1 versus Table A.3, a middle-income couple generally derives more value out of Social Security than is the case for a middle-income single person. This is true in both the United States and Canada.

For a higher-income married couple, as shown in Table A.4, the differences between the United States and Canadian systems become quite stark; the US Social Security tax is more than double that of Canada's, and the corresponding pension benefit is about 50 percent

Table A.3 Married Couple, 5-Year Average Earnings of $60,000 and $30,000

Provision	United States	Canada
Social Security tax in 2015	$5,919	$3,882
Monthly pension if age 65 in 2015	$3,481	$2,789
Ratio of pension to SS tax	58%	72%

Table A.4   Married Couple, 5-Year Average Earnings of $100,000 and $60,000

Provision	United States	Canada
Social Security tax in 2015	$10,524	$4,960
Monthly pension if age 65 in 2015	$5,038	$3,257
Ratio of pension to SS tax	48%	66%

more. It becomes clearer why the debate in Canada about enhancing the CPP rages on.

A closing observation is that neither Social Security system provides much value for the contributions (Social Security taxes) paid in. If the employer and employee paid the same amounts into a capital accumulation plan from, say, age 25, the ultimate pension benefit would be much greater. The basic reason for the lack of value is that the Social Security systems on both sides of the border are dealing with legacy problems that date back decades. The current generation is paying the price for underfunding these programs in the past.

Delving into this issue a little more closely, and starting with Canada, the CPP requires contributions of nearly 10 percent of pay from employers and employees combined, and yet the pension provided is actuarially estimated to be worth only 6 percent of pay. The extra 4 percent reflects continued payments into perpetuity to fund deficits created decades ago when past service benefits were provided at nominal cost to the early beneficiaries of the plans and the true cost was passed on to future generations.

In the United States, OASDI is expensive because it is funded on a pay-as-you-go basis, which is somewhat similar to a Ponzi scheme in that the early beneficiaries pay in less and reap greater benefits. The trouble is that the tax rate needs to continue climbing as the population matures and the number of beneficiaries grows. Otherwise, the existing fund will eventually be depleted.

High-Level Comparison of Retirement Vehicles

The retirement vehicles that are available in the United States and Canada are very similar in some respects but very different in one important respect. In both countries, the following is true:

- There are both group programs, which are available through the workplace, and individual retirement arrangements.

- To the extent that employers contribute to these arrangements, the employer receives an immediate tax deduction while the employee's tax liability is deferred until benefits are paid out, usually many years later.
- Defined benefit (DB) pension plans in private-sector workplaces are being replaced by defined contribution (DC) plans where the employee takes all the risk.
- In both the United States and Canada, the vast majority of public-sector employees are covered under DB plans where the employer assumes the investment and longevity risk.
- In the various retirement vehicles that are available to individuals, the investment income is tax-sheltered during the accumulation period.

The one significant difference is that tax-preferential treatment of retirement vehicles is skewed heavily toward workplace plans in the United States whereas in Canada, an attempt has been made to level the playing field and provide essentially the same level of tax assistance to all individuals. Another difference is that a special tax penalty is levied on early withdrawals (with some exceptions) from US retirement vehicles, but there is no such penalty under Canadian retirement vehicles.

Workplace Plans

In the United States, the predominant type of retirement vehicle available through the workplace is known as a 401(k) plan because it was established under Section 401(k) of the Internal Revenue Code. 401(k) plans are defined contribution arrangements, meaning that the contributions are fixed by a formula and the retirement income provided is whatever income the contributions plus interest can generate. Strictly speaking, the 401(k) plan is not a pension plan, though it serves that purpose for tens of millions of Americans.

The parallel retirement vehicle in Canada is the DC pension plan. Whether it is a 401(k) plan in the United States or a DC pension plan in Canada, employees are usually required to contribute a basic amount to the plan and usually have the option to contribute more. The employer often encourages additional contributions on the part of employees by making a matching contribution, where the matching percentage is typically between 50 and 100 percent of the optional contribution made by the employee.

The tax-deductible contribution limit under a US 401(k) plan and a Canadian DC pension plan is broadly comparable, but with the following differences: (1) contributions in Canada are limited to 18 percent of employment earnings, whereas there is no percentage limit in the United States, (2) the Canadian dollar limits are a little higher than the limits under 401(k) plans, and (3) employees over age 50 in the United States can contribute $6,000 more than younger employees, whereas there are no age-related differences in Canada.

Individual Retirement Vehicles

Outside of the workplace, the primary retirement vehicle available to individuals in Canada is the Registered Retirement Savings Plan, or RRSP. The general idea is that contributions plus investment income accumulate within the RRSP and when it is time to draw an income, the monies are transferred to another vehicle known as a Registered Retirement Income Fund (RRIF).

The individual receives a tax deduction for the contributions made to the RRSP and the investment income is tax-sheltered as long as the money remains in the RRSP, though the shelter remains intact if the amounts are transferred to a RRIF. Income tax is paid when the individual makes withdrawals either from the RRSP before retirement or from the RRIF after retirement.

Contributions to an RRSP are limited to 18 percent of earned income up to a fairly high dollar limit (over $25,000) that increases annually. To the extent that the individual contributes less or nothing at all in a given year, the unused contribution room is carried forward to future years. This carry-forward provision is not applicable, however, within a DC pension plan.

In the United States, the vehicle that most closely resembles an RRSP is the traditional Individual Retirement Account (IRA). It is subject to virtually identical tax treatment to an RRSP except that the contribution limits are much lower. In fact, the ability to take a tax deduction on IRA contributions phases out at fairly low income levels so as to make the traditional IRA practically ineffective as a savings vehicle for higher-income individuals.

A new type of savings vehicle was introduced in Canada in 2009, called the Tax-Free Savings Account, or TFSA. It is different from the RRSP in that TFSA contributions are not tax-deductible but the proceeds of the TFSA, whenever they are received by the individual, are tax-free, including the investment income that was earned within the TFSA. Even though they were introduced quite recently, TFSAs have already become very popular, with more than 10 million accounts now in existence. While TFSAs were not specifically earmarked to be a retirement vehicle, no doubt a substantial amount of the savings in TFSAs will be used to produce income after retirement.

The parallel vehicle in the United States is the Roth IRA. Contributions are not deductible, but distributions from the Roth IRA are tax-free, assuming certain conditions are met. Once again, the contribution limits are too low, and the income-related restrictions that are imposed make Roth IRAs ineffective for higher-income individuals.

A Tax Comparison

Income taxes are an important aspect of retirement planning.

Table A.5 shows the marginal federal income tax rates for single filers at various income levels. Taxable income is expressed in local currency.

Table A.5, of course, does not tell the whole story. Most US states and all Canadian provinces also levy a state or provincial income tax, and basic and personal exemptions vary by country and even by state or province. There is also a Medicare tax in the United States and a health premium in some provinces.

We will attempt to take this all into account by comparing the overall income tax bill, including state or provincial tax, based on the following assumptions:

- The US situation assumes residency in New York state.
- The Canadian situation is based on living in Ontario.
- Calculations are for a married couple, age 55, both working and filing jointly in the United States.
- Primary wage earner earns two-thirds more than the spouse.
- There are no dependent children.
- Contribution to retirement vehicles is 10 percent of pay.
- The Social Security (pension) tax is included in both countries.
- The Medicare tax in the United States and the health premium tax in Ontario are included in the calculation.

Table A.5   Marginal Income Tax Rates (federal only)

Taxable income	United States (single filer)	United States (joint filing)	Canada
$ 25,000	15%	15%	15%
$ 50,000	25%	15%	22%
$ 75,000	28%	15%	22%
$100,000	28%	25%	26%
$150,000	28%	28%	29%
$250,000	33%	33%	29%
$500,000	39.6%	39.6%	29%

Table A.6   Tax Burden by Country

Household earnings	US tax	Canadian tax
$64,000	$12,064	$10,901
$96,000	$22,528	$20,704
$160,000	$48,151	$42,758
$280,000	$97,403	$93,897

Applicable for tax returns filed in 2015

- Employment insurance premiums are excluded.
- No contributions to employer-sponsored retirement arrangements are assumed.

On this basis, Table A.6 shows the overall tax bill for working couples at various income levels.

It might be a little surprising that levels of tax in Canada are actually a little lower than in the United States. There are, of course, numerous disclaimers regarding Table A.6. Some states will levy lower state income taxes than New York, and some even none at all. The Social Security taxes are higher in the United States, but so is the coverage level, at least for pension benefits. More deductions are permitted in the United States, such as mortgage interest, which may not have been fully reflected in the table.

On the other hand, some provinces have lower income taxes than Ontario, and most provinces do not charge a separate health premium as Ontario does. Canada's universal access to health care provides broader and more comprehensive coverage than does the 1.45 percent US FICA tax for Medicare. Pension coverage under Canada's Social Security system is less at higher income levels but greater at lower income levels when one takes the Guaranteed Income Supplement into account. Finally, the tax deductions permitted for individual contributions to retirement savings vehicles are greater in Canada than in the United States.

Even if all the possible refinements were reflected in the tax calculations, it would not change the basic point of the table: The tax burden is significant but of comparable magnitude on both sides of the border. Another similarity, not illustrated here, is that both the United States and Canada offer further tax breaks to retirees, especially once they have attained age 65.

For these reasons, the various arguments that we use in this book to derive retirement income target, lump-sum savings targets, and appropriate savings rates, are broadly applicable in both countries.

B

Social Security in the United States and Canada

Reference is made throughout the book to Social Security benefits, a term we have been using generically to refer to pension benefits under government-sponsored programs in both the United States and Canada. The summary in this appendix describes both the differences and the similarities between the Social Security benefits of the two countries.

Name of Social Security Pension Plan

In the United States, the government-sponsored pension is known as the Social Security or Old-Age, Survivors and Disability Insurance (OASDI) benefit.

In Canada, it is the Canada Pension Plan (or for Quebeckers, the virtually identical Quebec Pension Plan). Canada also has another program known as Old Age Security (OAS) and the companion to it, the Guaranteed Income Supplement (GIS). OAS and GIS will be described later on.

Purpose of Social Security

In both countries, the Social Security program is intended to provide a basic level of retirement security to everyone who had employment earnings, including the self-employed.

Neither plan is intended to be sufficient to meet all of a retiree's needs. US Social Security does a better job of providing basic protection to individuals who earn more than the national average wage, while the Canadian system is more focused on meeting the needs of lower-income workers, which it does effectively.

In Canada, the combination of CPP, OAS, and GIS is often sufficient to give low-income workers the same or better standard of living in retirement as they had when they were working. There is an ongoing national debate about the need to enhance CPP to better protect workers who earn more than the national average wage.

Earnings Base for Pension Calculation

The approach to computing pensionable earnings for pension calculation purposes is very similar in the two countries, in that it reflects employment earnings over a career but with three important adjustments:

1. Employment earnings are recognized only up to a given ceiling that changes annually, in line with wage inflation. In the United States, the OASDI ceiling is $118,500 in 2015 (US dollars). In Canada, the CPP ceiling is $53,600 in 2015 (Canadian dollars).

2. Employment earnings in each year are indexed by the change in the average national wage from that given year up to a year or years just before retirement. This adjustment eliminates the eroding effect of inflation over one's working lifetime.

3. Periods of low earnings are eliminated, which increases the average pensionable earnings. In the United States, this is done by taking only the 35 years of highest (indexed) employment earnings when computing the average pensionable earnings for pension calculation purposes. In Canada, it is done by dropping out up to 8 years of low earnings as well as years in which one was a homemaker with children under age 7.

The result of the calculation is known as the Average Indexed Monthly Earnings (or AIME) in the United States and as the average of the Year's Maximum Pensionable Earnings (YMPE) in Canada.

How Pension Is Calculated

The OASDI pension calculation divides the AIME into three tranches (known as bend points) and applies a different percentage to each tranche to determine the pension. The pension is:

1. 90 percent of AIME up to the first bend point (which is $826.32 in 2015), plus
2. 32 percent of AIME over the first bend point up to the second bend point (which is $4,980 in 2015), plus
3. 15 percent of AIME over that second bend point.

Thus, someone who had attained age 66 in 2015, with the maximum AIME ($9,066), would have a monthly pension of $2,685.50. This is known as the Primary Insurance Amount (PIA).

In Canada, the pension is basically 25 percent of the average YMPE in the year of retirement and the preceding four calendar years. The reason the formula can be simpler in Canada is the existence of the OAS and GIS, which provide disproportionately higher benefits to low income individuals.

How the Plans Are Funded

OASDI and CPP are both funded with equal contributions from employees and employers. The funding approach, however, is quite different between the United States and Canada.

OASDI is funded on a pay-as-you-go basis. This means the contribution rate that is needed to pay benefits tends to increase over time as the population ages. As a result, the ultimate contribution rate needed will be substantially higher than if benefits were prefunded. The OASDI contribution rate is currently 6.2 percent on the part of both employees and employer (12.4 percent for self-employed), but this rate will have to rise eventually if benefit levels are to be sustained.

In Canada, CPP used to be funded on a pay-as-you-go basis, but this was changed effective in 1997 and contributions were gradually raised to a level that would partially prefund benefits and stabilize the contribution rates in the process. The CPP contribution rate is 4.95 percent and applies only on earnings above $3,500, an amount known as the year's basic exemption, or YBE.

The CPP contribution rate has been the same since 2003 and projections of the fund over 75-year periods that are made regularly by the chief actuary of the CPP indicate it will probably not have to be increased. What could change this conclusion would be a lower than expected investment return, a drop in the fertility rate or a greater increase in life expectancy than is already built into the actuarial projections.

One other difference between the United States and Canada is that the amount paid into the plan by the individual is called a "tax rate" in the US but is referred to as a "contribution" in Canada. The choice of terminology perhaps reflects the differences in funding approach.

Normal Retirement Age

The age at which full pension is payable under OASDI is currently 66 but is rising gradually to 67 for people who are born in 1960 or later.

The normal retirement age under CPP is 65, which is making Canada somewhat of an anomaly among developed countries, as 67 or 68 is becoming the norm to receive full pension elsewhere in the world (often after a long phase-in period). There is little impetus to change it in Canada since CPP funding is currently stable with normal retirement at 65, though the commencement age for OAS and GIS is scheduled to rise gradually to 67 by 2029.

Early Retirement Age

One can receive OASDI pension as early as age 62. The reduction on early retirement is generally five-ninths of 1 percent per month that pension starts before full pension age, but the calculation is complicated by the slow transition to 67 as the age for full pension. For someone whose full pension age is 66, for example (meaning they were born in the 1943 to 1954 period), the pension starting at age 62 is reduced by 25 percent.

CPP pension is payable as early as age 60 but subject to a reduction of 0.6 percent (as of 2016) for each month pension starts early. For someone starting their pension at age 60, then, the reduction is 36 percent and if pension starts at 62, the reduction is 21.6 percent. A slight complication is that the dropout period is different if pension starts at 62 instead of 65, which could affect the pensionable earnings base but not the reduction.

Delayed Retirement

In both countries, the retiree can delay commencement of pension up to age 70. The starting pension would be increased as a result to reflect late commencement and a shorter collection period. The increase under OASDI is two-thirds of a percent for each month (8 percent for each year) that commencement is delayed after normal retirement age. Under the CPP, the increase is 0.7 percent per month, or 8.4 percent for each year.

As a result, someone who was born in 1954 and entitled to a full pension at age 66 under OASDI would have his or her pension increased by 32 percent by delaying commencement until age 70. In Canada, the pension starting at age 70 would be increased by 42 percent.

Only 0.6 percent of Canadians start their pension at age 70, which is surprisingly low, given that surveys show that the prospect of running out of money in retirement is of great concern to retirees, second only to worries about health.

Indexation

During one's working years, pension benefits that are being earned are indexed to wage inflation, which tends to average about 1 percent a year more than price inflation. After retirement, pensions being paid are indexed annually to price inflation. This applies to both the United States and Canada.

Other Government-Sponsored Pension Plans

In Canada, CPP is considered to be the second tier of government-sponsored pensions. To round out our understanding of the pension benefits from government sources, we also need to take into account the first tier, which is known as the Old Age Security (OAS) pension. In this book, Social Security pension in a Canadian context includes both tiers. OAS is a flat amount (generally) and provided to all Canadians who have met the residency requirement.

OAS payments start at age 65, though there is now the option to delay the start date up to 70 and receive a 6 percent increase in pension for each year the start is delayed. Pension benefits are indexed to the inflation rate with adjustments made quarterly, a throwback to the days of high inflation.

The benefit amount as of January 2015 is $563.74 a month. OAS is not quite a universal benefit, since payments are subject to a *claw-back* if retirement income is over a threshold ($71,592 in 2015). Because of the claw-back, no OAS is payable at all if retirement income exceeds another threshold ($115,716).

The companion program to OAS is the Guaranteed Income Supplement (GIS), which is also considered to be part of the first tier. GIS is payable only if one is receiving OAS and if income is below a given threshold. The maximum GIS in January 2015 is $764.40 a month for a single person and $1,113.72 a month for a couple (if both are receiving OAS).

No comparable universal program exists in the United States, although some attempt is made to recognize the greater need of lower-income citizens by providing a higher benefit accrual rate on the first tranche of earnings under OASDI, as was described earlier.

Taxability

Social Security pensions are generally regarded as taxable, although in the United States the portion of Social Security that is taxable depends on the household's total income. The test involves determining how much total retirement income excluding Social Security plus one half of the household Social Security pension exceeds a base amount (which is $32,000 for couples and $25,000 for singles). In general, between 50 percent and 85 percent of Social Security is subject to federal income tax.

Table B.1 provides a side-by-side comparison of the US and Canadian Social Security systems.

In Canada, OAS, GIS, and CPP pensions are all taxable, though there is a tax credit on up to $2,000 of pension income on sources excluding OAS and GIS.

In both countries, little or no income tax is paid by retired households with modest income as a result of various age exemptions, the basic personal exemption, and other exemptions or credits.

Table B.1   Summary of US and Canadian Earnings-Related Social Security

Provision	United States	Canada
Name of plan	OASDI	CPP
Who participates	Everyone with employment earnings, including the self-employed	Everyone with employment earnings, including the self-employed
Pension formula	Varying percentage (90% / 32% and 15%) on 3 tranches of average indexed monthly earnings over the 35 years with the highest earnings	25 percent of average pensionable earnings in the year of retirement and the previous 4 calendar years
Pensionable earnings in a given year	Employment earnings up to a ceiling, indexed by the change in wages from the given year until the third last calendar year preceding retirement	Employment earnings up to a ceiling, indexed by the change in wages from the given year until the year of retirement
Ceiling on pensionable earnings (local currency)	$118,500 in 2015	Based on the average national wage; 2015 ceiling is $53,600
Normal retirement age	Age 67 (by 2027)	Age 65
Earliest retirement age	Age 62	Age 60
Latest retirement age	Age 70	Age 70
Inflation protection after retirement	Annual increases equal to 100% of change in CPI	100% of change in CPI

APPENDIX C

Retirement Income Targets under Other Scenarios

In Chapter 4, we established retirement income targets that varied from 40 percent of final income up to 70 percent, depending on the extent of the "investments" people make with respect to their children and their home. People who never raised children and never paid a mortgage will tend to spend more on themselves during their working lives and would naturally want to continue to do so after retirement. They are the ones who are more likely to have a retirement income target of 70 percent. Most people with above-average income will have paid a mortgage and raised children, and as a result they will have spent less on themselves. Their retirement income target will be closer to 50 percent.

In this appendix, retirement income targets are shown under alternate scenarios. To keep it simple and to maintain a semblance of consistency, each alternate scenario will involve one variation from the base scenario. The variations that we will explore here include:

- C1: Continued to spend money on children up until retirement age (the parents' retirement age, that is)
- C2: Retired at age 60 instead of 65
- C3: Did not start to save seriously for retirement until age 40
- C4: Divorced at 50 and retired single
- C5: Participated in a pension plan since age 32

To be consistent with the other scenarios in this book, the base scenario will be as follows:

- Two-earner couple making $160,000 a year in the final 5 years before retirement or a single person earning $100,000
- Raised children and owned a home on which they paid off a mortgage (child costs of 4 percent of income and mortgage payments of 20 percent of income until retirement in their last 5 years of work)
- Saved for retirement on their own, starting at age 32
- Retired at 65 with mortgage paid off and no more child costs

With 20 percent of gross income going toward mortgage payments and 4 percent toward helping out the children, the base scenario does involve significant cash outlays that we assume end at retirement. While many households spend less in these two areas in their last few years before retirement, some spend more.

Scenario C1: Continued to Spend on Children until Retirement

In the base scenario, I assumed that if there were children in the household, the brunt of child-raising costs would have been incurred before the parents turned 60 and that the costs from 60 to retirement age amounted to 2 percent per child up to a maximum of 4 percent of the parents' income. In this alternate scenario C1, I assume that the parents continue to dedicate 10 percent of their gross income toward child-related costs.

There are many possible reasons why spending on children can continue at an even higher level than this, right up until the parents reach retirement age:

- Parents had their children fairly late in life
- Helped finance higher education for the children
- Helped the children with a down payment on their first house
- Provided ongoing financial assistance to grown-up children until they found well-paying, permanent jobs

The resulting retirement income targets and the savings rates needed (starting at age 32) to reach those targets are given in Table C.1.

Note how low the retirement income targets are. The higher savings rate needed in the case of a single parent reflects the fact that the cost of living for two people is less than it is for one person.

Table C.1   Scenario C1: Child-Related Costs Continue (at 10%) until 65

	Couple	Single Parent
Retirement income target	38%	37%
Savings rate needed	5.7%	6.6%

Savings rate excludes Social Security contributions.

Table C.2   Scenario C2: Retiring at 60

	Couple	Single Parent
Retirement income target	41%	40%
Savings rate needed	11.8%	12.8%

All other assumptions match base scenario.

Scenario C2: Retiring at 60 Instead of 65

To retire early, one needs to save at a higher rate since there are fewer years to save and a given dollar of savings does not buy as much retirement income as if one retired at 65. This is reflected in the results in Table C.2.

Apart from retirement occurring at age 60, Scenario C2 is identical to the base scenario, which means we are back to assuming child costs in the last 5 years of employment of just 4 percent of income instead of 10 percent as in Scenario C1. The retirement income targets are slightly higher than under Scenario C1. The savings rates needed, however, are much higher.

In the case of the single parent, the savings rate needed is probably understated. That is because there would have been a divorce along the way and the couple may well have been saving less than 12.8 percent of pay for retirement before the divorce.

Scenario C3: Start Saving Late

It is not realistic that everyone will save significant amounts on a regular basis starting as early as age 32. Many families may be tempted to get other major expenses under control first, like saving for a down payment on their first house or paying for daycare. In Scenario C3, we will assume that saving starts at age 40, but with the other assumptions being the same as the base scenario. The results are shown in Table C.3.

Table C.3   Scenario C3: Start Saving at 40

	Couple	Single Parent
Retirement income target	42%	41%
Savings rate needed	10.2%	11.8%

Table C.4   Scenario C4: Divorced at 50 and No Remarriage

	Higher-income spouse	Lower-income spouse
Retirement income target	44%	47%
Savings rate needed	9.4%	5.7%

Comparing Scenarios C2 and C3, we see that starting to save at age 32 and retiring at 60 requires a higher level of annual contributions than starting to save at 40 and retiring at 65. Nevertheless, a drawback with starting to save late is that it restricts one's retirement options. It may no longer be possible to retire early and forced early retirement that is initiated by your employer or your health situation will mean you will fall short of your wealth target.

Scenario C4: Divorced at 50 and Stayed Single

The scenario of divorcing in mid-life and having to pick up the pieces is unfortunately quite common. At the point of divorce, I am assuming that the couple's assets are split evenly. Following the divorce, I assume joint custody and also assume that both spouses will continue to work but with ongoing financial support at the rate of $1,000 a month provided to the spouse with lower income until the higher-income spouse reaches retirement. The results are given in Table C.4.

The even split of assets at the point of divorce puts the higher-income spouse behind in retirement saving and the lower-income spouse ahead. That is one reason why the higher-income spouse then needs to save more from age 50 on to catch up. The other reason is that higher-income individuals generally need to save more than lower-income because Social Security pensions are a smaller proportion of their overall retirement income.

Table C.5   Scenario C5: Participated in a Workplace Pension Plan

	Couple	Single Parent
Retirement income target	48%	47%
Savings rate needed	3.9%	5%

Note that divorce puts both spouses behind the standard of living they would have enjoyed had they stayed married. As was explained in Chapter 12, the cost of living per person in the case of a couple is less than the cost to provide a similar standard of living for a single person.

Scenario C5: Participated in a Workplace Pension Plan

Participating in a workplace pension plan generally means you do not have to save as much for retirement because your employer is making contributions to the pension plan on your behalf. This means you should have a little more disposable income available to boost personal consumption, which translates into a higher retirement income target. All things being equal, a pension plan participant should have a higher standard of living both before and after retirement than individuals who have to save for retirement on their own.

In Table C.5, it is assumed that the employer was contributing 5 percent of pay each year from age 32 on behalf of the employee. Everything else is the same as the base scenario.

D

About the Assumptions Used in the Book

In this book, we have used examples to estimate (1) what your retirement income target should be, (2) future retirement savings, and (3) how past savings would have grown under certain conditions. This appendix gives more details on these assumptions.

Thoughts on Conservatism

Let me preface the following summary of assumptions by confessing that we actuaries are naturally inclined to being a little conservative in our choice of assumptions. We are sometimes tempted to build surreptitious buffers into our calculations even when no one asks us to. It is no surprise, then, that the calculations in Chapter 4, for example, are on the conservative side (i.e., produce a higher retirement income target). Erring on the side of caution is deemed to be a good thing provided one does not go overboard. Here are some ways in which that conservatism manifests itself:

- In the calculations, retirement income is assumed to start at age 65 instead of an earlier age. This is conservative, since it allows one to save a lower percentage of pay for retirement. A lower saving percentage leads to more personal income and a higher retirement income target.
- Retirement saving is assumed to start at age 32, which is younger than when a great many people start to save on a consistent basis. A longer saving period leads to a lower saving

rate, hence more personal consumption and ultimately a higher retirement income target.

- I assumed one encounters no major setbacks along the way such as divorce, serious illness, or periods of prolonged unemployment. These types of events interrupt our saving for a while, or even deplete what savings we have, and when that happens, we need to save even more when we get closer to retirement and so we tend not to get used to a high rate of personal consumption.
- The ultimate retirement income target is deemed to remain the same in real terms throughout one's retirement years. In fact, it is a little overstated, since it will almost certainly decline starting at some point in one's 70s and possibly earlier. This will be studied in a subsequent chapter.

Perhaps I should be mildly troubled by this propensity to be conservative. After all, we want to achieve the right retirement target, and an excessively high target is not the right one since it limits our ability to spend in the middle part of our working careers when, frankly, we probably have the greatest need for the money or at least the greatest capacity to enjoy it. Yet, nearly all of us tend to be a little ant-like when it comes to estimating how much we will need for that long winter. Perhaps this tendency is a survival instinct. After all, we always know in the present moment how much deprivation we can endure, and it is within our control (provided we have employment earnings) to manage it. What we do not know is what financial challenges we might create for ourselves in the distant future by not being sufficiently conservative today.

Assumptions Used to Estimate Personal Consumption

In Chapters 3 and 4, I broke down gross pay into various categories of expenditure, including child-raising expenses, paying the mortgage, employment expenses, and saving for retirement. From this, I calculate income tax, and what is left over is deemed to be used for personal consumption. Once we know personal consumption during our working years, we then have our retirement income target, assuming we want to maintain the same personal consumption after we retire. Here are the basic assumptions that were used to break down gross pay.

Employment Earnings

For married couples, I assumed both partners were working with one partner earning 60 percent as much as the other (e.g. $60,000 and $36,000). I assumed these were current earnings rather than historic or future. Past earnings were estimated by deflating current earnings at the rate of 2.25 percent from age 65 down to 55, and at the rate of 3.5 percent from age 55 down to 30.

Retirement Savings

I assumed all amounts that were saved for retirement were eligible for a tax deduction and that the investment income on savings were sheltered from income tax during the accumulation period. In the main calculations, retirement saving on a consistent basis was assumed to start at age 32. If a later age had been used, the retirement saving percentages would have been higher and the retirement income targets would have been lower. An earlier starting age would have the opposite effect.

In the scenario where mortgage payments ended at age 60, an assumption had to be made about how much of the resulting increase in disposable income would be directed toward retirement saving, since the model would use this information to recalculate the right amount to save up until age 60. It was assumed that 20 percent of the amount that had been allocated to mortgage payments and child-raising expenses would be spent on one-time expenditures that would not carry on into retirement, and the rest of the amount would be split between personal consumption and retirement saving. The exact split would depend on what level of retirement saving was necessary to permit personal consumption to continue at the same level.

Employment Expenses

I assumed a constant 3 percent of pay for all expenses related to employment, such as additional transportation costs.

Child-Raising Costs

Based on outside sources, the cost of raising a child averages about 10 percent of the parents' gross pay for a period of 21 years. Unlike in my previous book, this offset to personal consumption is ignored in the calculations, since I assume that the children would have reached 21 by the time the primary breadwinner is age 60. After the 21-year period, though, I assumed that parents would continue to help out their children financially in some fashion, and to this end I quantified this support as 2 percent of pay per child up until the parents reach age 65.

Mortgage Payments

For households that owned their home, two scenarios are described in the book. In one, mortgage payments are assumed to continue up until age 65. In that scenario, mortgage payments were assumed to be 20 percent of gross household pay each year. In the other scenario, the mortgage was assumed to be paid off by age 60, in which case it was assumed that payments represented 25 percent of gross income in the years when payments were made.

Retirement Income from Savings

I assumed an annuity would be purchased at age 65 and that payments would be guaranteed for 10 years. The interest rate underlying the annuity purchase was 2.5 percent, which is lower than the long-term norm for nonindexed rates but higher than rate that insurers would use currently for indexed annuities.

Assumptions Used to Calculate Future Retirement Savings

Actuaries sometime make assumptions about the future that eventually come back to haunt them. Any assumption about how economic factors will unfold will always be at least a little wrong and sometimes spectacularly so. The error often involves putting too much weight on recent years' experience and not enough on long-term trends.

In the projections made in Chapter 13, I attempted to give proper weight to long-term experience. This is why some assumptions, such as interest rates and inflation rates, may look a little high relative to what we have become accustomed to in the past 10 years. The assumptions used are summarized as follows.

Inflation

One of the key assumptions is the future inflation rate. I have assumed 2.25 percent, which is higher than what we have been experiencing for the last number of years but still lower than the long-term average of 2.89 percent, which is what Canada experienced during the period 1923 to 2013.

I was tempted to go lower, given the arguments about the dampening effects of an aging population and real-life example of what has been happening in Japan (which has a two-decade head start on us when it comes to aging) since the early 1990s.

On the other hand, there is still the possibility that the efforts of central banks to keep interest rates so low will eventually lead to much higher inflation, but those fears are diminishing with each successive year of low growth, low wage increases, and continuing low inflation.

Ultimately, I was persuaded that a lower assumption would be putting too much weight on recent experience and that some reversion to the historical norm still seems possible.

Wage Inflation

In the individual examples, I assumed the average wage increase until age 55 would be 3.5 percent, which is 1.25 percent more than inflation. Some readers will be skeptical that such a high rate of increase can be achieved in the typical case, but remember that this includes individual merit and promotion.

A common error is to assume that the average wage increase for an individual employee will match the average wage increase for a larger group of employees. This ignores the fact that in the larger group, the higher-paid older employees will be constantly retiring and lower-paid younger people will be hired. Experience studies consistently demonstrate that if you track the increases for individuals in a larger group, those increases will be substantially higher than if one looks at the average increase of the entire group.

If anything, the 3.25 percent rate of increase is too low for the first two thirds of most careers. In the final stage of one's career, the period from age 55 to 65, I assumed that increases would simply track inflation at 2.25 percent. Once again, this reflects the typical situation where older employees are lucky to have increases that even match inflation.

Investment Return

The return on an investment portfolio that is invested 60 percent in equities and 40 percent in bonds has been estimated to be 5.25 percent. Actually, it was estimated to be 5.75 percent, but 50 basis points were deducted for investment fees. There was a time when 5.25 percent would have seemed inordinately conservative but the low current rates reflect lower inflation (2.25 percent assumed versus the 50-year historical average of 4.1 percent), lower risk-free interest rates on fixed income investments, and a slightly lower equity premium. This is consistent with the arguments that were made in Chapter 8 about why interest rates will stay low for a long time.

For the purpose of converting lump-sum account balances into a stream of retirement income payable for life, it is more appropriate to be using an annuity factor that reflects the investment return offered by insurance companies rather than the 5.25 percent return. For this purpose, I assumed the underlying interest rate that insurance companies would be using for annuities would be 2.5 percent, for reasons mentioned above.

Assumptions Used to Estimate the Historical Accumulation of Savings

In Chapter 13, I estimated the level of retirement income that a fixed savings rate would have generated over prior 30-year periods. Even though this was an historical rather than a prospective exercise, some assumptions about the individual circumstances and the economic conditions of the time were still necessary to perform the calculations. Table D.1 summarizes the assumptions that were used.

Couple Contemplating Long-Term Care Insurance

In Chapter 11, we use an example to show the impact of being insured versus not insured. The couple's estimated income needs at the point of retirement are $65,000. It was assumed that half of this comes from Social Security pensions and the other half is funded by retirement savings. Since the second half is not indexed to inflation, the overall income will rise by half the CPI each year, which means that at age 71, their income will be $73,600 (if CPI rises by 2.25 percent a year for 10 years). By age 86, their income will be $88,600.

Table D.1   Actuarial Assumptions Used in the Historical Simulations

Couple's earnings	Combined earnings of $96,000 (in present-day dollars) at the point of retirement. This would be categorized as a little above average (but not by much), given that many households have two incomes.
Historical earnings	Earnings in the final year of employment in past periods are estimated by deflating current earnings by the average increase for Canadian salaries in each prior year. For other years, those earnings were projected backward by deflating earnings at 65 by inflation rate between 55 and 65 and by inflation rate plus 1.5 percent for merit and promotions before age 55. The 1.5 percent component reflects the tendency for salary increases to be higher at younger ages.
Investment return	Based on the return that could have been generated historically by 30 percent in a Canadian equity index fund that tracks the S&P/TSX index, 30 percent in a US equity index fund that tracks the S&P 500 index but expressed in Canadian dollars, and 40 percent in a Canadian long-term government bond index. The annual fee on the index funds was assumed to be 50 basis points.
Annuities	Annuities were assumed to be bought from an insurance company at age 65. The annuity rate was approximated by the yields on long-term provincial bonds less 25 basis points, further reduced by 50 percent of long-term inflation that would have been expected at the point of retirement. The reduction for 50 percent of inflation assumes the annuity would be partly indexed. Full indexation was not deemed to be necessary, nor could it be purchased from an insurance company in any event. The form of annuity was joint and survivor, with 60 percent of the pension continuing to the surviving spouse of the primary annuitant.
Mortality	The mortality table used at the point of retirement approximated the mortality rates for insured groups at that time. Hence, it starts with the 1971 GAM table from the late 1960s until 1982, the 1983 GAM table from 1983 to 1993, the UP-1994 table (without projection) for 1994–2000, the UP-1994 table with projection to 2005 for retirees for 2001–2005, the UP-1994 table with projection to 2010 for 2006–2010, and the UP-1994 table with projection to 2015 for retirees after 2010.
Annuity	The form of annuity was deemed to be payable for life only, with a 5-year guarantee.
Social Security pensions	It is assumed that government pensions were available in their present form since 1967, the first retirement date in the accumulation period. The couple's pension benefits from Social Security were estimated to be 33 percent of their final 5 years' average pay. This is based on current rules for CPP and OAS. In the United States, Social Security would have provided about 40 percent of final average pay.

Morneau Shepell Retirement Solutions practice

If the income needs for one spouse living alone is 65 percent of that for both spouses, then regular income needs for the household needs reduce by $25,760 at age 71 and by $31,010 at age 86. For the example, we rounded these numbers off to $25,000 and $31,000, respectively.

Also in the same examples, it is assumed that if the all-in cost of LTC is $80,000 a year now, it will rise to $100,000 in 10 years' time (at age 71) and to $140,000 in 25 years (at age 86).

Assets Needed to Cover Long-Term Care (LTC)

In Chapter 11, I show the additional amount one should be adding to their dollar target to cover an LTC claim of moderate length. A description of how I derived those amounts is given here. Note that this applies only to upper-middle-income households, since lower-income and middle-income households are better off relying on publicly funded solutions while upper-income households will have the financial means to cover the cost of LTC in any event. I will define upper-middle income households as having final employment earnings (for both spouses combined) between $150,000 and $300,000 a year.

Based on Chapter 10, a stay in a better LTC facility costs about $80,000 a year in current dollars, which translates into about $116,000 a year in 15 years' time. To the extent that the LTC claimant no longer has outside spending needs, regular household expenditures should decline, which will partly offset this cost. I will assume they decline by 35 percent.

This has the curious result that the net cost of LTC for a couple whose retirement income is $75,000 a year is higher than for a couple whose retirement income is $150,000. We therefore modified the cost of an LTC solution so it rises with retirement income as follows: With retirement income of $75,000, it is $70,000 a year for LTC in current dollars, at $100,000 income it is $80,000, and at $150,000 it is $90,000.

On this basis, the net cost in current dollars of a 3-year stay in an LTC facility is about $120,000 in all three cases. The net cost of a 6-year stay would be about $240,000.

About the Author

Frederick Vettese is chief actuary of Morneau Shepell, the largest company in Canada offering human resources and consulting and outsourcing services. Frederick has spent his entire career providing retirement consulting and actuarial services in respect of workplace pension plans. Much of his professional time these days is spent in the public eye, speaking at professional conferences and writing on retirement issues for national newspapers and other media. In his spare time, Frederick struggles enthusiastically with both his golf game and his piano. He was born and raised in Toronto, Canada, where he continues to reside with his wife, Michelle.

The Essential Retirement Guide is Fred's second book. In 2012, Bill Morneau and Frederick co-authored *The Real Retirement*, a book that explained why Canada was not suffering a retirement crisis.

Index